THE BLIND SIDE OF EDEN
THE SEXES IN PERSPECTIVE

The BLIND SIDE *of* EDEN

THE SEXES IN PERSPECTIVE

CAROL LEE

BLOOMSBURY

First published 1989
Copyright © 1989 by Carol Lee

Bloomsbury Publishing Ltd, 2 Soho Square, London W1V 5DE

British Library Cataloguing in Publication Data

Lee, Carol
The Blind Side of Eden: The Sexes in Perspective
1. Men. Interpersonal relationships
with women.
I. Title
305'.3

✓ ISBN 0-7475-0076-2

Typeset by Cambrian Typesetters, Frimley, Surrey
Printed in Great Britain.

Did feminism want to take masculinity to the cleaners? Was the book of Genesis the work of a vengeful mind? *The Blind Side of Eden* explores present-day relationships between men and women in the Western world through modern and ancient eyes. It does so through the microscope of 'manalysis' and through the telescope of a long look back through the pages of Biblical history.

This book describes what women and men feel about themselves and each other by looking at relationships from many perspectives. It also analyses these within the context of prevailing influences. This century has seen Freud, Jung, atomic weaponry, mass-communication, feminism and education all affect what men and women want from each other. Their expectations are often high and occasionally they are contradictory.

It was in someone's vested interest to create a system of sexual opposites which has provoked the longest war in human history – the battle of the sexes. But is this a just war? Are women and men really the opposite sex? Do they see each other through entirely different eyes? Will sexual desire diminish if men become less aggressive and women more assertive? Carol Lee brings a deftness of touch and a breadth of experience to these and many other issues in this timely and thought-provoking book.

Carol Lee is a journalist who has been an agony aunt, a columnist for the *Daily Mail*, a feature writer on the *Daily Mirror* and has written for the *Guardian*, the *Observer* and the *Sunday Times*. She has spent more than a decade working with groups of teenagers and adults in the area of sexuality and relationships. She is the author of two highly acclaimed books, *Friday's Child* and *The Ostrich Position*.

TO VERA PETTITT WITH
LOVE AND GRATITUDE

CONTENTS

ACKNOWLEDGEMENTS

Many thanks are due to everyone at Bloomsbury, especially Liz Calder, and to Esther Jagger. I would like to thank five friends: Veronica Sperling, Brian Matthews, Peter Martin, Tony Rudolf and Moris Farhi for reading all or part of the manuscript and for offering assistance beyond the call of duty. I would also like to thank the many people who agreed to be interviewed, those whom I have worked with in groups, and all who have generously given their time, ideas and their words.

Excerpts from *The Sea of Faith* by Don Cupitt and *Men: An Investigation Into the Emotional Male* by Phillip Hodson reprinted by permission of BBC Enterprises Ltd; excerpt from *The Wisdom of Insecurity* by Alan Watts reprinted by permission of Pantheon Books; excerpt from *Outrageous Acts and Everyday Rebellions* by Gloria Steinem reprinted by permission of Jonathan Cape and Henry Holt, Inc; excerpts from *Murder in the Dark* by Margaret Atwood and *Einstein's Monsters* by Martin Amis reprinted by permission of Jonathan Cape Ltd; excerpts from *The Female Eunuch* by Germaine Greer and *What a Man's Gotta Do: The Masculine Myth in Popular Culture* by Anthony Easthope reprinted by permission of Grafton Books; excerpt from *The Golden Fleece* by Robert Graves (Century Hutchinson) reprinted by permission of the executors of the estate of Robert Graves; excerpt from *The Wild Girl* by Michelle Roberts reprinted by permission of Methuen, London; excerpt from *Thou Shalt Not be Aware: Society's Betrayal of the Child* by Alice Miller, Copyright © 1985, reprinted by permission of Pluto Press; excerpt from *Beyond God the Father* by Mary Daly (The Women's Press) reprinted by permission of Charlotte Cecil Raymond; excerpt from *Pornography and Silence* by Susan Griffin reprinted by permission of The Women's Press Ltd; excerpt from *The Sadeian Woman* by Angela Carter reprinted by permission of Virago Press; excerpt from *The Painted Witch* by Edwin Mullins reprinted by permission of Secker (Martin) & Warburg Ltd; excerpt from *The Sceptical Feminist*

ACKNOWLEDGEMENTS

by Janet Radcliffe Richards reprinted by permission of Routledge &
Kegan Paul; excerpt from *Jung and the Story of Our Time* reprinted
by permission of Chatto & Windus; excerpt from *Monuments and
Maidens* by Marina Warner (Weidenfeld & Nicolson) reprinted by
permission of Peters, Fraser & Dunlop; excerpt from *In the Name of
Love* by Jill Tweedie (Jonathan Cape) reprinted by permission of
Curtis Brown; five lines from *True Stories* reprinted by permission of
Jonathan Cape Ltd and Macmillan Canada.

Introduction

When I began this book I imagined I would be dealing with new attitudes. Initially I set out to describe and analyse what women and men in the industrialized west feel about themselves and each other as the end of the twentieth century approaches. Relationships and attitudes have obviously undergone considerable change due to many important influences. Feminism is the most recent of these. However, as the digging got deeper, it was obvious that many up-to-date opinions masked archaic prejudices. This is why *The Blind Side of Eden* takes in both modern and ancient themes.

The book evolved from listening to men and women talking about relationships, from feminist literature heralded in by writers like Simone de Beauvoir, Kate Millett, Betty Friedan and Germaine Greer, and from interviews. It also draws on my work with teenagers in classrooms as a sex educator, and at conferences and workshops with groups of adults. Clearly a great deal of anger, uncertainty and resentment lay not far beneath the surface. This was true from the ages of seventeen to the seventies. The talk grew vociferous as soon as the subject of male/female roles and relationships was opened up. While heterosexuality was not presumed in any of this work, it became the purpose of this book to illustrate the strange condition of being 'the opposite sex'.

My initial aim was to catch the words, but the enterprise quickly began to look like an archaeological dig. It wasn't a net, or a tape recorder, that was needed − but a bigger shovel. For the words themselves revealed pictures of hidden empires supposedly long dead. The Roman soldier, however, is alive and unwell and living in the heart of the journalist with a fortress mentality. How come the executive who said she'd left seventeenth-century Cinders behind at the fireplace was still looking for Prince Charming? And, on a modern note, why did the couple who enjoyed each other sexually suddenly switch off when they discovered the word 'sexism'?

In finding out what underwrote some of the perplexing anomalies in modern relationships the ancient rites of passage began to surface.

Many prevalent attitudes – even some feminist ones – date straight back to biblical times. I have called these attitudes Old Testament, fundamentalist or biblical. They are as pervasive now in their disguised forms as Noah, Jonah or Eve.

The changes in relationships after the advent of feminism and in the wake of Freud have been colossal. However, modern ills should not, in the main, be left at their door, for many of the culprits are at least two thousand years old.

There, for the moment, the shovel rests.

1
The Writing on
the Wall

Before Germaine Greer's *The Female Eunuch* hit a largely unsuspecting populace well below the belt in 1970, women and men commonly described each other as 'the opposite sex'. For decades Hollywood had offered us the full technicolour version of screen images of a five-foot baby doll blonde being swept off her feet by a six-foot, dark and definitely not baby doll hero. While there had been cosmetic changes to this scenario, like the blurring of man's macho image in the sixties, nothing had occurred to shake an intrinsic acceptance that *real* men and women had complementary and opposite qualities. This is the way it was meant to be: men were men, women were glad of it, and vice versa. The missionary position was archetypal of this attitude, at least in western culture: the dominant, potent man; the undominant, receptive woman; and their piecing together like a jigsaw through opposite parts.

Feminist thinkers then arrived on this scene – in which, it has been claimed, you at least knew where you stood – and in the millions of words that followed, their message was unequivocal: 'So far, so bad.' Feminism's own analysis was that the female had been the eunuch in the exercise not so much of heterosexual relationships, as of a system of injustice called patriarchy. It set about rescuing this eunuch from the jaws of such a fate. Germaine Greer's words: 'Most women have very little idea of how much men hate them',[1] were instructive. From the eunuch's point of view lying underneath a man who loved you was one thing, but playing possum to his naked aggression was beginning to seem dangerous.

So the battle began. Feminist writings were the spur, giving women not just support, but intellectual frameworks from which to argue. At its simplest, the argument described women as wrong-done-by and patriarchy as systematized wrong-doing. It declared that women's skills, ideas and contributions to society, like child-rearing, were undervalued and taken for granted. Feminism declared that the undervaluing and denial of woman's intellect and sexuality were not accidental, but part of a systematic process designed to keep her from

1

important knowledge about the world and about herself. Feminism set out to examine and expose the workings of this system, and either to free women from it or fundamentally to alter it by making women its equal participant instead of its victim.

The word 'system' is important, because the central arguments have been about patriarchy as a system, not man as a person. To argue against the system of patriarchy is not to be anti-male, although both feminists themselves and their opponents have frequently not made this clear – some feminists are anti-male in any case.

In order, therefore, to clarify what is meant by the term 'feminist' I have taken as a guide Janet Radcliffe Richards' definition in *The Sceptical Feminist*. Ms Richards' book, first published in 1980, was essentially a pro-feminist work which revealed the gaps and inconsistencies in feminist thinking. 'In saying that feminism has a strong fundamental case,' she wrote, 'what I mean is that there are excellent reasons for thinking that *women suffer from systematic social injustice because of their sex* . . . I shall be taking that proposition as constituting the essence of feminism, and counting anyone who accepts it as a feminist.'[2] A little later she added:

> However, more subtly, feminism should not even regard itself as a movement to *support women who suffer from injustice*. This is because many injustices suffered by individual women have nothing to do with their sex, and could equally well be suffered by men. If, for instance, there are men and women in slavery, it is not the business of feminists to start freeing the women. Feminism is not concerned with *a group of people it wants to benefit*, but with *a type of injustice it wants to eliminate*.[3]

Initially feminism did not talk of freeing men too from the bonds of patriarchy. For a while confusion reigned between patriarchy as a symbol and man as a person, and men were the potential enemy, deemed guilty unless they proved themselves innocent. Their burden was that, in being raised in a patriarchal system which denied women and favoured men, they behaved accordingly. But Ms Richards' work brought feminism firmly into the area not only of justice but of heterosexual relationships. Through it man also could be seen as a victim, for although patriarchy gave him more ostensible power it left him emotionally vulnerable. The system, with its hierarchical structure, allowed only few men to be powerful in any case – at least in the eyes of other men. In the competitive male world of business and of class status not many made it to the top; the rest had to make do. But in the eyes of women men looked different. They were domestically 'the boss', by being traditionally head of the household and by virtue of supporting it with their income.

Feminism helped to change this situation, or at least made it possible for change to take place. In encouraging woman to find a new identity for herself, it gave man the same possibility. For if one side decides to stop behaving like 'the opposite sex', the other side is automatically in a different relative position. However, credit for the release of men and women from their set positions of big strong/small submissive has not usually been given to feminism. This is because many men were frightened of the prospect of a gender reversal. Man feared that if he let go his traditional power he would become feminism's eunuch – he was scared that the female eunuch of the patriarchal system would be replaced by the male eunuch of a matriarchal one. Weren't most feminists ball-breakers, anyway? he thought. These fears have been scoffed at by feminists, not so much because they have no theoretical substance, but because they underestimate the power of the status quo. It is the people who have sought to change the system of patriarchy who know at first hand how powerful it is.

Woman, too, feared gender reversal because, while part of her wanted to be 'free', part of her also wanted something from man. That 'something' is the elusive commodity called 'masculinity'. Most women did not want 'freedom' to result in metaphorical castration. If men were dismantled of the armour of male conditioning, might they not be left weak and spineless? While one half of a woman wanted the tyrant to surrender, the other half couldn't imagine what heterosexual life would be like if he did. Others, however, gleefully took feminism as a sign that, after centuries of being the other way round, women were now right and men wrong. Men could have a taste of their own bad medicine.

The personal battle was conducted around these kinds of fears and protestations. Heterosexual relationships entered a period in which the one thing you couldn't be sure of was masculine or feminine behaviour or identity. What did it mean to be a woman or a man? With gender stereotypes in the melting pot it wasn't easy for anyone to find a quick, off-the-shelf, ready-to-wear substitute for the old Me-Tarzan-You-Jane costumes. In the midst of all this, the word 'person' was reborn.

Man was now in a tricky position. While woman had been asserting herself, man's traditional image had been revealed by the zoom lens of feminism as so much window dressing. But how and where was he to find new clothes? Man, who for so long had considered himself the superior sex, now found himself, like the Emperor, naked in public – and at a time when the people doing the scrutinizing were women. For one of the starkly new factors thrown up by feminism was woman as *public* participant and scrutineer.

Man could not turn to other men for support or inspiration, because it was the traditional drapers who had sent him out in this condition. Nor could he trust the new public, woman, to clothe him instead. She was in particularly mischievous – some would say malign – mood, and was quite likely to revenge herself on the dirty trick she called patriarchy and suit man to her own designs, just as he had fashioned her. She might even do something really mean and send him out dressed as a woman. The fear that the 'new man' is an emasculated version of the old one is not unfounded, on the part of either sex. Neither is the notion that he is a toothless pet dinosaur strung along on numerous feminist leads. There was a strong fear that feminism's subversive purpose in the seventies was to take masculinity to the cleaners. No – if man was to be his own person, his own *man*, he had to find his own way. But how, when so many men were emotionally reserved and reactionary?

Woman had problems of a different nature. While she had used the writings, affection and shared experiences of other women to discover a modern identity for herself, an identity which frightened many men, that identity had not necessarily helped her to be a *heterosexual* woman. Sometimes it had actually hindered this process: the knowledge, for example, that only men could be bishops, newspaper editors and airline pilots made her furious with gender elitism. And this was even to suppose that most women had changed. Most hadn't, but feminism had changed the atmosphere in which relationships were conducted, so that its messages, even if not agreed with, were nevertheless on the agenda. So for both women and men the old and the new existed side by side, sometimes within the same skins. It meant that women's needs from men were often conflicting and even contradictory.

Some women, on the other hand, couldn't understand why men should want to hold on to the ultimately arid and brittle structures of the 'old man', and wondered why men didn't grasp the opportunities that feminism offered them. At a group seminar which I attended, for people learning to be counsellors, a young, successful businesswoman asked: 'Why aren't men pleased to have life made better for them? Why aren't they pleased that women can now earn a living, help with the admin, be capable of shouldering their share of the mortgage, and in general free men from the burden of being the sole breadwinners?'

A male administrator replied that most women *didn't* relieve men of burdens – that they wanted to have their cake and eat it. If they earned money, they counted it as their own, to do with as they pleased, and they still left men to do mundane things like getting the car serviced.

Another man, a social worker in his early thirties, said something quite different:

> I don't think you realize how much in his deepest heart a man wants to be a hero. I was brought up on it – fantasies of doing incredibly brave things, or of managing in the face of impossible odds – while inside I was a mass of nerves and fear. For me being a boy was like this – the fantasy of being heroic lived with the disappointment of not being. I think upbringing and conditioning do that to us – or at least did.
>
> I know what you mean about men not being pleased to be offered a much more interesting deal. But you women only see it as what you give, not what is taken away. If women can now do things men can do, what are men for? Our whole idea of ourselves, of our place in the world, of our value, has taken a battering. The reason we're scared of the good life is because we haven't made it ourselves. We're not its architect, and I don't think we believe in what we haven't made or engineered. In one way we haven't a right to, because we think we have to work for what we get, and in another way I think we're scared of something that's offered by a woman.

The demise of man as hero or architect of accepted ideas left a vacuum in the condition of masculinity and of being male. It had been hardly a flash of a feminist's pen since man was God, breadwinner, knight, prince, and in all these the answer to a maiden's prayer. Now the maiden was on the rampage. It seemed only five minutes ago that man had been opening doors for women which were now being slammed in his face. Instead of asking to be cosseted or spoiled, modern woman was asking for things like positive discrimination and non-sexist behaviour. She was also asking for much more.

One of the facets of a feminist woman is that she has high expectations. She wants an interesting job, maybe children when she's ready for them, a partner who understands her and whose politics, both sexual and otherwise, she approves of. She expects sex to be good, and is herself knowledgeable enough to say so if it isn't. She has needs and expectations that would not have been voiced before the advent of feminism.

In this sense the arguments between male and female partners can no longer be dismissed as domestic squabbles. They are often about political and moral issues which seek for and presume freedoms, comforts, choices and rewards that were hardly glimpsed at the beginning of the twentieth century. These in turn are reflected by larger issues.

This century has seen Freud, Jung, technology and feminism all play enormous roles in changing people's ideas about what it is to be human, moral, male, female, a child, a parent. At the same time many contradictory influences exist side by side. Sophisticated travel has made it possible to marry someone who lives ten thousand miles away, and to die from AIDS through having intercourse with someone who lives down the road. Science and technology have made it possible to have only the children you want. They have also made it possible for most children and adults to be killed at the touch of a nuclear button. People having relationships with each other as the end of the twentieth century approaches do so with all this in mind, even if not consciously.

Woman's place in this modern picture has been on the upbeat. Man's has been on the down. His so-called brave acts and achievements have taken a battering not only from feminists, but from ecologists, environmentalists and modern thinkers like E. F. Schumacher, author of *Small Is Beautiful*. In a shrinking planet there is no room for man the expansionist dinosaur. Man the inspired inventor of the modern car, the genius who split the atom, the adventurer who travelled to the moon, the cowboy who killed Indians is not a hero any more. Woman is today's adventurer in the recently charted area of the emotional world. For man it feels as if feminism has turned the tables on him, and is now kicking over the traces. Man has suffered a terrible loss of status. Germaine Greer issued challenges like: 'The first significant discovery we shall make as we racket along our female road to freedom is that men are not free, and they will seek to make this an argument why nobody should be free.'[4] The contemporary American novelist Paul Auster has a different view of man's loss of status, and writes: 'Most men abandon their lives.'[5]

The mass abandoning of men's lives has usually taken the form of war. Traditionally a man has been asked to prove his courage on the battlefield, or in conquering natural obstacles like Everest or the South Pole. Now he is being asked to show bravery in a different way, not only by women, but in a world which needs seemingly unheroic but vital things like clean air, clean water, uncontaminated food and the preservation of the ozone layer.

The problem is that man has usually been in conflict with the natural world. He has seen himself as superior to the randomness of nature and has taken somewhat literally the instruction in Genesis to 'fill the earth and subdue it'. This was previously a common attitude towards women also – keep them pregnant and docile.

In this way man has been the boss, and as the boss has traditionally portrayed himself as the 'big provider'. Women was the 'small provider'. She took care of the domestic bits and pieces like child-rearing – and of a full range of human emotions! Man provided the 'important' bits: the house, the money, the status and all the things that made the world go round.

Man's world stopped going round the way he wanted it to when, following precedents set by Freud and Jung, feminism started investigating male psychology. Instead of man the big provider it found a needy person. In their book *What Do Women Want?* Luise Eichenbaum and Susie Orbach write that woman provides for man more than man provides for woman, and also more than woman provides for other women. They take the view that, through the mother, a man's or a boy's dependency needs are better met than a girl's. As well as taking the Freudian stance that the boy has the hazardous task of separating from a different sex-person – his mother – and finding his masculine identity in the role model of an absent and therefore not very helpful father, the authors assert that heterosexual men who initially have their needs met by a mother may look forward to a return to this kind of relationship when they find an adult female partner. Men have their dependency needs met by their wives. This enables them to go out into the world and do things.

Women, on the other hand, are in the difficult situation of not having their needs met by an absent father and of being reared by a mother who shapes them to meet *other* people's needs, not their own. A woman's needs are further thwarted when, as an adult, she has to relate to a male who is looking to *her* to minister to *him*.

In describing relationships in this way, Eichenbaum and Orbach answer the question that is the book's title by saying that women want their needs met by being with a partner who can both sustain them emotionally in the way their fathers couldn't, and can be part of a two-way interchange of emotional needs. At present boys are brought up with the expectation of having their needs met by a woman, and women are brought up by other women to expect to have to do this. The system is thus a self-fulfilling prophecy.

However, viewed only this way the story would not be complete, for it ignores the petrifying business of what it must feel like to believe as a boy that you have to find another woman before you can function properly. The Old Testament and Freud had both described *woman* as not complete, either because she was not intended to be equal with man or because she doesn't have a penis. Man as incomplete was a new picture. Whether it was an anti-male picture depends on one's perspective, for it is not necessarily so at all. In seeing man as needy and afraid one can either feel compassion and empathy or say angrily: 'Serves him right.' In the early eighties compassion for men, who were eventually seen to be as vulnerable as women, was subsumed by anger that patriarchy *in the shape of men* had kept women under for so long.

Until feminists took issue with the role of man as ostensible provider, emotionally needy man was *not* ostensible, at least not publicly. Traditionally it was a woman who needed a man in order to be taken care of by his strong arms, his bank balance or just his God-given way of being the superior sex.

Eichenbaum and Orbach's thesis, while pointing out men's vulnerability, particularly emphasized the raw deal suffered by women – for women, it seemed, lost in every way. They were depicted as weak, yet their services propped up the very system which kept them as such. Since their dependency needs were not met they found it difficult to be independent, for one needs a secure base from which to adventure; but at the same time as women are not independent they were providing the secure base from which men ruled the public world.

The danger lies in seeing this as the only way of telling the story. True as it is, what it doesn't discuss is woman's collusion. For woman has known privately for a long time that man is not the only powerful one – in fact he is not necessarily powerful at all. She has known that the Lord of the Manor is also a needy little boy who comes to her lap for comfort. She has also known herself to be powerful in ways that please her, and to have the added power of being the custodian of what is secret and arcane. This powerful secrecy contains her position as keeper of the 'home truths' – the ones that don't get washed in public. These truths are the private lives of men, which shape their public actions.

She has also known the truth of the cliché: 'Behind every strong man there's a good woman' ('trying to get out,' the feminist graffitists add). This is one of the reasons why she didn't make a fuss sooner. The feminist explanation – that women didn't complain because they were so oppressed that they didn't have the power to be writers, politicians and trade unionists – is not complete without the coda that woman's position wasn't all bad, any more than man's was all good. It is also not complete without the understanding that the status quo was kept in a tenuously balanced state by a collusion of weak woman with strong man and strong woman with weak man, and that within individual relationships this was something that sometimes worked extremely well.

It was, ironically enough, man's strivings through the industrial revolution, and developments in science and technology, which radically shifted the position of woman in any case. The industrial revolution was a major factor in bringing about the end of the extended family as men moved from home to find work in the new centres of industry. With family life changing, so woman's role and place within it changed too. In this century science has given woman control over her fertility, a revolutionary change which culminated in the widespread use of the birth pill from the 1960s onward. Meanwhile technology brought the gadgets which meant that doing the housework and the laundry ceased to be a full-time job. A woman's life was no longer house-, children- and husband-bound. Since then, woman's efforts have rocked the cradle to its foundations.

Suddenly, as a result of that freedom, women began to discover themselves and each other: the concept of sisterhood was born. 'No, other women were not enemies, not competitors in the race to get yourself a man,' said one woman recalling her experiences in the early seventies. 'They were sisters, and no wonder men felt the draught.' The new sisterhood decided to empty its lap of the cuckoo male and catch up on centuries of having its talents ignored. Strong women were out in force. In his book *Men: An Investigation into the Emotional Male*, Phillip Hodson looks at the effects of all this on men and on their relationships with women.

> Manly man's plight remains profound. He cannot ask a woman what has gone wrong with him because you don't confide in subordinates. And in any case there is no guarantee that women are still prepared to listen. Sisterhood is not only powerful, it is a darn sight more interesting than ministering to men's wounded vanity. Neither can he confide in men-friends because their knee-jerk reflex would still be to put the boot in out of self-protection. In an age of transition, this is where the agony lies.[6]

The 'new women' no longer want the 'old' traditional men and constantly lambast them for their chauvinistic views, though

9

usually underplaying the point that chauvinism traps men as well as women in roles which they may not want.[7]

Men have so far invested minimal resources in making themselves desirable to the new generation of women. Instead, they continue to risk their lives and prosperity by holding stubbornly to the old manly stereotypes.[8]

But the manly stereotype was shored up by woman, who did not tell the world that her Lord and Prince suffered from whimperings in his sleep, from sweats occasioned by nightmares and from childish cravings to use baby talk in the privacy of his bedroom. This is one of the reasons why the search for the 'new man' is so perplexing, for woman was part of the conspiracy that held the 'old man' together. In stepping out of this role without so much as a by your leave she left the status quo of marriage looking like a house of cards. To add insult to perfidy she then blew, and she blew, and she blew the house down.

The consequences for men are not initially bright, for most don't, as Phillip Hodson says, have a friend in other men, at least not this side of death and war. Antony Easthope writes of this in his book *What a Man's Gotta Do*. 'In the dominant versions of men at war, men are permitted to behave towards each other in ways that would not be allowed elsewhere, caressing and holding each other, comforting and weeping together, admitting their love. The pain of war is the price paid for the way it expresses the male bond.'[9] There have always been the standard brothers-in-arms myths to hide man's homophobia and the fact that, in life as a search for growth and meaning, man has traditionally had few friends.

Woman, as Phillip Hodson points out, has been man's subordinate rather than his equal, and although a conspirator and an ally in shoring up the 'male myth', not its advocate. When she upped and left the house of cards, or 'House of Mirrors' as Mary Daly calls it in *Beyond God the Father*,[10] it was bad enough that she walked out at all, but it was her reasons for doing so which really upset man. He complained enough about the ostensible reasons – such as her not wanting to be an unpaid servant any more – but the real reason was too much to take, for it was something that had always been inviolably his.

Woman upped and left the domestic hearth because, after all that time looking at the fire, she suddenly saw the light. As if thousands of years of conditioning had dropped away, she took up her bed and walked. It was this more than anything else which man found disturbing, because until this century (with a few hard-done-by

10

exceptions like Joan of Arc) man had kept the mandate on revelation. Woman now seized it from him, and her insights revealed the patriarchal system as a gigantic fraud designed to keep man in the limelight and woman in his shadow.

So not only has man recently lost in one fell swoop his pamperer (I won't use the word 'mother' here), his conspirator and his access-to-an-heir-for-his-personal-line-to-continue, and not only did this unholy trinity slope off without so much as a permission note or a doffing of her servant's cap, but she knocked the master's bowler off the hatstand on her way out. The word has been used many times: 'Sacrilege'. Some will mutter in response to this that the writing was on the wall, and had been for some time – which is true. But it had been on the wall at home, which is not where man was wont to do most of his reading.

The other piece of 'sacrilege' that woman got up to in packing her bags was to treat all this in general rather than in particular terms. In the past it had been man's province to generalize about woman and about the world; it was woman's personal role to be particular, and to be very particular about the house. By making her issues general, woman transgressed another sacred cow. As Marina Warner writes of Pandora and Eve in *Monuments and Maidens*: 'Their stories express an understanding that *they bear meanings ascribed to them by their creators, that their identity is perceived through the eyes of others, not their own* [my emphasis] . . . The female was perceived to be a vehicle of attributed meaning at the very beginning of the world . . .'[11]

For woman to take over the role of ascriber of meaning, and in so doing to become individual rather than symbolic, was not so much a knock to the system as a clashing of cymbals/symbols in the corridors of power. Now woman was saying not only that the man she was living with was a bit over the top at times, but that man in general had been over the top for at least twenty centuries. The result was a torrent of books, written overwhelmingly by women, on patriarchy, double-dealing and self-assertion. Many of them have reinterpreted the past, or at least shone a bright torch into the hitherto dark part of it which has been inhabited by the unknown women painters, thinkers, poets and politicians.

In response to this onslaught, which made the grassy banks of patriarchy look like a bunch of mole-ridden hillocks, 'men have re-thought next to nothing and have allowed [their] prestige to decline by default,'[12] writes Phillip Hodson, and again: 'If . . . men were beginning to look inside themselves at this time, then something

11

seems to have inhibited publication since the results to date have hardly troubled the bookshelves.'[13] In other words man has looked *outside* himself to define, name and alter, but the act of looking inwards he has not mastered.

It's true that the bookshelves have hardly been troubled by the adventures of man in the little-charted territory of his own psyche, for man the phoney adventurer has so far feared walking the plank from his outer, constructed universe into the shark-infested depths of his own subconscious. But the work is at least under way now, and some books written by men for men have appeared – undoubtedly because of pressure from woman. 'One of the primary reasons for the modern male crisis', writes Phillip Hodson, 'is the fact that women have been so successful in identifying the female crisis.'[14]

But there is further to go, because a crucial part of the female crisis, the part which is heterosexual, has not been properly or sufficiently identified. Matters got stuck for a while as the 'other' or opposite sex, woman, did her share of calling man 'other' as she named his achievements disasters and his reasoning folly. It would have been unrealistic to imagine that if woman ever woke up – not, like Sleeping Beauty, to the kiss of a prince, but to an urgent call from her own heart to be subject rather than object – she would view the world in anything other than an opposite light to man's naming. How could she not but see as sorcerer's apprentice the erstwhile King of the Castle who had made such an unholy mess of a supposedly given planet? If the earth was for husbanding, he had made a poor spouse.

So she switched man from king to sorcerer, from wise to foolish, and herself from shrouded to exposed, from silent to shouting. She turned herself from a guilty Eve into a discerning woman, and she saw man as the cause of the whole ghastly mess: the bombs, the deaths, the maimings, the lead poisoning and the lack of love. She switched from meek to accusing as she blamed man for the fact that the books had been written either without mention of her subjective existence or with poisonous pens which blamed her for the sins of Eve or the whims of Pandora.

Because man had made a generality out of the whole world without so much as consulting her, woman decided to make her own generalities. They equated man not with strength of character and resolve, but with myth-spreading and psychological weakness. This is why some men tried to dismiss feminism as bad form, as a bunch of harridans creating a fuss or a clique of ugly women who couldn't get a man in any case. Many men would gladly have bettered their partners' conditions without written requests; many men would have been happy to take more of an interest in the daily lives of their children once it was pointed out that this was important. What was much more difficult for man was to come to terms with the substructure or the underpinning of the change in woman, for she was literally naming the world as she saw it – opposite to what he was used to. And all of man's fears had come to pass.

First of all woman left him. His conspirator, tied to him through the tacky bonds of sexual activity and the even tackier ones of tradition, his friend/foe, companion/stranger, earth-mother/word-child, familiar/demon broke her ties with him. Then she did something even worse – she wrote her own myths; she went public. His feeling was probably that, if she left him at all, she could at least have left him alone – but she didn't. She wrote her own words in her own hand: large, blunt and blaming. His early gaze had been deriding, so he named her less; hers now was furious, and she named him culprit, though had she only done this she would of course have been wrong.

The role of woman as conspirator is one that Jill Tweedie talks about in her book *In the Name of Love*. In discussing the role of the poor little woman wringing her hands behind closed doors while the man she sleeps with commits unspeakable atrocities Tweedie writes of Teresa Stangl, the wife of the man who commanded the Nazi extermination camp at Treblinka, where a million men, women and children were murdered:

> [The journalist] Gitta Sereny put a question to her after her husband's death in 1971: 'Would you tell me what you think would have happened if at any time you had faced your husband with an absolute choice . . . "Either you get out of this terrible thing, or else the children and I will leave you." ' . . . Frau Stangl took more than an hour to answer that question. She lay on her bed and she cried and then she composed herself and answered: 'I believe that if I had ever confronted Paul . . . with the alternatives: Treblinka or me; he would – yes, he would, in the final analysis, have chosen me.'

Tweedie continues:

> Teresa Stangl, a small pretty woman from Linz, could have persuaded one of the nine camp commandants of Nazi Germany to leave his post and flee. It is impossible to tell what repercussions this might have had, how many others might have been given a flash of humanity, a burgeoning resistance, through this event.[15]

13

This illustrates something that feminists have been at pains to discuss and which has been at the forefront of feminist thinking – the importance of stopping the divide, the split between the personal and the political. There are many ways in which this divide needs to be bridged. In one sense it means stopping the division between political man and personal woman, between deciding male and domestic female. In another it means ending the system which makes it possible for a man to be a mass murderer during the day and a cosseted baby when he comes home at night. It also means that woman must become publicly accountable. Then she would not only become political as well as personal, but, in so doing, she would stop being man's familiar, his conspirator. Man could then no longer claim the support of his conspirator because she could no longer claim dependency, ignorance and being morally unenfranchised as extenuating circumstances.

Man's erstwhile prop was now involved in something that looked suspiciously like a conspiracy *against* him. But a woman who was heavily involved in feminist meetings, now a mother in her mid-thirties, denies that there was any plot of this kind:

> There was no plan to leave men out. It looked that way because of the enormity of what women were going through. For a while in the mid-seventies the earth could just as well have spun in the opposite direction. We were having such a great time. Women were for a change safe and warm, locked up in the women's room where it was all at – the meetings, the challenges, the howls of laughter, the tears and the warm smiles. It was those smiles I remember, those open, gut-wrenching, heart-warming smiles.

In the past women had smiled publicly *at* babies and *for* men. Now they smiled with, around, through and between each other, and for men this was a most discomforting prospect. A rugged-looking actor in his thirties made a wistful comment about it: 'The thing I most envy women is their smiles. You see two women meeting in a pub and they greet each other warmly, animatedly, and their whole faces light up. It's great to see women these days. They look wonderful because they've discovered something us lot haven't – each other.'

It was true that women were smiling for and with each other. They had discovered an outlet for their much-needed emotional world which married the emotional with the practical and professional in a way that had not, in the main, been allowed in their real marriages. Real marriages had corralled women safely in separate houses, busy with separate husbands who went out to communal places called

14

work. For centuries women did not have communal places. And with man being in practically constant short supply he had made himself into a scarce commodity. Even at the beginning of this century he might be killed at almost any time – wars, pit disasters, industrial injuries. Today he might be abroad on business for weeks on end, or away commuting, or on night shift at the local factory. Man might be many things, but he was seldom at home.

In this sense woman was a kind of army recruit, there to hold on to base camp and keep it going while man went foraging. And then, without too much public warning, base camp was suddenly deserted except for a bunch of strangers called his children who wanted their teas *now* and were going to fill their nappies or start screaming or play potty bombs unless their needs were met fast. Meanwhile the base camp corporal was out with the girls, and it was quite an extraordinary time they were having. For it was an era when a whole generation of women were in love with their girlfriends as well as their boyfriends. For some heterosexual women it was a painful time, too, as the mismatch between the world of the women they communicated with and that of the men they lived with stretched painfully to snapping point.

For many women, however, it was a time of celebration. Nothing like it had been written about since the Christian conversions during the life of Christ. The parallels between the two were pointed out when I asked four women who were practising Christians to discuss feminism and Christianity. The following is an edited version of the tape transcript of that discussion. The first woman said:

Let me make the analogy directly by putting it in the form of a modern parable . . . In the beginning of feminism, for those of us who experienced it as that privileged group called intelligent, middle-class women, there was a new word – and that word was 'female'. And it was very, very light. That light illuminated a picture of women as hard-done-by, shrouded people.

When you walked towards the Light and embraced feminism a shroud fell away. It hadn't seemed heavy, but it was there. And when it slid easily to the ground and you looked over your shoulder you saw it was crumpled and made of sackcloth. On the ground it looked nothing, and hundreds of thousands of women shrugged it off without even a backward glance. But it was worth looking backwards, if only for the memory of how big your own shadow was and how small the bundle on the floor was, helpless now without the support of your body.

15

The women who walked together towards the Light called Female began to join hands, and to smile at each other as they walked. The nearer they came to the Light the more they smiled, and felt supported by those around them. Sometimes they stumbled or cried, and those near to them came and dried the tears, helped them up and very often carried them. As each woman came to the Light she saw who she was without the years of conditioning and the centuries of wearing her shroud.

The women who saw the Light knew that the world was a dark place, and they wanted to make it better. They wanted to carry their Light to others, even to those who had followed a false system which had caused so much of the destruction. Women named this false system patriarchy, its source coming from the wrong and vengeful idea that men were more important than women.

One of the other women continued the story:

In actual terms what happened was that many women formed that crucial marriage between the personal and the political. You suddenly found yourself at dinner parties where there wasn't a man in sight. Instead there were fascinating women who were helping each other to be published or to grow or to get over grief or to better themselves. And for a while it was rapturous.

It was a wonderful feeling to experience the world in a different way. It wasn't just a shift in emphasis but crucial new knowledge and feelings that hadn't been experienced before. It wasn't only that your gaze shifted, but that the world became a completely different colour. Women discovered for a while that the world was not perilous and vaguely hostile, but that it was half peopled with women.

The importance of feminism, not only as a political movement but as a felt experience, cannot be underestimated. It is why, whatever its eventual political outcomes, or whatever successes are or are not laid at its door, it cannot be dismissed – because for so many women it was a personal revelation. What's more, it was a personal revelation that was also a shared one.

There *are* startling similarities and differences between this and Christian conversions. The similarities are that important baptisms took place, that they took place *en masse* and that they radically changed lives. The differences are that the baptisms were self- and co-operatively administered, and that they recognized the self as powerful within a supporting group rather than within the context of the importance of someone else.

And of course the really important difference is that all this was happening among women, for women and by women. Not only was a male priest not present, but it was his absence and his banishment that was crucial to the discoveries being made.

It's difficult for someone who is outside an important experience, like an awakening, to understand it. And I make the analogy between feminism and Christianity not to play havoc with either Christians or feminists – neither of whom will be pleased with it – but to show the dangers of denying an important experience just because you haven't had it yourself.

We have accepted in our history that Christians have conversions, and still do. Yet we also view personal transformation of any kind with grave scepticism. Resurrection is extremely difficult in the part of the world which has accepted only Christ as capable of this, despite the fact that His message would seem to be that spiritual resurrection is possible and necessary for all of us.

Therefore to say that as a feminist you saw the Light, which would be a true statement for many women, is seen as a danger to an existing order. In that order the light of the world has always been male, whether he be God, the sun-gods, the sun itself – or the man-made electricity grid. One way or another man brings, gives or dispenses light – at least the light of reason. The light of unreason, the shadows of moonlight, firelight and candles, has traditionally been linked with women. So one is handcuffed in describing what happened to women in the seventies as a mass conversion. Such conversions were man's business, not woman's.

The third woman took up this theme:

It was a conversion initially from being the victim of darkness, in the form of the fierce male light of patriarchy which has singed women's wings, to being a subject of one's own. It was a conversion from the slavery of conditioning to being a witness in one's own right, and of bearing witness.

And it was a startling conversion. It was a change from believing as a woman that you were only half a human to an understanding of being whole and independent. You were not a cripple, but able to walk unaided without the truss of a male God or a husband. For feeling only half a person wasn't just a matter of not being financially independent – it was about the deep feeling that *without a man around* you were only half a person. This is one of the reasons why women have always talked a great deal about

17

men. Men are the other half of themselves, without whom the world is not whole. To convert from being half a person to being a whole one is an extraordinary experience, and needs understanding as such.

Some of the slogans and clichés which have attended feminism, as they do every movement for change, have blunted people's understanding of the fundamental personal changes which took place. When one realizes their nature it is also easier to understand why some feminism overbalanced into separation and man hatred.

Despite the problems, for a while the world became once more an Eden of possibilities. Women felt the earth could be reclaimed from industrialists and arms manufacturers, and that with enough care and sacrifice it would be possible to create a world which revolved around co-operation and concern for nature and the future rather than exploitation and greed.

These women had wonderful evenings together. They were on a 'high', and it wasn't surprising that when they came home to husbands and male lovers who weren't a part of this new experience it was a little disappointing.

The fourth woman endorsed these feelings and went on to talk about the new concept of sisterhood:

We were strong, happy and delighting in our possibilities. Literally we danced in the streets, threw flowers round each other, hugged, and – yes – loved each other as sisters.

I felt as if my family had expanded to include every new woman I met. Sisters was the correct word. I was not and never have been lesbian. Yet I can say that I loved women. I still do. I went through an experience with other women at that time which is how some people describe the sixties. What I do know is that it was powerful, and although feminism has changed from those heady days into something quite different that was one of the major formative periods of my life.

One minute we were treading all over our pretty little selves to get ourselves a man. The next we were linking arms on the sidewalk, and the men were just out of it. It was like a honeymoon. Women shared practically everything there was to share. We talked about religion, fantasies, orgasms, men, jobs, politics, children, art . . . The feeling was that we women cared for each other enough to be generous with ourselves. We all gave a lot, and while things have changed – they had to – there isn't any of it that I

18

regret. It taught me more about how to be human than anything else I've ever been involved with.

I feel women have returned to being more guarded now, but I don't see that as a defeat. I think we feel that the honeymoon is over and the rest of the work is now to be done.

There was definitely a period in the seventies when women were conscious of this honeymoon period. There was also no doubt that men were left on the sidelines – but all four women agreed that it was not planned or plotted like that.

Feminism has certainly been a panacea for a certain kind of loneliness. It is the loneliness which, for a woman, comes partly from the fact that the world is not her own and partly from the fact that, although she was raised to think of man as filling this gap in life, he mainly doesn't. Feminism dispensed with the former because woman now had a reason for being alive, a validity, a new passport into direct experience with the world; and it dealt with the latter by providing spontaneously a huge pool of sisters. The word is clichéd, but it is an accurate description of the powerful bond that women had found with each other. So the tyranny of needing a man to fulfil daily needs was over. What I call the phallacy had ended. Or so it felt.

From a man's point of view this was a disaster. Woman had left, gone public with her criticisms and complaints, and then, instead of coming home bowed and contrite when she couldn't fill in her tax forms or work the computer, had learned to do this with and from other women! All the while she was smiling – but not for him. So man lost his ally in the worst of circumstances. She left without good enough public reason, denounced him and then flaunted around with *other women*. The keeping of women in separate homes, and the subtle producing of a culture which said that women were enemies of each other in the competitive enterprise of catching a man – and would scratch each other's eyes out to do so – was blown.

Women discussed all this. That's how they found it out. They used the women's room to talk with each other, and through this interchange of ideas and experiences developed an overview of women's lives and a powerful feeling of identification. Man, however, was outside all this, and often barred from entering because meetings were 'women only'. He had been accustomed to being in charge of the agenda for most meetings, whether business, sexual or domestic. Now he didn't know what the agenda was. As one woman described it, he was 'outside in the cold howling at the moon'.

2
Knock, Knock,
Who's There?

When I interviewed and talked with men on the subject of feminism many of them said they felt initially bewildered about what exactly it was, and what it was trying to achieve. The feeling of not even knowing what the feminist agenda looked like was described by a comedy scriptwriter in his late thirties:

One minute life was jogging along as usual, and the next there was a note on the table saying: 'Get your own supper. PS: The fridge is empty.' I knew something was up, but I couldn't for the life of me work out what.

I'd only just begun to get the hang of women anyway. My ex-wife would testify to that dreadful state of affairs. Then suddenly all the rules changed. Just like that. I had just worked out that women were people, like men – or at least not like men, but much nicer. I had got to the stage of knowing that if I swallowed my nervousness and treated women well they would be friends with me – and then all the old rules flew out of the window. I'd always led a perilous existence, but for fully a decade from about the mid-seventies to the mid-eighties I wandered round in a state of complete bemusement.

I mean, are you going to be offended if I offer to pay for this lunch? Are you going to think me a mean, stingy wimp if I don't offer to pay? Should we go dutch? Do I leave it to you to decide? Or do I make the decision? In the old days – it seems like centuries ago – these things were clear, and everything else followed on from them. Including sex . . .

Right now a man and a woman getting into bed with each other is a major triumph accomplished via dozens of landmines of social and sexual manners. Am I supposed to make the first move? Is she? If she fancies me and I *don't* make a move will I be branded frigid? And will she tell all her mates?

Yes, we're in the era of the frigid male, you know. At least we've been through it – I hope it's past now. Some of us were frigid with fear of doing the wrong thing, and some of us were so pissed off with women we stayed rigidly in the bar at night and hoped it would all have blown over by the time we staggered home.

Then you had medical manners, of course. There's AIDS to think about. Should I go to the hospital and get myself a health certificate? Or will that in itself look suspicious? Joking aside, it hasn't occurred to me to ask a woman about AIDS – but I've been asked twice. It doesn't feel very nice. But why should all this be left to women? On the other hand, I can hardly ask a woman who she's slept with lately.

I asked this man to go back to what it felt like in the early days of feminism. Had he felt threatened? He replied:

Not threatened, but totally confused. Though I wouldn't have been surprised to have switched on the radio one morning and found out that men had been declared redundant. You know – something like 'Downing Street announced this morning that the country has no further use for men. Would all chaps who are not gas fitters, milkmen or brain surgeons please report for recycling.' They could have made cat food out of some of us and cardboard boxes out of the rest – though half of us are only cardboard boxes in disguise anyway. If you take the lid off us you won't find anything inside, I promise you. We're empty.

When asked to explain this in more serious terms he said:

Men don't live inside themselves. They live outside. This explains their domestic habits – or lack of them. They always have to be out – at the office or in the pub. They don't like being cooped up at home because the domestic bits of them – things like emotions and feelings – they don't look at. It's almost as if they declare all that invisible, or believe that it will become invisible if they never pay any attention to it. Like a whining child. If you ignore him he'll vanish sooner or later. So men are like empty cardboard boxes, because what you see on the surface is all that most of them are.

I asked a large number of men the question: 'What does it feel like to be a man?' Many couldn't answer, and some gave replies which avoided dealing with feelings at all. But some answered fully, and one of these, a journalist in his early forties, drew a verbal map of his perceptions of male psychology. What he described was the result of many years of observing and talking with men.

Men find it difficult to answer the question 'What does it feel like to be a man?' because they haven't indulged what it feels like. They don't pay attention to the emotional life, so they don't actually *know* what they feel like. Men are a mystery to themselves – and therefore to women too.

One of the commonest requests women make of men – of husbands and partners – is: 'Talk to me,' meaning 'Tell me who you are and what it is you feel now and then.' He's completely mystified by this. He's told her what happened at the office, that he's going to play golf tomorrow, that he's fixed up the overdraft. What the hell is she talking about? He can't tell her, because he doesn't know himself!

One of the binds that brings this about is the seriousness with which men are obliged to regard themselves, their work and their careers from very early on. Young women by contrast have always had at the back of their minds the idea that there's an option. They might work or they might get married or they might have children. Men, even if they're going to become husbands and fathers, don't have the *option* of not working.

Because men's views of the world and themselves harden up so early they're very blinkered when it comes to discussing choices, roles, who they are and so on. It's like the army – it's as if they're conscripted by this thing called masculinity, which is a life sentence. They get very alarmed indeed at the idea of choice and wondering who they are – they're armour-plated by the time they start work.

And one of the reasons why women have this problem understanding men or talking with them is that men don't even have a language about their emotional lives. They've never afforded themselves it, which is what makes them such reactionaries emotionally.

When you put this together with one of the most prominent male fantasies – that the fully functioning male is self-sufficient and doesn't need anyone – you've got an idea of the problem. The greatest male fantasy is that of his own self-sufficiency. He can break other men – men and mountains. This is what makes him so isolated. It's what makes him so unreachable and makes the people around him so lonely.

This feeling of loneliness in the presence of men is one that many women have talked about. It is why the emotionally supportive content of feminism, the warmth and openness, was so important: it

22

gives women something they weren't used to having from most adult relationships. One woman described how she came to view her husband – they were both in their mid-forties – as a closed door with a room on the other side which she never entered.

> He was tall like a door, and I had an almost irresistible urge to knock on the letterbox – his mouth – and say: 'I'm sorry to disturb you like this, but please may I come in?' A kind of 'Knock, knock, who's there?' approach. It was very physical. I didn't exactly want to ask him to speak to me – though he seldom did – but more to *show* me, to show me round. He didn't. He remained a mystery to me until we parted.

The man who rarely spoke was accepted for generations as the outcome of hard work and the superior position of the male: 'Don't trouble your father. He's had a hard day,' combined with 'He's obviously having an Important Thought and I mustn't nag him.' Present-day knowledge acquired through psychology, psychiatry and general medicine tells us that the taciturn man is not a healthy, superior model but an emotionally anaemic one.

This dilution or repression of man's vitality was described by the journalist whom I interviewed as resulting from a combination of three influences. The first he called the 'shoulds' and 'oughts' of masculinity – the things that a man supposedly has to do in order to be manly. The second is 'the fixed script of masculinity', which is tied in with the 'shoulds' and 'oughts'. It is a set of rules that men are supposed to follow in order to fit in with other men. The third is the way man has to make up or invent another kind of script as he goes along. This last script is the personal one, the one which would make him an individual if he could discover and develop it. It is his emotional identity.

But the absence of a personal, male guide in the form of a communicative, warm father confounds men in their search for personal identity. So for safety and a false sense of security they stick together in a collective personality which is a caricature of masculinity.

> The whole business of *becoming* a man is so difficult because there's so little to go on. Fathers, traditionally, are absentee parents in so far as they don't preside over the formative years. And even when they are about the home they're so low on self-disclosure that their sons have a hell of a hard time working out what a man is.

There's so little emotional substance to go on. All you get are directives like: 'Act like a man.'

Maleness is a school of acting. You learn the way men laugh, or tap their pipes out on the heel of their shoes, or rattle their keys in their trouser pockets when they're talking with other men. So, to become a man all you can really do is copy all this male behaviour. Otherwise, you simply have to make yourself up as you go along. Taking no reference from what you feel, you subscribe merely to an *idea* of what you are and should be.

The 'shoulds' and 'oughts' of masculinity are fantastically powerful, whether you're talking about machismo or what a proper man should do. So the man sees himself as having a fixed script, but the woman doesn't see herself like that at all. She's now ready for something else, and some of the most exciting women I know are like this: 'I'll take on the whole bloody world now!' Then they find themselves married to men whose views are amazingly conservative – who, when the matters of choice and options come up, actually think: 'What on earth are they talking about?'

As regards marriage, men aren't self-sufficient either in terms of making a home of the environment they live in – they're too lonely for that – or in providing for themselves in ways like cooking nutritious meals. So they need an emotional and practical support, and the woman performs this function for them. It's like the man who behaves professionally in a way that isn't too moral, but he gets his repair from his wife. Which doesn't make him a moral person. It just winds him up to go and do it all over again.

These remarks contain echoes of Gitta Sereny's interview with Teresa Stangl – the idea that an immoral man relies upon the domestic and emotional services of a woman, and might capitulate without them. He continued:

Basically women have to call men out, to challenge them, to let them know that men must find their own moral centre. Women have to do it because men will do terrible things unless women call them to order and let them know that they will not treat with beasts.

One of the roles men have relied upon in women is their virtually uncritical support. That's the inequality of the relationship. That's what makes tarts and creeps of women. They will flatter the brute, accommodate the beast, congratulate and repair the bastard. It's difficult for women, because the hardest thing in the world is to discover that you are treating humanly with someone who is a brute.

Women really work as field hospitals to keep this type of man functioning. Men require women to make it better for them, to make it possible for them to carry on. And they think it's their due that women should do this – should make their dreary lives bearable.

Did you know that the unhealthiest person in society is a bachelor? They die younger, go madder. The healthiest is the spinster. A woman is actually worse off when she's married, and a man is better off – which I think says something about the bad state he was in in the first place. He's not self-sustaining, he's not self-sufficient. He requires a life support.

Women work as emotional batteries for men. Men think that's what they're there for. 'Don't you dare to presume to have problems of your own – your function is to make *me* feel good!'

A man does this out of bloody-mindedness as well. There's rage attached to it, and here I tend to get a bit Freudian. In the main – emotionally, certainly – men are their mothers' sons, and in order to become a 'proper' man you have to put your blinkers on and push all that behind you.

That puts young men in a very parlous state, emotionally and healthwise. You still require the old attention that your mother gave you in the first place to keep you going, to back you up – and you try and find it in females of your own age.

There's that moment in the street when you're ever so pleased to see your mum – and then next week when your balls have dropped, or you learn how to spit, you're fantastically embarrassed by her. You don't want to see her, because all that has to be put behind you. A man will tell you about that period of embarrassment if you ask him outright. It's the moment when he decides to go the other way, when he decides to become a *man* rather than just another human being.

In doing all that men are not only putting down the female outside, they're also putting down the female within themselves. So ask a man the question 'How do you feel?' and he doesn't know, for in the script it says you must shut down.

This shutting down and denying the mother deprives men of their emotional stock – both literally and metaphorically. Instead of emerging from the primordial soup of early childhood fortified by their experiences and influences, men shake them off. This brings about emotional anaemia. The attempt to cut off from their beginnings causes the loss of a vital blood flow, which constricts the heart. In psychological terms this fresh blood keeps the veins and arteries of self-knowledge, vitality and repair going. It is essential to an emotionally healthy, vigorous person – without it the arteries close up and premature ageing, stiffening and pain set in.

This is the condition of the male ego: a heavy-handed, tyrannical apparatus set up by the ailing male to try and get by, to try and carry on. This is why the ego is damaging. In order to make itself bigger and more important it squeezes hearts so that they can't function properly. It sets itself up in opposition to the 'child', to the essential emotional stock of childhood.

The journalist went on:

You don't deny your own feelings, as men are supposed to in order to shape up to life properly, without doing yourself out of emotional faculties. Men render themselves emotionally stupid. The masculine script does that to them. It's why manliness itself remains a core mystery. There's a kind of hole at the centre, where the heart should be.

Men don't develop the emotional equipment, not only to recognize themselves, but to recognize other people and what's going on. They understand what's happening literally – they know what's going on in the newspapers. But they don't know what's going on aside from, underneath, around that. Most of the time they're mystified, so unless they take charge of a conversation and there's lots of women listening and nodding to what they're saying, they're totally baffled. Men lack emotional intelligence. After a dinner party, for instance, the man will have understood all the stories, all the jokes, but for the major plot – what was actually happening between the people there – he'll have to ask his wife.

Men don't understand nuance and intuition and what *real* humour's about. It's why men tell jokes – formal jokes. Laughter is the one emotion men allow themselves freely enough, but even laughter has to be socially coded into jokes. It's part of camaraderie. That's not the same as friendship. Friendship exists for its own sake. But camaraderie always has an ulterior motive: winning the war, beating the other firm, smashing up the away team's supporters. Likewise jokes are ritualized because the chief point of male camaraderie is to celebrate maleness. Young men especially enjoy yarns about Great Blokes who are never actually present – those mythic, ideal men who drink more, screw more,

26

earn more. It's a religion – probably based on longing and on absentee fathers. It's lonely in there, inside a man. Which is why cameraderie is essential. It's a buttress against the loneliness. Hear the hollow laughter, the jingle of the car keys in the trouser pockets. It's so *desperate*. It's a kind of emotional homelessness. It probably explains why men remarry far quicker than women do.

Men are emotionally damaged, yet they still think they're the principal characters and that they're entitled to go about indulging themselves as they see fit – when actually what they are doing at this point is only paying attention to anguish. They're responding to the anguish caused by them having done this damage to their emotional selves by saying no to it, and by kicking the whole ragbag of feelings into touch.

All this means they're emotionally unavailable, but they need their anguish seeing to. One of the responses you'll get if you ask a man what he feels is that he'll go crying all over a woman's shoulder because he needs her to put it right for him.

At a conference called Men Too, organized in the mid-eighties by the Family Planning Association to try to involve more men – and men more – in the area of emotions and sexual responsibility, I ran, jointly with a male colleague, a workshop called Men, Sex and Relationships. The men who participated said it wasn't that they didn't discuss emotions and sexuality at all – they just didn't discuss them with other men; they *did* discuss them with women. The men in the group saw this as a vindication; the women didn't. One woman said: 'I'm sick of men hiding behind this. Men can go on discussing themselves with women and using women to dump on without ever changing a single thing about themselves. Until men discuss these things with other men, nothing will change. Men will continue to behave as if emotions are not really a part of them and only "happen" on special occasions.'

What no one discussed that day was that emotional servicing needs to be a two-way process. The journalist whom I interviewed commented:

While men feel free to look for instant therapy, they can't provide the same service in return. They can't help women. They can't listen to women, for the moment they listen to someone else resonating it churns up all this damaged, neglected emotional life that men have got. It makes them sick, mad, drunk. They're terrified.

It's very unhappy because the fiction on top of all this self-denial, this sickness, this emotional stupidity is the myth that basically there is nothing wrong with men. They won't have it. They'll kill, murder, rape, rob, think of people in terms of profit and as objects. That's men's crime. It's a crime to regard yourself and others with so little pity. But they've gone past the point of pity – they've neglected themselves for too long.

My experience is that if a man comes to have a drink and a joke with me I'll see him again within a month. If he comes and talks about how he feels and tells me about himself I won't see him again for six months. He can't bear the vulnerability. He's terrified I'll use it against him.

Phillip Hodson and Antony Easthope have both written of the man who has no friends in other men because he doesn't make the emotional connections with people of his own sex in the way that women do. The women at the Men Too workshop expressed similar opinions. The men that day did not discuss sexuality at all, either among themselves or in larger groups. This fear of public disclosure, even in a one-to-one situation, is mirrored in man's behaviour in bed. The journalist analysed it like this:

It's to do with control. It's to do with who's in charge. It's to do with his sense of prowess and his duty to be the one who provides the performance, who provides the enjoyment, who provides the orgasms. He's the mechanical partner, and he remains mechanical because he won't relinquish control. It's why men don't have orgasms.

I've taken a bit of stick from time to time for maintaining that men don't actually have orgasms. The stick has chiefly been dished out by the sort of lazy women who have a vested interest in men remaining as they are. They don't want the whistle blown. It is, after all, daring a man's whole emotional repertoire for him to have an orgasm and not just an ejaculation. The sexual act, the idea of joining in, the idea of passion and of entertaining your own sexual feelings for long enough and broadly enough to achieve orgasm – a man has to *dare* to do this.

He's very literal, you see. If you move yourself so thoroughly into your own ego not only can you not join with another person, but the other part of that tragedy is that you're denying yourself the whole emotional repertoire. The maintenance of the ego is the denial of emotion. It brings about sex in the head. Christ, it's all up there!

KNOCK, KNOCK, WHO'S THERE?

Any man who's witnessed the female orgasm couldn't possibly maintain that what he experiences is in the same league. The graph of the female orgasm goes on and on like a sea swell. The man's – well, there's this little spike on the graph. And maybe because the male orgasm is so comparatively limited explains why men go bunny-rabbiting around still. Us chaps, we buy all this superdong mythology and we have orgasms which rate alongside the average Chinese takeaway.

But you can't have what you can't feel. Is all.

A female teacher whom I interviewed in the early eighties for a magazine article about women and sexuality described how fed up she was with being asked by her partner if she had had an orgasm yet. She said: 'First of all I thought he was putting pressure on me and blaming me for being slow. Then I realized he wanted me to have an orgasm to make *him* feel better. He wanted to know that what he was doing was right, that it worked. It was a mixture of a desire to please – to be sexually heroic, if you like – and a desire to have his ego fed by the knowledge that he was a good lover.'

The journalist I interviewed expressed man's resistance to the good aspects of feminism in a different way:

It's hard for him to take on something as new and riddled with choice as feminism. He hasn't yet learned that living with an equal partner is far less of a strain than living with someone he views as an inferior. The fear in bed, and out of it, is deeper than the fear of failure. It's fear of the disintegration of ego, of the abandonment of ego, and abandonment of the upper hand in terms of what he regards as the proper relationship of him being a man and her being a woman.

In Britain this is getting worse because we're in an economic decline and everyone is looking inward. I don't mean inward in a healthily introspective sense. I mean inward in that we've become greedy and turned inwards like in-growing toenails. Which is why Thatcherism is so successful, in that it appeals to individual fear and greed as opposed to what we might be as a community.

In these circumstances the old male things can reassert themselves: 'If I don't get on and do it, if I don't get out and do unto the next man and all the rest of it, I'll go to the wall and so will my family.' That legitimates any greedy or immoral behaviour, because we now live in fear in a way that we didn't when the economy was more expansive and we had an idea of the promise of the future. I grew up in a time when there was no question you would have a job. A job was something you could have for ever if you applied yourself. Now all that's shattered.

And in a curious way that's especially critical for men, since the work ethic is so inextricably tied up with a man's idea of himself. So with everyone's heart contracting from fear it's harder and harder to know about the emotional life of a man. He's even more closed down than he was fifteen years ago when we weren't living in such a terrified culture. Man's emotional life is a no man's land. The man doesn't live there – or if he does he's not very conscious of his feelings – and if he does become conscious he knows it's his duty to shut down against them. So men can't tell you about themselves because it actually feels quite hollow in there. Most people don't realize what a contrived fiction being a man is.

For many men this fiction results in a sense of unreality, which can be summed up in the cliché: 'Life passed me by.' That's why some people have viewed men strangely – as emotional deserts, doors, and empty cardboard boxes. But there are terrifying consequences in acting out of what is almost an emotional vacuum. For if the man himself doesn't feel, or at least doesn't allow himself to feel, then he doesn't understand feelings in others. He therefore cannot guard against wide-scale pain and destruction.

The journalist took up this point:

What isn't a fiction is the results of this madness, this despair, this lack of pity. Because men paralyse themselves they then have to paralyse others.

The bomb already paralyses people's aspirations, their capacity to function. That's the extent men have gone to to overwhelm life, because they regard natural life – as opposed to order – as male-threatening chaos. So they've come up with their own threat to sort out all of that.

That's why it's the ultimate weapon. Because we can't even breathe in and out. We can't ask questions about who we are or how we are with that menace there.

It's always been there. They used to call it hellfire and damnation. And that was a function of male psychology, too – the idea of damnation. Now we've created that damnation ourselves.

As for what can be done, it's up to woman in a sense – although you have to be careful when you say that because you can't assume it's your responsibility to re-engineer and rework another person. Women are always trying to do that.

30

KNOCK, KNOCK, WHO'S THERE?

One of the classic things they do is that they marry men as if they're raw material and can be shaped and modelled to suit thereafter. If a man won't do it on his own account – if he won't make a decent human being of himself – a woman tries to civilize him. Women try to make men take an interest in marriage, togetherness, children, fathering, society. But men put themselves outside of that.

A low opinion of male behaviour was one of the overwhelming themes that cropped up when I interviewed men. This is the sense in which women have been on the upbeat during the seventies and eighties and men on the down. Women felt differently about female behaviour: they thought women had grown and developed during this time. But many men are still acting in the dark.
The journalist ended up:

It's terribly difficult – because until men understand what they're doing they can't face up to it. And until they face up to it they can't change it.
Basically men compartmentalize their lives so they don't see the other bits. They never have the whole picture in view. It needs this to happen before men and women can wrest a more human exchange with each other. At the moment it's difficult not to look at a man and see someone who's so self-caricaturing that you can't deal with him humanly. It's very difficult dealing with someone for whom the scripts are that fixed. How do you challenge him?
But I think we're getting to the stage when some men are beginning to understand that the whole thing is also unfair on them – on us. It's not only unfair on women that they can't have responsive, emotionally adult partners – it's also unfair on men. It's unfair on *ourselves* not to be responsible and emotionally viable. We miss out on so much that could enliven and – yes – entertain us. But, lacking pity for ourselves as much as we do for others, we don't dare imagine this is our due. We give ourselves a hard time. That's the script. It's why the map of manhood is so hard to dig up.

3
The God-Father Myth

The map of mankind is deeply rooted in history and myth. It is particularly rooted in something which, for want of a better term, I have called fundamentalism, or biblical attitudes. I use the words to describe a certain kind of biblical interpretation which treats Old Testament myths literally, using them to downgrade women and to reinforce a crime-and-punishment mentality. This mentality views the Garden of Eden story as proof that woman is a temptress, that man is weak, and that punishment is necessary to combat human nature.

Since the majority of people do not read the Bible frequently, let alone on a daily basis, it is tempting to imagine that Old Testament folklore went out with the Ark. But notions of justice, for instance, are still biblically based. Unless witnesses in court state they are non-believers, they are asked to swear on a Bible before Almighty God that they will tell not only the truth, but the whole truth. A barrister whom I asked about this said that very few people choose to affirm in court rather than swear in the traditional way.

Biblical psychology, however, runs far deeper than courtroom etiquette. Without realizing it, we accept, like breathing, that human nature is essentially flawed. We accept 'dog will eat dog', and that the base side of us means we can't help being destructive and essentially selfish. We make headlines out of people who aren't: Mother Teresa of Calcutta is a notable example. We also accept, like breathing, that life has become complex and that there is little we can do about issues like unemployment and over-industrialization.

My argument is that the retention of Old Testament values led us into this labyrinth, while modern influences – like so-called sexual licence – get the blame. The Old Testament is not, as we believe, dead. We ingest it with our daily bread.

But even before the Bible was written, something between women and men had already created a gender imbalance. Why did man get the upper hand in the first place? Certain feminist writers such as Marilyn French have postulated envy as the reply; not woman's envy of man's penis, as Freud wrote, but man's envy of woman's child-bearing capacities and his fear that, without tying himself to one woman, he would not know who his children were. In other words, man became the dominant sex in order to redress a balance in which it seemed that *woman* was favoured.

She was favoured because she could not only produce what he couldn't – a child – but she could also feed her children. The drawback was that, while pregnant and breast-feeding, woman was less agile than man. So a system evolved by which the woman stayed at home and the man went afield, hunting and exploring. She provided milk for the babies; he provided meat for her. This system has been referred to as matricentric. Looked at practically, woman was the centre and man went round her – she the pivot, he the compass point.

In giving birth, the woman's body was responsible for what we still consider to be the highest form of production. While in monetary terms a far higher value is placed today on a Ming vase or a Van Gogh painting than on a human life, these do not have the power of recreating others of their kind.

Since through mating with a man woman is responsible for the higher form of production, it is a startling fact that in human history someone else has laid claim to an even higher achievement. That 'person' is God – or, to be precise, man in God's name. For man has claimed, through fundamentalist interpretation of the Bible, that the great mother is male.

Even in the light of Old Testament, creationist ideas that the world was *made*, why is the maker male? Why not female, or a 'marriage' of both female and male? And a creator of *either* sex is of course an extraordinary concept in the light of Darwin's theory that the earth and its creatures have evolved over millions of centuries. It is also an extraordinary claim in the minds of feminist writers – some of them practising Christians. In their book *Dispossessed Daughters of Eve*, Susan Dowell and Linda Hurcombe argue against what they call the sexist, patriarchal notion of a male God. For them, true Christianity involves an acceptance and integration of female and male qualities. Eve was not a temptress, and neither are her modern counterparts in the shape of women, who are all her gender daughters. The authors argue that those who oppose the ordination of women still think of the female sex as less spiritually acceptable and reputable than males, and that this in itself is unacceptable and disreputable.

Man has claimed that God produced the first man and woman, thereby beginning the human race, and that as our developmental 'womb' He gave us earth while He resided in the infinity of Heaven. This God took life as we know it – life as given by woman – away from us. He said that it was only short, and fraught with trials and tribulations; it was a preparation, a test, for His life, one that would last for ever. So the life given by woman is one of woe, and that offered by man through God is a life of bliss in a place called Heaven.

You render the mother secondary if you construct a male, invisible God and a series of rules which say that man is superior to woman and must be obeyed, in the name of the male God. She may produce life and feed us; He actually started all of life. She may feed from the breast; He feeds from the sky. She may have milk; He created the whole world and all the plants and animals – food far more varied than hers. He even created *her*, and therefore supersedes the inalienable truth that all people are born of women.

The mother may influence her children, especially since they recognize her; He influences everyone, and demands even more than simple recognition, for in being invisible He requires the bonding of faith. She has the power of rejecting a child or a man if she is angry; He has the power not only to be angry, but to decide at the day of judgement who shall enjoy the kind of life she cannot offer – eternity. She is the gateway to finite life on earth; He to the infinite Kingdom of Heaven. She may be crossed or blamed; He may not. Nor indeed may He be questioned, for He has the ultimate diplomatic immunity – invisibility.

If you must go one better than a potent mother, an omnipotent father is a force to be reckoned with. Many other creations were possible if it was purely a myth that was needed: fairy stories are full of them. There could have been a genie or a giant – even an animal, either real or invented; there could have been a queen fairy, an exacting witch, a sleeping beauty or an omnipotent mother. Since women were life-producers, what more natural than to extend the existing role of the mother into myth? And what more natural, as the biblical story stands, than that she should give birth to Christ?

Had only a mythic figure been needed, then it would have been slightly more relevant and pertinent to accept a giant mother than a creationist father. If the earthly male wanted to restore the balance of the female's superior powers, then a mythic father makes sense.

However, if that had been the intention the story would have been differently written. Omnipotent father as balance to potent mother is already weighting the scales. A male deity, with a male son, male disciples, male scribes, male Pope and male Church hierarchy, is not balance but paranoia.

It would seem that the reason for such an order must have been utter determination, dire need, to better the visibly believable mother.

With God the Father belief rests, and has to rest, in his *in*visibility, for there would be no test of faith if this were not the case; and without the test of faith – the test of believing in what you cannot see – where would the Christian religion be? We need to believe in God the Father not *despite* the fact that we cannot see Him, but *because* of it.

The story of God the Father as written also depended on something else – our readiness to believe in the existence of Hell. If it were not for the notion of Hell the God-figure would not have worked, for we could have taken the promise of Heaven with a pinch of salt if we had felt like it and gone our own ways. The prospect of a share in the sky was appealing, but would not have been sufficient inducement for most people radically to alter their lives on earth for the promise of possibly attaining it. In order to accept a God-figure people needed the goad of fear and punishment, and it was given.

So two major ideas were brought into existence, Heaven and Hell, the twin opposites of bliss and eternal damnation. These 'places' were also at opposite ends of the universe, Heaven being a movement upwards into the skies and Hell a movement downwards into the bowels of the earth. These constructs were postulated long before people realized that the universe is not shaped like a big box, with a top, a bottom and finite sides.

Heaven and Hell then led on to other things. Once the set of opposites had been created, a whole lot of others tumbled into being. The ones that related to male and female followed on directly from the idea of Heaven as a male province and earth as a female one. They looked like this: God and Mother Nature, intellect and body, master and servant, clean and unclean, strong and weak, ordained and unordained, absent and present, invisible and visible.

These polarities contained the seeds of an earthly division as stark as the one between Heaven and Hell. This was the split between culture and nature. Culture is used here as a way of describing the predominant shape and trends of a civilization – not the high culture of music, art and literature. It is worth noting that the word 'civilization' carries the meaning of putting something in order – which is what civilizations have done to nature.

The divide between culture and nature says that man as a thinking person must order and subdue the chaos of the natural world. He built factories, invented cars and aeroplanes, and cleared forests so as to build roads and houses. For a while this was not a problem, since nature was abundant. But the earth has now been asset-stripped to such an extent that the human race itself is endangered from problems like acid rain, lead pollution and Agent Orange, to name but a few. Culture got the upper hand through not keeping a balance between technology and nature.

In a similar way man has used his intellect to suppress his own personal nature – by keeping a lid on his emotions. He has also done this in the past to woman, for the split between male and female has associated male with culture and female with nature. This division was scripture's legacy. As the female person was called less important than the male in the Old Testament, so her macrocosmic counterpart, Mother Nature, was also seen as less important, as existing only to be ruled over by man. The danger today lies in over-reacting to this interpretation by calling all culture bad and all nature good. What is needed instead is a 'marriage' between the two, so that the needs of both are considered and balanced.

The divisions between male and female that have come to be accepted from the fundamentalist viewpoint mirror the creation of opposites that Christianity imposed, with a male God in Heaven up above and a female mortal down below on earth, subconsciously thought of as the possible gateway to the Hell of even further down below. Our first model for this is the Bible's first woman, Eve.

It was Eve's curiosity which brought down the wrath of God and banishment from what is described as the bliss of ignorance and the Garden of Eden. While Adam was banished too, as the guilty partner, in the way the story was written and handed down it is Eve who was the main perpetrator. Adam was more a victim than an equal party to the deed. However, a woman who is not curious, who does not seek knowledge but instead bears her lot without questioning it, is the Virgin Mary, chosen for her meekness and purity.

These two major biblical figures bring us very nearly the dichotomy of the virgin and the whore, for although Eve is not whore, she is temptress, and the intellectual steps between the two are short ones. Mary, mother of Jesus, is chaste; she brings us culture's or scripture's son, and through Him offers us the entrance to eternity. Eve, mother of the whole human race, is a fallen woman of a kind. We all have to follow her as, steeped in original sin, we hope to expiate ourselves through good deeds and regain the paradise our forebears lost us.

The virgin/whore dichotomy is important in that it contains woman in a split mould, which the Bible strongly supports by giving us two starkly different pictures of women in Mary and Eve. But real life is not like this. Women are neither pure as driven snow nor damningly lascivious in their search for sex or knowledge. In her book *Pornography and Silence* Susan Griffin gives this false biblical picture another twist.

To her, pornography is not mainly about nasty pictures but about deep-rooted attitudes, many of them derived from the scriptures. She traces these attitudes back to the Church Elders, who viewed sexuality as dirty. It is this that she describes as pornographic, because it splits body and mind and prevents the integration that is necessary for good, healthy attitudes. The other false tension is in romantic fiction, in which the woman's resistance has to be built up, then broken down: not a million miles removed from the idea of rape.

Griffin's definition of the pornographic mind is one that sees sin in the faces of young children, dirtiness in human bodies and division within each person. She describes how this kind of mind relies upon division in order to gain both the impetus and the control that it needs. The division is between culture as an institution and nature as an equally unavoidable institution or fact of life. 'The pornographer's triumph . . .', she writes, 'occurs when he turns the virgin into a whore.'[1] In other words, considering that women are neither all virgin nor all whore, the pornographic mind is at its craftiest not only in making women appear so, but in turning them from one into the other. As a result, instead of two separate categories of women – which in itself is bad enough – it creates a single category: the virgin who has no way out of virginity except into whoredom. In other words, once a woman becomes sexual, she is automatically bad.

The Old Testament took the first steps towards this conflation of female nature with Eve, because she was the original virgin. Then she became a temptress and a fallen woman. Eve long predates Mary in biblical history, and was not born of another woman but made by God Himself. Yet the mother of the human race is not worshipped, because unlike the mother of God's son she fell from grace. It is from Eve that we are tainted with suffering, the pain of childbirth, the sweat of daily labouring and original sin. Every child born into the world is doomed because of her, but may regain paradise by following culture – or to be precise scripture – rather than nature. In her book *Thou Shalt Not Be Aware* Dr Alice Miller questions Eve's fall from grace: 'What kind of Paradise is it in which it is forbidden – under threat of loss of love and of abandonment, of feeling guilty and ashamed – to eat from the Tree of Knowledge, i.e., to ask questions and seek answers to them? Why should it be wicked to want to know what is happening, to want to orient oneself in the world?'[2]

The biblical distortion of women was uncovered in feminist works like Mary Daly's *Beyond God the Father* and Susan Dowell and Linda Hurcombe's *Dispossessed Daughters of Eve*. But the full-scale creation of a system of opposites also distorted man. For while man gave himself the dominant position, supposedly thereby bettering himself, the combination of trying simultaneously to live up to it and to contain woman in a position of obeisance has taken a heavy toll.

The Old Testament division between God and Satan or good and evil not only created the arena for the battle of the sexes, but also created the inner arena for perpetual conflict between good and bad. Instead of being born pure and trusting our God had us born into original sin, guilty until we proved ourselves otherwise through good deeds or self-denial – or preferably both. The possibility of self-exploration and understanding was thwarted here, at birth, by the idea that we could achieve grace only through looking outside ourselves. He made us a microcosm of the fight between good and evil, and as He is in our hearts, so is Satan, ready to pounce and gain control if we are not vigilant.

The Old Testament interpretation of religion says that each human is a war zone engaged in a lifelong battle with the enemy both within and without. War, therefore, is a condition of the human heart as well as a fact of being mortal. The 'battle of the sexes' is the war which most closely shows the links between the enemy without and the enemy within, for in it man and woman fight both the opposite sex without and the opposite – and banished – sex within. For since man and woman have been invested with opposite roles, they have also been invested with opposite qualities. So the meek woman fights not only the strong man opposite her, but the strong person in herself who would have her be more than uni-faceted; the strong man not only grapples with the meek woman, but fights back the tears in himself which are supposedly weak and womanish.

A personal interpretation of this idea was contained in a piece that I wrote for *Cosmopolitan* magazine in 1986. The article was an attempt to describe the process of being conditioned with Old Testament values, as seen through the eyes of a child. The child was myself, and the conditioning was heightened by an upbringing in the East African bush.

There, I wrote, Mother Nature held sway of a kind that she doesn't in the urban environment in which most of us in the western world live. The starkness and dramatic quality of bush life led me to formulate rather unusual ideas, one of which was that God and Mother Nature were husband and wife. The picture I had was of a prototype marriage, which people on earth tried to copy. This explained to me why, in our tiny circle of European friends, people had two children – because God and Mother Nature had two, Adam and Eve. My parents did rather badly here, because I was born a long time before my brother, and he should have been born first. But at least they got the numbers and the genders right in having two of us, one of each sex.

By keeping my ears and eyes open I was always coming across clues to fit my rather outlandish theories. It was, for example, obvious that, as God was more important than Mother Nature, so men were more important than women. The men dished out the orders, and the women obeyed. My father went out to work and had Important Thoughts, while my mother stayed at home doing menial things like looking after us children. This reflected what happened 'up there', where God ordered the whirlwinds, and Mother Nature carried them out.

I also learned that in some way women were less 'good' than men. As I wrote:

> I knew all marriages were made in Heaven. I also understood that women had to be angels to keep them there. This made a fall from grace inevitable, and as one who had fallen from grace many times in a young life I rued the fact that I and other females were not the angels we were intended to be. We couldn't help, it seemed, being naughty girls. Men were different. They were descended in a direct line straight from God and, although they might seem wayward at times, in their case there was obviously a good reason for it, if only we could understand what it was.

This piece of vital information was surprisingly easy to come by. My mother and the woman who lived up the track often talked about how they didn't understand men, and my father sometimes scolded my mother for this lack. 'Look, you just don't understand these things,' he would say as he marched off to have another Important Thought.

My picture of the Big Couple was informed by the spoken and unspoken allusions around me. I was told that you could not question God because He was above such things. Mother Nature, however, was different. If I dared to question my actual father I was told off, but my mother was the long-suffering recipient of a string of daily questions. The contrast between the male and female line became obvious one morning after the violent goings-on of an African night had put paid to my best friend at the time. The baby deer I had hand-raised when she was orphaned after a shooting safari was with us no more. I wrote:

In the lengthy and unwise explanations that followed my anguish-
ed discovery of a bunch of bones where Bambi had once stood no
one came out well, but Mother Nature fared worse than most. The
unacceptable face of nature formed by that macabre cluster on the
ground left a stain on the character of whoever brought about such
things, and it was Mother Nature who picked up the tab.

God was kept out of it. He had far more important things to
worry about than the death by lion or leopard of one deer on a
plain then teeming with wildlife. But he still got the kudos for the
better bits, for of course my friend had gone to the green park in
the sky where all animals live happily ever after.

In their attempts to still my hysteria my parents turned to
simplified accounts of the natural order of things and the food
chain. In other words Mother Nature was red in tooth and claw.
When I was a younger child she had been a sort of Universal
Aunty, like the ladies who met you off planes to make sure you
didn't fall foul of the local amenities. But I was growing up fast!

When you add to the deer's demise the case of seven baby ducks
gone to a marauding mongoose Mother Nature was coming up
scarlet all over the garden. To the sobbing questions: 'Why did it
have to be *my* Bambi and *my* baby ducks?' the answers were
explained via the mysteries of nature and the fact that the natural
world was like that – random of course. In other words, doing
things with no good reason.

So a general impression was cemented. God beamed over all his
good children and Mother Nature was his earthly zoo-keeper and
mucker-out. Thus it was that the dear Mother found in my
countenance something she did not like, an examination of her
actions. Let her expect no gratitude from me for administering a
despotic and capricious order where one is forced to accept
without question what she doles out without reason.

My thinking on the matter was simple and profane. If by Mother
Nature's house rules lions ate defenceless deer and mongooses ate
tiny baby ducks then she wasn't a very nice person. And there was
nothing in my by that time growing rule book which said you had
to obey someone who wasn't very nice. Except Him of course who
was above such mortal questioning.

So mutiny against the bountiful was upon me. My actual mother
began to have a difficult time. If my father told me to do something
I would jump to it. If she did I was sulky and obstinate.

At the end of this article I drew another analogy between God and

Mother Nature, male and female, by discussing the different form and colour that the two have taken on. God is presented either as invisible or, if he has a colour at all, it is a neutral grey or white. Mother Nature is multicoloured. In my childhood men wore sombre colours and women wore bright ones. This further fixed in my mind an impression that men were more serious than women, especially since I sometimes heard brightly decked women called 'hussies' in a we-wouldn't-want-to-be-one-of-those tone of voice. I also felt that men were more interesting than women. Being allowed to go on safari with them was infinitely preferable to cooking lessons at home with mother.

The traditionally visible and invisible qualities of females and males respectively have played a large part in the myth that man is more spiritually respectable than woman. The difference between what is visible and what is invisible is one of form. A religion based on an invisible male and a visible female in Mary, Eve or the natural world states implicitly, whether we choose it or not, that to be female is to be more of the body and to be male is to be more of the spirit. The problems of body-centred woman defined by brain-centred man, of culture riding roughshod over nature, are manifest in control systems which dictate that the head should govern the heart or the torso, that the invisible should govern the visible. When man created an invisible God in his own likeness – a figure invested with man's projections and fantasies – something came about which affects vision itself. For the difference between the body and the head is that the head contains the eyes.

4

The Tyranny of the Eye

For any child fed the traditional Bible stories there are many intimidating things about God. He can see you wherever you are, He can see whatever you are doing, and He can also see inside your head and heart. There is nowhere you can hide to escape His gaze, and no thought you can hide either, because He knows about all of them. This God of the X-ray eyes is so extraordinary that He can see not only millions of people at the same time, but everyone everywhere at all times. This is the God myth, that God is all-seeing.

In *Monuments and Maidens* Marina Warner analyses the kinds of mythic and symbolic women which adorn our banks, public squares, museums and cathedrals. She describes how women are seen rather than seeing, and the objects of desire rather than desiring. Of Pandora and Eve she writes: 'Woman is an occasion of sin and an agent of fatality through the desire she inspires, not experiences',[1] and of Pandora, Eve and Helen of Troy: 'Their identity is perceived through the eyes of others, not their own. This is the condition of beauty and of being the object of desire, a form of profound Otherness that Simone de Beauvoir analysed so inspiringly as the condition of the Second Sex.'[2] In the introduction to her book *The Nude Male* Margaret Walters makes a closely related point: 'The nude athlete, his body moulded by exercise, incarnates virtues that were regarded as distinctively Greek; . . . the Venus exists simply to be looked at – as an object of desire.'[3] Later she argues:

> Many men still seem afraid of being looked at by woman, as if her gaze might have a Medusa-like effect, paralysing and petrifying its object – or perhaps more accurately, softening and weakening it . . . Women are not encouraged to express their sexuality by looking at all . . . There is still a rigid division between the sex that looks and the sex that is looked at. The dichotomy is bound to breed perversion in both sexes: in the man voyeurism, hostility and envy, in the woman masochism, exhibitionism and hypocrisy. Both men and women are deprived and impoverished.[4]

THE TYRANNY OF THE EYE

The masochism in woman takes the form of a de-eyeing (and de-I-ing), so that the tools she was born with – which, if she is to lead a full life, must inform her – are blunted. Until recently, woman did not look the world full in the face. Instead she saw the world through lowered eyelids and obliquely through half gazes. By doing this she not only saw less and only partially, but she also learned to deny what she saw, even when it was clear that things were wrong. She is the guilt-ridden mother who has stood wringing her hands outside bedroom doors while fathers have beaten children sometimes into unconsciousness. She is the wife of the commandant at Treblinka. She has turned a blind eye to the moral outrages that have made up the world in which she lives, and even many times to the bruises on her own face.

The woman on whom the evils of war, greed and destruction have depended is the woman who claims she didn't see anything. She has not been a witness to life for herself or for anyone else because one of her five senses, and the most far-reaching one, has been denied her through received Old Testament prejudice and her own continuing actions. She has been tutored not to inspect the gaze of man, but to present herself for inspection. She has not looked at life, which is why life has in so many ways passed her by.

The filter to her gaze which culture and scripture gave her has sent her into the world physically veiled but morally naked. If wealthy, she has been able to see the world through rose-tinted sentimental spectacles; if poor, she has had to keep her head down and her gaze near. She has often behaved as if she were invisible, as if then she might be spared 'being' at all. She has certainly wished to be spared being accountable, for she would not have known how to cope with the responsibility. As a result, the physical development of the world has been left to someone else, and it is still true that, when presented with things outside themselves – with objects – men are more enquiring about them than women.

Women, on the other hand, are more enquiring about each other. This may have arisen because when one sense faculty is blunted the others frequently become more sensitive and acute in compensation. Woman's abilities to relate may therefore be partly caused by her de-eyeing, as in lowering her gaze from the canvas of the world at large she has concentrated on discovery through the microcosm of close relationships. Women have traditionally been good listeners, and they talk much more than men about the emotional world.

The idea that men and women see the world differently, and that it is difficult for them to see things from the other's point of view, is the product of a system in which one is the viewer and the other the viewed. This concept filtered through to the judicial system, for even though there was no law which said that women could not sit in judgement on others it wasn't until after the Second World War that women became jurors in Britain. Before that one had to be a householder to be eligible to sit on a jury, and in practice householders were men. The law has now been changed in any case – to include, for jury service, all adults barring exceptions like the insane or the incapacitated. But it wasn't until women started becoming householders that they began to gain the right to sit on juries and therefore to 'view' or weigh up evidence. Women have traditionally been 'protected' from seeing so much of the world that a belief that they couldn't be witness to what occurred in it was a natural consequence.

Neither have women been allowed to be witness to deeper issues. The Church has 'allowed' women throughout the ages to have heavenly visions – Teresa of Avila, Thérèse of Lisieux and Hildegard of Bingen, to name but a few – but it has not entitled them to the authority of high office, and therefore to the position of full witness. They are still only sparse in the 'meaning of life' areas like philosophy and the Church hierarchy. Even though the 1988 Lambeth Conference voted to allow women to become Anglican bishops, such was the resistance to this move that a commission was set up to try to limit the 'hurt' it created. The Bishop of London, Dr Graham Leonard, was the author of this concept of hurt, and has declared many times that he would not be 'in communion with' women bishops.

The moral ramifications of woman being visually curtailed can be seen in a convoluted document called *Positive Steps*, issued by London's Metropolitan Police to help women avoid being attacked. In August 1987 the Commissioner of the Met., Mr Peter Imbert, launched this strange document along with a video of the same title. The booklet includes the following advice:

Avoid walking home alone late at night. Don't stop to investigate road incidents. Don't carry housekeys and your means of identity together in your bag. Put your cheque book, correspondence and credit cards into separate coat or trouser pockets. Keep your hands out of your pockets so you're always free to defend yourself. Don't take short cuts. At night, park in a well-lit place. Lock up, putting any valuables in the boot. And when you get back, remember to check the back seat before getting in. Have a good pocket torch handy and the keys ready in your hand for a quick getaway.

THE TYRANNY OF THE EYE

Consider carrying a personal alarm with you.

On travelling and working late:

> Try to arrange a lift rota with a woman friend or someone you know. If you think you're being followed [while driving] try to alert other drivers by flashing your lights and sounding your horn. Or keep driving until you come to a busy place, a police, fire or ambulance station or pub.

According to the *British Crime Survey*, published by the Home Office in 1984, the majority of victims of street attacks are in fact young men below the age of thirty. But as the Fawcett Society, a women's equality group founded in the nineteenth century, wrote to the Home Secretary at the time: 'If a booklet on personal safety was prepared for this section of society [young men] we very much doubt that it would contain advice on keeping to busy, well-lit streets, or not walking home unescorted. Therefore to place restrictions on women's civil liberties seems no proper answer to crime.'

A *Sunday Mirror* reporter saw the video and asked some questions:

> Are we women really supposed to avoid eye contact with strangers? Does this mean there are never to be any more complimentary smiles? We are advised to avoid getting involved in jokey conversations. So when a taxi driver says 'There you go, darlin' ' should we be alarmed? And if a stallholder at the local market tells you cheerfully, 'It's a nice day for it' while doling out two pounds of his best golden delicious should you run or blow your whistle?

When I was researching an article on self-defence for women more than a decade before this was written, police advice was, indeed, to avoid eye contact with strangers. The eyed and de-eyed aspect of the situation was further compounded by the suggestion that you should use your fore and middle fingers to poke an attacker in the eyes. At a self-defence demonstration for women in Manchester I said I didn't feel this was good advice, as I could never imagine being able to do it. I was told it could be done, and was something women must overcome their squeamishness about.

The continuing suggestion that women should avoid normal daily intercourse with the world is not a cynical exercise. Its misguidedness comes from a warp in consciousness, constructed into an invisible God-figure and the resultant male hierarchy, whose rules state that the man must be the gazer and the woman the gazed-upon. By lifting her eyes the woman elevates herself to a position of equal responsibility, and thereby challenges man's moral and sexual supremacy. From the moral standpoint, if she sees the world properly she becomes responsible for what she sees – in other words, she bears witness, and in doing so *becomes* witness. Her challenge to man on a sexual level comes about because his sexual myths have always depended upon her blindness, and because in woman's biblical role as temptress she might, as Margaret Walters states, Medusa-like turn man into stone – or more likely jelly. She might melt his resolve to be strong and steadfast, and lead him into the paths of sexual temptation.

Man greatly fears woman as hypnotist: woman therefore courts disaster through becoming visually equal. It has been said of her that she issues an invitation if she looks at a man, and leads him on by doing so. What *Positive Steps* actually tells us is that a woman may be at risk of being raped if she establishes eye contact with a stranger, and must therefore curb her world view.

Any woman who lives on her own these days knows not to look a strange man in the eye unless the circumstances are relatively safe. Establishing accidental eye contact with a male stranger in a park or in the street *can* on the odd occasion lead to danger. If you go to the police to say that a man followed you home and has been threatening you, you are more likely these days to be heard sympathetically, but you will also be questioned. If you say that you wish to lead an ordinary life and that in the process you said 'Good morning' to this man at the newsagent's round the corner, you will be warned of the dangers of such behaviour. If you say that you are new in the neighbourhood and smiled at this man in the cake shop, you will be told that it is not safe to do so. If you ask what the long-term consequences are of all women treating all unintroduced men as potentially dangerous, you won't get an answer. Crime prevention doesn't reach that far.

In fact the prevention of crime against women, and therefore the blame for a crime being committed when it is, rests in the main with the woman rather than the man. This is particularly clear in the case of rape. There is no doubt that through pressure groups like the Rape Crisis Centres public attitudes towards women who are rape victims have altered. Instead of being regarded with hostility, as if it is their own fault, rape victims are now more likely to be taken seriously. Police attitudes have also altered: the Metropolitan force has set up special rape units at which women who report rape can be treated sympathetically and examined, where possible, by a female doctor.

But the onus of trying to avoid rape still rests with women, and the victim doesn't get public sympathy because she isn't named. Her anonymity has been seen to be essential, yet adult victims of other serious crimes are not anonymous, and receive public sympathy for the injuries perpetrated on them. The perceived need for anonymity results partly from the fear that women will not report rape unless offered this protection; the real reason, however, why women need anonymity is because rape is a crime whose victim suffers humiliation and the risk of being further ill-treated. Many women feel sullied for years by the act of rape and are ashamed.

By contrast, the man who rapes is seldom caught and therefore less frequently blamed or punished. He is once more the invisible factor, and it is only the visible woman who is there to be gently scolded and reminded that she really must keep to the rules. By trying to reduce crime statistics through persuading women to become invisible by staying at home all the time, or through pretending that men are invisible – in other words don't exist – is surely short-sighted. The more absent women are, the more they will be craved and the more conspicuous they will be when present.

Women have been used to being looked at, to parading, and to attracting the attention of men. This is the way they have traditionally found husbands, and it is also the way they have attracted rapists. Women have sat in courts while judges have admonished them for dressing provocatively, for trying to get to know men, or for assuming that the person who offered them a lift home from the party was decent rather than not. The woman who wants a reasonably normal social and business life, and wants also to avoid assault, has a difficult path to steer.

So does the judge – and he, like the woman, sometimes fails, for his ability to be reasonable is sorely tried by a rape case. He knows there is a collusion between man and woman called sex, and it is difficult to separate the symbolic from the particular. While he may avoid the conscious snare of thinking about rape as the updated version of Beauty and the Beast, he may not be able to avoid the unconscious pitfalls. One of these is that no one has a more intimate link with violent man than woman. Peter Sutcliffe, the man whom the press referred to as the Yorkshire Ripper, was married. Ian Brady, while not married, had a long-term relationship with his 'Moors Murderer' girlfriend Myra Hindley. Women have slept with murderers, married them, and in some cases shielded them.

There are twin traps here. First, if woman is being asked to view all unintroduced, and even some introduced, men as possible rapists, then she is being asked to view man as symbol. Man is a symbol of possible violence. If she is fortunate she will be able to transform this symbol, without being its physical victim, into man as lover. But it's asking a lot. Second, if woman is viewed both as temptress and as shielder/lover/mother of violent man, then she colludes with him. In symbolic form she is both his victim and his nurturer.

These two symbols then feed off each other and increase the likelihood of man becoming violent. He will do so if rejected by woman and outcast by her so that he doesn't have normal social intercourse. He will also do so if he lives under the symbol 'violent', for, as woman showed in her pre-feminism days, the weight of symbolism means that a person will fulfil his or her symbolic value. So if woman is told to act on the symbol of man as violent and ignore him, man will become more violent and woman – and man – will become more endangered.

A judge and jury in a rape case need therefore to avoid coming to conclusions based on the protagonists' symbolic rules and act instead on individual details, one of which may be that the woman did not use good judgement in trusting the defendant. Many men think – and the thought is a cause of great annoyance to them – that women are extremely undiscerning, particularly regarding other men. I've frequently heard men say in an exasperated way: 'Women seem to *want* bastards!' While this kind of statement contains an element of men being highly critical of other men, as I suggested in Chapter 2, there is also an element of some women being under-critical.

One of the reasons why intelligent women fall for unreliable or callow partners may well be that, until recently, woman has not been trained to examine man critically, so she is still a poor judge. It is only when she is older and can look back over a number of relationships that she can spot what she's been doing. At the time it's happening, in her twenties, she goes out with a string of unsuitable men, believing every one of them to be wonderful until he clearly proves himself otherwise. Woman *is* still remarkably undiscerning about men in general, their habits, customs, patterns and shades. It is difficult for her to judge between the smooth words of a trickster and the slightly staccato utterances of a decent man who finds the whole business of looking for a partner difficult. But when a woman does find a partner her curtailed field of vision renders her prone to minute criticism. Man in general she might be a bit hazy about, but if she is not careful she will get to all too critical grips with a particular man.

THE TYRANNY OF THE EYE

Although feminism *has* made man squirm under the microscope of general 'manalysis', which has found patriarchy such a can of worms, an individual woman does not go round eyeing man, appraising him and studying him. Her behaviour then traps her. Her purblindness means she doesn't spot danger. Her apparent lack of interest also means she can be thought of as a stuck-up bitch. Caught both ways. Man may then think she needs to be brought down a peg or two – and there is nothing like rape to achieve this.

Woman also runs the risk of being thought either irritatingly obtuse or actually mad, for the form of gaze avoidance which she has practised makes her mistress of the dubious art of being unfocused. Since eye contact with strange men might lead to danger she attempts to avoid looking at them, and so adept have some women become at visually disengaging when a man looms large in their retina that it is like a reflex action. The way such a woman avoids seeing what is directly in front of her can sometimes make her look disturbed – at the very least she is annoying company to be with because she is so unrestful and 'busy'. She makes a lot of agitated movements and gestures, turns her head a lot, flounces her hair, glances sideways and looks round things rather than at them.

The process that Wordsworth called 'the tyranny of the eye' has its counterpart in the oppression of the de-eyed. It is why many women still feel they are invisible if not seen – if not accompanied – by a man, and why they behave in such a mannered way when they are. It is why some women are so visually busy and demanding and so ill at ease when alone in a public place. It is not only the fear of molestation or unwelcome attention, but a form of crippling self-consciousness. This is the eye's corset, the clasp which fastens a woman to the constructs of herself. Trim a woman's vision of the world, give her blinkers, prescribe for her spectacles through which she sees men as twice their normal size, and you have corseted her view of the world so that she becomes her own totem pole, her own fetishist. She will rush up and down herself to make sure not so much that she is all there – for she isn't – but that she is correctly uniformed for inspection.

If an invisible creator encourages people to develop the 'inner eye', to understand that seeing is not necessarily believing, that all which glisters is not gold and that handsome is as handsome does, then the creator has indeed served us well and well might we serve in return. If an invisible creator would have us listen quietly to inner voices, pay attention to dreams and be witness to the richness and importance of inner invisible worlds, then that creator is crucial to us. For without these experiences we are substantially animal and our decay would be unavoidable and eventually unimportant. If an invisible creator is a sign that the human eye is a tool, not a weapon, and that to seek inner beauty and harmony will bring meaning into lives that sometimes seem meaningless, we should not seek to live without such a creator.

However, if it is insisted upon that the invisible creator is only male, and if his scriptures make the kinds of divisions they do between black and white, good and evil, male and female, then through them we inherit and perpetuate a divided world. In this world we may not question an invisible Father – or an absent one – but we certainly blame a visible mother. In this world, too, it is predictable that the man will become the eye – and the I – through which things are judged. There are no better circumstances for looking as long as you like and as hard as you like than invisibility and God-given domain over what is being looked at.

The eye of the beholder is different from the eye of the beheld, for it searches keenly and makes choices in a direct link with the physical world which it orders and designs. As Antony Easthope writes: 'This kind of visual dominance, seeing and knowing everything, comes from a particularly masculine perspective . . . To keep in sight means to keep under control.'[5]

The eye of the woman, however, is the eye of the looked at or the subject, which is why her gaze is often cast downwards. In that saccharine pornography called romantic fiction it is why she looks up at him through lowered eyelashes, and it is why the colour of her eyes is often a surprise to him when, emboldened through mutual passion, they meet full frontal for the first time. You don't need to take your clothes off in romantic fiction, because its main sexual organs are there, visible all the time. His eyes are like organ stops and hers like limpid pools; his probe hers fiercely and hers learn to receive his gaze.

Woman's masochism, exhibitionism and hypocrisy (for, after all, she does *have* eyes to see) are matched by qualities in man which make him an eye-junkie. The eye of the beholder has created visual nightmares called nuclear reactors and inner city slums, and this eye continues to need some kind of satisfaction. The male is so eye-dependent that it is much more difficult for him to trust what he cannot see, for sight and ownership are inextricably linked. His eye-rule of the world in which he has claimed land as far as the eye can see, and the woman next to him, has made him a predator *par excellence*. Whether it is pornography or sitting glued to the TV, he needs a great deal of eye satisfaction. He is certainly, as Margaret Walters states, voyeuristic; hostile, because he exists in a position of domination over his visual surroundings; and envious, because someone has caught him out.

Her name is beauty. She is the most fulsome antidote there is to the idea that invisibility through the God-figure is a superior state. It may even have come to pass that the God-figure has X-ray eyes *because* of her, because man's gaze does not look to recognize, or even to describe, but to dominate.

5

The Enemies of Beauty

In common with many children I often felt sorry for the King Kongs of this world. Although they initially frightened you, as they were meant to, by the time the dénouement came and they shed giant tears over the beautiful woman with whom they invariably fell in love you grieved for the poor creatures. The heated off-screen arguments which followed, about whether they should have killed him or whether he was really just a poor animal, showed how well our young heart-strings had been played on. He had, after all, fallen for beauty, and didn't that make him more than animal?

We never gave much thought to beauty herself, even though a recurring theme of these monster movies was to use her as bait. King Kong might tear down tower blocks and decimate whole cities, but a truly beautiful woman, kind of temperament and loved (usually by a handsome hero), stopped him in his tracks and brought him to his knees (where the CIA could zap him). The unrelieved Hollywood nightmare of it all was the idea of turning beauty into a highly saleable commodity. Even a monster of the magnitude of King Kong could be tamed by her.

It seemed only a few flickers of a television screen later that this important subliminal realization was seized upon fully. If beauty could move the heart-strings of a beast, she could certainly move the purse-strings of a nation. And so she did, and the ad men's dreadful lie of the beautiful-life-out-there swept like a tornado through living rooms. At first beautiful women, and then beautiful men also, became advertising's life-blood, and the consumer society began in earnest with beauty pinned to its mast-head.

Before the industrial revolution man still possessed beauty. Since ancient times the idea of personal beauty, in clothing and adornment, had been shared by both sexes. Nature, in the form of rivers and mountains that had to be crossed, or ferocious weather which had to be endured, was on the whole regarded as a force to contend with rather than a source of beauty. By the late eighteenth century the concept of natural beauty had at last been discovered by the Romantics, but the burgeoning industrial revolution was to be doubly destructive. First it started to take away the beauty of the natural landscape; then men began to dress soberly in dark colours, for practicality, and handed over to women the bright colours and frills and ruffs with which they had hitherto beautified themselves.

But there is another important factor to consider, too, because even before he became a company director rather than a country squire man still held the power of the beholder – he painted woman, which was also his way of defining her. In his book *The Painted Witch* the art critic Edwin Mullins visits some of the western world's major galleries, prompted by Germaine Greer's comment in *The Female Eunuch* that 'Women have very little idea of how much men hate them.' Taking Freud's view that the artist's gift is 'to express as a kind of reality fantasies which in all of us lie repressed', Mullins 'turned to art as the principal historical witness to what men have really felt about women, and . . . tried to elicit what sort of evidence it offers'.[1]

Wearing the bi-focals of his previous vision of art with Greer's vision on top, he found that much of what feminists had been saying was true. The old masters, for example, tell us that a good woman is a non-sexual one, that women are a scapegoat for men's feelings of self-disgust, and that they are vessels outside the male body in which men can dump what they do not want to own themselves. What he describes as 'a banquet of emotions' is portrayed on these canvases – 'love, desire, affection, need, tenderness, admiration, friendship'.[2] But 'quite another set of values is often seen to lie hidden . . . nourished by an emotion generally more pervasive than all others when men have come to paint women. And that is . . . fear.'[3]

That fear is expressed on several levels – at its most extreme it shows women 'as destroyers of men, as voluptuous sacks of evil, helpless fodder for sadists, rapturous victims of martyrdom'.[4] But more frequently it is seen

> as a range of anxieties that are to do with man's estimation of himself as a creature who is strong, dominant, decisive, good, virile, and wise. The accompanying anxieties are about how this vision of himself can be made to hold once he stands alongside his most natural partner, woman. It is in the most elaborate contrivances of art – the posturings, the mythologies, the grandiloquent allegories and sermons – that these anxieties commonly break through; the awareness that alongside woman he may cut a quite different figure, be submissive to her will, morally weakened by her, rendered impotent by her appetites, generally reduced, humbled, even made evil or destroyed, in fact not worth all that

much at all. Hence the over-riding need . . . to corral her, cosset her, control her, reduce her to manageable stereotypes. Viewed from this standpoint, so much art comes to look like magnificent camouflage behind which the dominant sex hides horrible doubts about his fitness to dominate.[5]

Because the male eye was the beholder and the male hand held the brush, man became the arbiter of beauty rather than its follower or disciple. For during the industrial revolution man actually gave away his own beauty and made its recipient or custodian woman. He excised from himself the traditional beauty that was epitomized by the classical Greek male nude and decided he was too busy for all that, especially as industrialization gathered pace. He then became much more acquisitive about beauty. There was work to be done, and all this business about classical thought and looking at sunsets wouldn't build you another factory. But the profits from the factory might buy you another Renoir.

Man was already afraid that his ability to dominate woman was some kind of lie, which through a series of twists he translated into misogyny. He now dumped on her something that his subconscious knew was precious and fearful, but which his conscious mind regarded as a luxury – beauty. In transforming the landscape of nature into the profits of culture, man has been in headlong flight from the fear of vulnerability. In so doing he has made himself ostensibly free of beauty but actually more vulnerable to her. Hence the hostility and envy, for he forgot that she is crucial to his existence, and while part of him still fears beauty part of him also envies those who don't – and those he perceives as women.

He also forgot that beauty, like truth whom she represents, is the hardest of task-mistresses. Without due devotion to her self-destruction is hastened, for her opposite is not only ugliness but annihilation. Without beauty in attendance and being tended man may feel falsely and insanely impervious to the consequences of his actions, and may buy, build up and eventually bury all he sees. He has done it before in many civilizations.

Beauty provides the opportunity for a split in the armour which everyday life often requires us to wear. It furnishes the necessary tears, flashes of insight and unspeakable but essential longing and desire. As it startles, surprises and replenishes, so it also sears, saddens and humbles. It will always catch you out and trounce your emotions when you would rather forget you had any. More than pain itself or grief it is the most cauterizing and unavoidable predicament, for without it we are not human at all. It is not containable, and the wish to avoid the pain of it, in particular the pain of losing it, can have a crippling effect on what we will allow ourselves in thoughts and actions.

I had a conversation about beauty with a woman teacher in her late twenties, shortly after a very important relationship of hers had ended. She found that the notion of beauty was crucial to her understanding of what had happened, and said:

In my dreams I would remember the beautiful bits. I would come gasping and heaving out of these dreams with the feeling that my heart would literally break. They say you only remember the good bits, which isn't the same at all as only remembering the beautiful bits. I don't think I could bear the strain of having all that intimacy and delicacy brought back to me and then realizing the nightmare that it was no longer mine, that the person who was instrumental in the beauty happening, in my feeling beautiful, would never be with me again.

I struggled for many months between despair and a minimal kind of coping, and eventually I talked about it with a woman I barely knew. She said she had had a similar experience and felt strongly the need at the time to turn her back on it all – to deny beauty if you like, to say that it didn't belong to her because it was so painful. She was struck by the thought of denial and what that had meant in terms of Christ's life and death – she was a Christian – and felt that if she denied what was hers and what was painful she too would in some way die.

So she didn't. She allowed the painful memories to live on, and eventually they stopped racking her and began to soothe instead. She used a lovely phrase: 'Beauty had at last come home.' I knew instinctively what she meant. She was saying that beauty will always terrify us because we can't own it and because it's so powerful, but that if you're woman or man enough to face the terror then in the end you'll be more complete – and ultimately less afraid.

It is this completeness that man misses by having given away beauty, and woman misses by being the custodian, not of beauty itself, but of image, symbol or stereotype.

A woman poet in her early thirties described how, cycling along one day at the end of an extra-long winter and the beginning of a late spring, she unexpectedly saw a phalanx of snowdrops in a garden.

I suddenly burst into tears. Thinking about it, I realized they were tears of relief that this symbol of spring should have broken through winter at last, and also tears from a reservoir of sadness because the winter had been a bad one for me. I wonder if this is the reason why we've created so much ugliness – we can't take beauty because she's too powerful? We're petrified that she could literally do us in.

There is another aspect of beauty which gives Old Testament man problems: it requires something from the beholder. Genesis tells a different story and gives man reason to believe his eye to be the centre of the earth and himself lord over all he sees:

And God said, Let us make man in our image, after our likeness; and let them have dominion over the fish of the sea, and over the fowl of the air, and over the cattle, and over all the earth, and over every creeping thing that creepeth upon the earth.

So God created man in his own image, in the image of God created he him; male and female created he them.

And God blessed them, and God said unto them, Be fruitful, and multiply, and fill the earth, and subdue it; and have dominion over the fish of the sea, and over the fowl of the air, and over every living thing that moveth upon the earth.

The idea of ruling over what he sees and subjugating it has been taken very literally by Old Testament man.

Beauty, however, is not to be ruled. Unlike people, or even money, it cannot be made to work for you. Perhaps that's why the Puritan consciousness has had such problems with it. For the Puritan believes that beauty is the enemy of work, and work is his reason for being alive and his passport to Heaven. Puritan or fundamentalist man believes beauty is a temptress that could lead him off the straight and narrow into the seductive bushes of the senses. He also knows something else about the relationship between beauty and work, because in some vital way *beauty works the person*, not the other way round. He therefore fears becoming beauty's slave, rather than God's servant.

A human being is a possible prey to beauty in that it can move someone who hasn't asked for it. A man might be moved to tears by the sudden glimpse of a beautiful sky, and might have his head turned round by a beautiful woman. He might, in other words, lose control and be un-manned.

On the other hand beauty, paradoxically, cannot be relied upon to work at all. It isn't like that. You can't buy a picture of a stormy sea or a mountain scene, look at it when you're feeling miserable and guarantee that you'll feel better. While beauty *can* uplift and make the heart soar or bring back hope, it can also produce tears, longing and sadness. What it can't achieve is doing any of this to order. It is essentially a relationship with the world and oneself, which allows in the unexpected, and is prepared to journey and to be adventurous. Almost by definition it allows one to be startled. Essentially beauty is in the eye of the beholder, and even more so in the heart.

In *Pornography and Silence* Susan Griffin describes how in the fundamentalist mind women and beauty are inextricably linked in morbidity, which it is culture's task to avoid or overcome. She describes how the Romantics linked beauty and death, and how the feeling has always existed that woman will use her beauty to ensnare man and bring about his downfall. Culture views the notion of beauty as frightening and potentially evil. Beauty is seen as weakening man's resolve to lead a pure life along the route which leads from outcast, original sinner on earth to redemption in the bliss of Heaven.

In this self-denying, hair-shirt scheme of things beauty is petrifying. For a start it is called 'she'. She is the fully decked temptress come to lure the most stringent and ascetic of men from his self-inflicted course. She is frightening precisely because she works through his senses, his emotions and his sexuality. Without her, flagellatory man could lock himself in and build, step by bitter step, the staircase between here and his appointed place next to God. Griffin writes: 'The beauty of women, and even the beauty of flowers, the Christian theologians warn us, can lead to hell. The revelation of beauty is dangerous . . . To understand the sacred meaning of the revelation of beauty, we must then understand the deeper meaning of perdition in the psyche.'[6]

Griffin draws a picture of perdition or Hell as a place where people are tormented in a physical way for their physical cravings. She writes of Hell as the ultimate manifestation of physical frustration. It is a place where desire is fanned with flames, and even more flames, and deliberately increased, never to be sated. Her statement is that Hell is a punishment of bodily needs and cravings, and in what she calls the 'Christian' imagination it is the temptress or the beauty in women which leads man to damnation. And this damnation is reached through the 'other' self.

Here is the self Freud called 'subconscious', a self accessible only through dream, or poetic raving, or madness or perhaps through the experience of ecstasy in the spirit of the body. And here is *beauty* again. For this ecstasy arrives through that window into the soul, and the body, which is opened when we feel an overwhelming beauty . . .[7]

Griffin goes on to describe how beauty and childhood are linked, in that childhood is the time when the world is at its most beautiful for us, and also at its most enchanting. She says that in the pornographic mind it is the memory of this enchantment which must be quashed and denied.

And when pornography punishes the vulnerable, when pornography punishes our memories of infancy, when pornography punishes the breast, and humiliates our body's knowledge of this world, pornography punishes this child. This is the deeper meaning behind pornography's obsession with the rape of virgins. And with the molestation of children.[8]

This is some of the nastiness of the business. While man has given beauty to the 'other', to woman, when as human he knows he intrinsically needs it himself, woman has something man wants. In his eyes she many times holds him to ransom for it, and even if she doesn't, she has the power to do so. In giving beauty away, man resents the woman who isn't beautiful – because that is what she is for – and fears the woman who is.

Much of the woman-hatred I have heard comes from the idea of a beautiful-looking woman making a fool out of men, who are like helpless putty in her grasping, thieving hands. Woman becomes a thief in man's eyes while she has what he needs: not sex, but power – the power through beauty to twist him round her little finger and empty his pockets while he falls on his knees in front of her. Why does man succumb? He will answer that he was blinded, deranged, robbed of reason by her beauty; and while – yes – he will be called a fool, he is somehow an understandable one.

The idea of woman as gold-digger and nasty bitch 'robbing men blind' carries the feeling that, whatever women say about men having the upper hand through brute force, it is actually women who carry the whip. This is why, however hard they try intellectually, many men cannot identify with the feminist description of woman as victim of a 'male system'. A woman (his mother) once meant a giantess who for a short time was his world. She ruled it in early childhood and then kicked him out, while he was still vulnerable, to join the brutalizing agents of the boys' gang. Man has genuine difficulty reconciling this experience with woman's declared powerlessness.

It is equally difficult for woman to be receptive to the idea of the male as victim of the unwise mother. For she knows what it is like to be brought up in a system in which she feels so clearly object rather than subject, and in which culture has taken a massive toll on nature. What about the unwise father? Woman is tired of the argument that it's all mother's fault. She rejoins that if men fathered rather than just sired, and contributed to a society in which parenting was regarded as valuable instead of one in which greed is encouraged, we wouldn't be in this mess. Woman is tired of mother being the whipping girl in a long line of moral outposts stripped bare by forces like 'success' and 'achievement' and, yes, bombs — bloody, life-negating bombs.

For man, female as object doesn't ring true in a *felt* sense when he has been so much in woman's power both as a child and now as an adult, and he personally didn't choose the bombs any more than she did. I've heard it said angrily and enviously many times by men: 'Women have it all ways.' A computer analyst in his late thirties described it like this:

A man is a much bigger fool than a woman, and you need to be a man to know that. Right from the start boys know girls are superior to them. It's documented that when they're younger girls are brighter and get on faster. So the boys start a form of warfare based on jealousy and fear and the macho myths which *insist* you must be better than girls, whatever the cost.

When I was at school the most degrading punishment you could get as a boy was being told to sit with the girls, where the other lads could scoff at you. The worst thing you could be called was a girl.

It's where the male dominance starts. Girls are cleverer, so let's crush 'em. By the power invested in us through the myth of male supremacy, us boys are the superior sex, so if there's somebody cleverer than us in the way they must be wrong. We were going to claw our way ahead of them or batter them down to our level, little sods that we were.

Men have got a lot to answer for . . . which is why we're fools. We start fucking it up practically from the time we climb down from our mother's knee, because we're jealous of women. We're jealous because we don't have access to the kind of containment they have. It's laughable that men set themselves up as the contained sex. Women are that, and a man is born into a male system where he is a fool if he joins in and an outcast if he doesn't.

59

A woman is born into a system where she's a nurturer and, while feminists have fought this role, I tell you it's the prize, for through it women nurture themselves and other women. It makes them contained, and the reason why men hate feminists is because they think feminism is going to mean that pretty soon men won't get any of that care, any of that 'making it better'.

There is no doubt that feminism has involved women making it better for other women by supporting and assisting them, and that men have suffered because of this. In the main it would be reasonable to echo the words of the woman in Chapter 1 who said that this exclusion of men was not deliberate on the part of most women. It is also reasonable to assume that it did not feel this way to men, and may indeed have felt like a plot to cast them out from the 'hospital services' they had been used to. Would they be able to manage without them? The computer analyst continued:

Some self-protecting mechanism tells us that without it we won't survive, because we can't do it for ourselves. We're not any good at it, except superficially. We're so jealous, and brought up to be so nasty, that we'll make sure that if we can't have a decent life on this earth no one else has it either. We're like that. It takes a man to think up a scorched earth policy, and to carry it out, because we do it psychologically all the time.

The scorched earth policy referred to here, as well as having literal historical precedents – for example during Napoleon's invasion of Russia and more recently in Vietnam – has the psychological dimension of destroying your own childhood territory. A scorched earth policy in its literal sense renders land useless so that others cannot benefit from it. In psychological terms, if a man's childhood territory is not only ignored by him but 'scorched', then it is no longer accessible either to himself or to the 'enemy' – in this case a woman who tries to find out who he is. While the actual doing of this would take a pathological mind, the symbolic doing of it, in the way that childhood is forbidden if not actually scorched territory, is not uncommon. It may be the reason why this man talks of women killing, both literally and metaphorically, in a different way. For a woman is still more likely to be in touch with both the internal and the external child, considerations which would render her less likely to use scorched earth policies.

Yes, women kill too, but differently. A woman will kill *now*, and kill perhaps more cleverly than a man, but she'll leave the earth alone for the next generation.

You want to know about the battle of the sexes? It comes about because of Christianity, which feeds it.

Like many people, including Susan Griffin, this man uses the term 'Christianity' to describe what I have termed Old Testament, biblical or fundamentalist values. I have used these terms in order to distinguish between the positive aspects of the scriptures and their destructive side. To my mind it is the New Testament that bears the message of Christianity which, like Taoist thought, is educative, whether or not one wishes to practise it as a religion. By contrast, the Old Testament myths serve their own self-defeating ends and reflect man at war with himself in a perpetual battle with personal authority. The analyst went on:

Imagine putting a dozen men in the City on a truth drug and asking them to tell you their feelings about women and girls from boyhood up – not their stated feelings, but their *actual* ones. It wouldn't work without the drug, because they're so used to holding up the world single-handed – look at Charles Atlas – that they wouldn't recognize a feeling if it killed them. Which it does, not infrequently.

Men don't die of heart attacks from overwork at their desks or from having too much sex – it's from the massive effort of damming up feelings so that they're inaccessible to anyone, particularly women, and especially themselves. I don't think men are a lost cause, but they're a dangerous one. Men are walking time-bombs, and they're as likely to unleash themselves on the first woman who tries to help them as on the 'enemy'. A man's problem is that in most cases these two are the same people. A woman is both helper and enemy, so men have to go to the 'other side' to be helped out.

He then went on to explain how some men try to avoid marrying 'real' women at all. He described these 'unreal' females as 'priceless Victoriana' – the kind of people who are much more concerned with image than with affairs of the heart or soul; women who are much more interested in marrying a 'good catch' than in being plagued by the messy business called love.

No wonder some men are marrying priceless Victoriana from Sloane Square or wherever mummified princesses live these days, rather than real flesh and blood women. They've got to. I mean, in their situation, wouldn't you? The man has to marry the 'virgin' not because she's pregnant but because *he* is – pregnant with enough bloody ammunition to do the lot of us in. And what better foil to a highly charged time-bomb than a cool, ice-like woman?

It's womb envy, really. Since a man can't carry a baby inside him he makes something else to carry. It's part of his jealousy at women's containment – the fact that they can nurture themselves while he can't.

He went on to say that he couldn't understand why womb envy wasn't an accepted fact of life, like breathing.

The original difference between men and women was that a man had a prick and a woman had a cunt – surely not too much to argue over, you'd have thought. But when you add on to that the fact that a woman can give birth *and* feed a baby – she can actually produce and feed another human, and he can't – then there's a hell of a difference.

I've already told you what jealous little sods we are. 'You make a baby, lady. We'll build something much cleverer than that. You want a tower block? You want a bullet-proof tank? Look what we can do. Babies, pah – they're just useless, mewling, puking little things. You take care of those, lady – they're boring. We've got much more interesting projects up our poor jealous sleeves. You stay at home and be boring, and we'll spray like tomcats all over the world so that soon there'll be no place on earth where you can't see one of our marks. Now isn't that clever and grand and important of us? . . . And did our sons grow up behind our backs? Give them to us now they can talk, and we'll make men out of them.'

Is there anything you can tell me that makes that picture not true?

The act of diminishing something you are jealous of by claiming it to be valueless is something that all children do at one time or another. When adults do so they have the power to make the diminution widespread and eventually commonplace. Man did so by making beauty into one of life's luxuries instead of an absolute necessity. He decided that beauty was a frippery which the women could play with. He needn't burden himself with carrying it round with him, but would pass on the bundle to someone who had so little to do she could afford to sit down all day doing nothing else but looking pretty.

In this way woman became the keeper of the treasure chest containing beauty, and man achieved the reverse – unusual in the natural world – of turning round sexual attraction. He brought about a situation in which the female was far more decorated than the male, and this created a power imbalance in relationships – the woman had to attract the man, not the other way round. But because she was not allowed to hunt him as a male might a female, and because any sign of obvious sexual display would have branded her a harlot, she was left with the task of working out how to become a man-trap while seeming to be the opposite. This is the hypocrisy of which Margaret Walters writes.

It was bound to be woman's lot in a system which gave the male higher value than her, making him therefore more desirable than her. But the fact that man had dumped beauty clinched the matter. It was now up to woman not only to scheme and plot and scratch out the eyes of her best friend or sister for that scarce commodity called a man, but also to primp and perm and pamper herself. She stepped straight into the trap. Why not? she thought. Compared with going to the factory or the office, wasn't it nicer to stay at home spoiling herself, dressing up in lovely things and having soothing lotions rubbed into her? While only a wealthy minority could afford these luxuries, trends impose themselves, like God, from the top. Women who were lower middle-class will have emulated the rich, and working-class women will have longed for their indulgent way of life.

Having stepped into the trap, it perhaps isn't surprising that woman was then called a trap herself, and man feared being lured into her waiting snare. Woman as trapper of unwary man is a concept going back to Eve. It plays havoc with the question of who wields the power in modern relationships, because it interferes with the roles of tyrant and victim. Modern man actually feels victim himself – and when his symbols are called tyrannical, with *woman* as their victim, he feels doubly put upon.

It was man who gave beauty its added power over him by giving it away and making woman its repository. In this way he victimized not only himself, but also woman, for until recently a woman who is not beautiful has been beneath his contempt. Some men have gone so far as to say she should be grateful for *any* attention from a man – even rape.

63

The reason why a woman who is not beautiful evokes such rage in man – and rage it is – is that she fails to keep safe his jewels for him. These jewels are his 'other self', and besides beauty they include qualities like gentleness and meekness. Without woman as the shadow of his other self, man is separated from the sun and he breaks up in anger or revenge. When he unconsciously misses beauty, to find it he turns to the woman next to him. Heaven help the woman who can't oblige, for if she is plain of face or not conventionally attractive there is no reason why she cannot mask this and at last adorn herself beautifully, which is what she has been expected to do. When for a while feminists decided they would duck out of this role, and dress plainly in dungarees and baggy sweat-shirts, woman-hatred reached its peak in comments like: 'Ugly old cows – couldn't get themselves a man in any case!' The wish to be comfortable, and the wish to avoid being man's plaything any more, hit him deep, for woman was not just a plaything but Mistress of the Keep.

The concept of beauty is highly complex and is as much in the individual eye – or heart – of the beholder as anywhere else. In physical terms it changes, both through fashion and within the individual eye, heart or mind. Someone who was once thought beautiful may appear no longer so, and conversely someone formerly considered plain can suddenly be transformed into a beauty. Feelings and opinions inform the concept of beauty just as much as physical planes and angles.

On the physical level, a top model will be thought of as plain by someone who doesn't like angular faces or thin women. It would be fair to say, however, that in any age there are certain women who are generally considered beautiful, like the sixties' fashion model Jean Shrimpton or the actress Elizabeth Taylor. Meryl Streep, on the other hand, both is and is not beautiful.

On the personal level, there are at the same time people who will always be beautiful to those who love them, but who may seem quite unremarkable to those who don't. Very often a woman will be considered beautiful because she has a lovely smile or is a kind person. For some the words 'beauty' and 'attraction' are virtually synonymous; for others, attraction means only sexual attraction; while for others again any face is utterly transformed by what lies behind it. For these people, conventional beauty is either subverted or redescribed by aspects of a person that are not physical.

Even though one has to work with the premiss, therefore, that beauty is partly a generally accepted image which changes as fashions change, and partly very personal, it is still the case that beauty in its

64

many forms is powerful. It derives some of that power from the very fact that it is not always concrete.

With all this in mind, my argument is that it remains the general case that women who are not perceived as *physically* attractive do not hold as much power over men as those who are. It is women whom men perceive as physically beautiful who have the power to make men craven and bring them to their knees.

As men become more discerning about themselves and about the nature of relationships this should alter. For if beauty is invested in men as well as in women, and is part of an exchange of relationships, it will have lost its enemy. For the enemies of beauty in its many forms – whether physical, artistic or emotional – are those who have given beauty away.

6
Smile, Please!

Part of the uniform woman must wear as the keeper of man's treasury is a smile, at least for him: the smile is the entrance to the treasury and signals consent. The woman who is beautiful or attractive and does not give a smile runs the risk of inciting male rage in comments like: 'Stuck-up bitch.' The smile seems to be requested or asked for in phrases like: 'Give us a smile, luv.' But in fact it is often an instruction, and there can be penalties for not delivering.

A woman in her early thirties described her experience of this instruction in the following way:

I thought I had a particularly stern face. Although what I should have worked out about ten years sooner than I did was that people accused me of having an over-friendly face as well, because I suffered a number of assaults. But on the times when my face was obviously in its stern mode I used to get men in the street saying to me: 'Give us a smile, luv', or, 'It can't be *that* bad', or 'Cheer up, it might never happen', to which my automatic response was: 'It already has.' I never came across a man who spotted the irony in that, even when I said it really grimly.

I took all the comments literally, at face value, and imagined, as I say, that I looked harsh. I would go home, look at my face in the mirror and think that because it was rather long and thin it could easily look severe – and this was exacerbated, so I thought, by the vertical frown-mark between my eyes. I vowed to lighten up, and I swear I didn't frown in public for at least a dozen years. During that time I was also assaulted five or six times.

On these occasions I didn't look at my face. I was too wretched. But I accepted the anomaly, put to me by women as well as men, that I smiled too much, and by so doing encouraged these strangers. It was only a year or two ago that I worked out I was battered from all sides. If I looked serious I was told to smile. If I smiled I was assaulted. And when I was assaulted it wasn't just my body that hurt, but all of me.

SMILE, PLEASE!

I can give you almost the exact date when things changed – it was in the late summer of 1987. I read an article about women and smiling, and how women were always being told to do this, and it all fell into place. It was happening to everyone, not just me. Suddenly women I had known for years and with whom I had discussed the most intimate things – orgasms, episiotomies, break-ups of marriages etc. – were discussing these smiles.

It was as if, twenty years after the second wave of feminism, we had suddenly discovered something. We'd known about the wolf whistles, and how you ignored them, and what to do about the other bits of sexism, but we hadn't known that this 'Give us a smile' business wasn't personal. We still felt it happened to us individually because of what we were doing, rather than because of what we symbolized. To a woman we'd searched our own faces and our own behaviour for the reasons.

When I said in a group of friends that my face was rather long and thin they just fell about laughing. Not one of them, they said, would have described it that way. And apparently I was the only one who knew about the frown-mark – it was so faint that no one else had even noticed it. I tell you, it was salutary.

Man depends upon woman's smile to make life better for him, to let him know that his investments are safe and that he can draw on them when he needs to. The times he most needs to do so are when the world looks at its bleakest. When sitting in a plant-filled office with a few personal knick-knacks around him man has his needs safely at bay most of the time. However, his needs are not safely at bay in the grey, concrete world of the building site, where beauty is at its most absent. In the unrelieved dirt and mess of a labourer's work the need for relief is often perilously near the surface.

The antithesis of this aesthetic desert is a mirage in the shape of woman, who is soft, cuddly, warm, beautiful – and necessarily friendly. For if she is not willing to be friends with him then the mirage becomes not relief, but torment; and man is already tormented enough. His symbolic cry to a woman is something like: 'My world is a dull, miserable, boring place. A hangover's bad enough, but please don't do this to me. Please smile, luv, and make me feel better.'

Men don't pester plain-looking women for smiles, because it is beauty they want back. At this point man is dying for it – not for sex, but for beauty. But she mustn't taunt him by not being available. If she does, the fragilely constructed system might snap and he will have to hit what he so much needs. This behaviour is a form of inconsolability.

Consolation is a necessary salve to a wound or hurt of any kind. We talk of giving people – particularly children – 'consolation prizes' for not having won the race, for not having got what they really wanted. The act of consoling or of being consoled is necessary if small disappointments and major hurts are to be recovered from. There are, however, times when people are inconsolable either because their pain is temporarily overpowering or because they wilfully put themselves outside consolation. People behave in inconsolable ways when they destroy the very thing or person that could bring them comfort, or when they ignore danger signals and put themselves beyond help – not waving but drowning.

The man who hits what he needs is behaving inconsolably because he is damaging what he wants – that which would console him. There can be an element of envy here, too, for he might well also be damaging what someone else wants. This inconsolable behaviour happens frequently.

One of the unpleasantest stories of this kind told to me personally was by a woman who happened to be physically very attractive and had had her nose broken by a lorry driver. She was walking along a very busy, congested road when a man started whistling at her from his slow-moving lorry. First of all he shouted, and when she turned to look at him he winked and said, 'Getta loada that!' She turned her head away and continued walking. The lorry driver went on wolf-whistling and making comments while the traffic crawled along at no more than walking pace. Then his attentions stopped. The woman relaxed and breathed a sigh of relief. Suddenly her arm was swung back from behind, and for only a fraction of a second she glimpsed the lorry driver's apoplectic face before his fist hit her. For a moment or two she remembered nothing else. People came to help, and someone shouted that the man had run off into the traffic. No one thought to watch for a large vehicle suddenly moving off.

Another woman had her eye blacked by a van driver. He had been 'playing' with her in city traffic, as happens to attractive-looking women who drive alone. He had been flashing his headlights at her in the rear-view mirror, and when she ignored him had overtaken her, then jammed on his brakes so that she too had to brake sharply to avoid going into the back of him. After that he drove off slowly so that she had to overtake him, and as she did so he had another look at her – and so it went on. Eventually, as she was leaving the city, the van forced her on to the verge. The driver got out. She wound down her window to yell at him, and as she sat at the steering wheel he hit her. She was too stunned to take his number or to remember clearly anything about him. She didn't phone the police. There seemed no point, since there was no prospect of catching her attacker.

I used to think of incidents of this kind as being connected with male ego, which in part they are. Many male drivers do not like women – or men – drawing away first at traffic lights, and will risk the life and limbs of themselves and others to ensure that they don't 'get away with it'. But what is it that *women* are supposed to be getting away with? It's not just a matter of men's need to be superior, because women whom men think of as plain don't suffer this kind of treatment so often. No – if beauty drives off without him, man is left not standing but kneeling. Too much is invested in woman for her to gather speed under her own steam and then vanish from sight.

To an ordinary, decent, caring man, the thought of a lorry driver breaking a woman's nose, and the hatred sometimes spat at women for refusing the demand to 'Give us a smile', are incomprehensible. He would probably not believe such stories coming from a woman, unless it was a woman whom he knew well and trusted. He would see them as the exaggerated ravings of a gender which, after all, does suffer from a persecution complex. The problem is that he's applying the complex to the wrong sex. In the following story, isn't it the *male* figure who is feeling persecuted?

It concerns a woman who, after some difficulty, had split up with a man. He was fifteen years older than she was, and she'd discovered, at the age of twenty-three, that while she had been looking for a father-figure (which she hadn't found in him) he had in fact got a mother in her. She said:

> I initially got cold feet because of his relationships with other women. Then I began to feel really creepy because when he told me about them he started putting in all the details. He began using me as a sort of mother confessor. He would end up by saying that it was of course only *me* who was important to him.
>
> After a while I decided to leave. He didn't believe me at first. Then when he saw I was serious he suddenly flipped. He turned into some kind of animal. In the past he had always told me I was beautiful. Now he turned on me like a snarling beast. I was absolutely petrified. He tongue-lashed me so that every single compliment, act of love, piece of confidence that had helped build me up was stripped off me. I can't remember the words exactly, but they were things like: 'Who do you think will have you after this?

69

You're not as pretty as you think. You're already as lined as some women twice your age.'

He stripped me of every piece of tenderness that had ever passed between us. I had been a shy, rather gawky person when we met. He was only the second man I'd slept with, and he'd built up my confidence. Now he was taking it all away because I was leaving him.

I didn't have orgasms for years after that because I was afraid I was ugly. Then I began to see how this not only hurt me, but divided women against other women. Because if I was saying you only deserved orgasms if you were pretty then I was saying that only attractive women deserved love. I still catch myself out sometimes wondering how a plain woman has 'caught' such an attractive man. It's a nasty business.

Man's paranoia is generally more concealed than woman's. It has to be. Man has been brought up to be big and brave so that he can rescue or defend little, timid woman. It is only recently that woman has jumped out of this mould.

Because of man's general heroic role the persecuted male personality is not a common historical figure – except of course in the crucified figure of Christ, who was different in that he suffered at God's command. Otherwise the persecuted male has been presented only as a joke, a foil to the big bossy women in seaside postcards and mother-in-law jokes. As a serious modern entity man is supposedly not persecuted.

However, in psychological terms the picture looks different. Man has been encouraged to see other men as enemies or rivals, therefore as threats. This is why learning to be friends with other men is proving difficult. In giving away beauty and in ignoring his own emotional stock he is also beginning to feel paranoid about the fact that there might be empty spaces inside him which do not exist inside other people – women. In fact woman seems to store strong ammunition inside herself in the spaces where man feels at his weakest. So the idea of the persecuted male *has* become serious.

The irony of this lies in the paradox that man as literal persecutor of nature is himself symbolically persecuted by lack of attention to his own personal nature. This, the world of feelings – emotions – was not important enough to worry about, which is where the present paranoia stems from. For man decided that woman could take care of all this lot – beauty and that ragbag of bits and pieces – but that he would still exercise control by fashioning it, in woman, to his own design. In other words, this is the myth of external creation, of being able to make another person outside yourself.

The man who turned into a 'snarling beast' in the story above took a gawky Eve and made a woman out of her. He clothed her not only physically but emotionally, giving her the confidence to blossom into a woman. He did not, of course, do this for *her* – otherwise he would have had no need to take all these things away when she left him. He built his own woman to his own design, and the paranoia implicit in that became obvious when his creation threatened to leave him. For why should you be paranoid if your creation leaves you unless she is taking half of you with her?

On a larger scale, the idea of beauty needing to be controlled so that it will do as bid manifests itself in the pressure we put upon it to be available, and ultimately to be unenduring. The notion of Beauty or goodness as short-lived (only the good die young) killed off by the 'Beast' of war, treachery or greed, is a reworking of the biblical story of Genesis. It perpetuates the idea that humans are intrinsically bad, and that however much we are punished or saved by God the Father we must eventually return to destroying goodness and beauty. We must fall.

In biblical terms we have to fall, for if we didn't there would be no need for God to save us or Heaven to lure us, and we might indeed create that most sacrilegious state – peace on earth. Then there would be no need for the good to die young, killed off by the Beast of our nasty selves, and Beauty could walk free and inquisitive. As it is, Beauty and the Beast form another collusive opposite like Heaven and earth, ordained and unordained, above and below. Only this time the opposites are turned round. For in this scenario of man as Beast, it is woman who is 'above' and heavenly and who is 'ordained' (with beauty), and it is man who is 'below', hellish and unordained (into human behaviour).

As Beauty and the Beast, however, their essential quality is their oppositeness. Which way round the opposites lie is not always important to the main theme, which is the playing out of opposite roles in dramatic incidents – just as if life is indeed a stage with an unseen audience judging the performance. Beauty and the Beast perform another variation of the old plot that humans are puppets dangling on the strings of the great puppetmaster (God), and are here on earth to give command performances of His one great theme – the struggle between Himself and the Devil. Whether it is man fighting woman, man fighting man or man fighting dragon, the battle must go on.

71

In the case of Beauty and the Beast a bad fairy turns a handsome prince into a beast and says he can only become himself again if he can get a beautiful woman to agree to marry him. What a tortuous and seemingly impossible task! However, in this moral tale Beauty wins out, because we learn that, although dark of countenance, Beast is gentle, as is Beauty, and his plight eventually moves her to marriage.

Unfortunately the real Beast – in the form of the maw of inconsolable behaviour which is the Old Testament's donation to humankind – *must* ravish Beauty. The day Marilyn Monroe died Alistair Cooke wrote an article for the *Guardian*, a piece sympathetic to the complicated life Monroe had lived. In it he said she was '*cursed by physical beauty* [my emphasis] to be dazed and doomed by the fame that was too much for her'. Towards the end of the article he wrote: 'This orphan of a rootless City of the Angels at last could feel no other identity than the one she saw in the mirror: a baffled, honest girl for ever haunted by the nightmare of herself, sixty feet tall and naked before a howling mob.'

The Beast got to Monroe, and maybe it was the Beast who killed her. He must kill Beauty, because even when he tries with all his might to be gentle, and even when he adores her, the mere act of picking her up will crush every bone in her body. Beauty and the Beast are locked in tragedy as Romeo and Juliet are, because in real life the Beast kills Beauty. That is his destiny. He either relinquishes her and grieves, or he crushes her and is in turn killed for his crime. In one of the versions of the King Kong story the hit men didn't need their bullets or bombs: it was the one where the Beast dies of a broken heart.

This is the Old Testament view of the human condition – that of mourning and the continual infliction of suffering on ourselves and on others. The condition asks us to accept that we were brought to life by a Maker who was disappointed enough in His creation to deem us all flawed – in other words, born in original sin. As His 'children' we therefore suffer the anguish of having caused disappointment to the person who gave us life – our Father. We also suffer the pain of being rejects in that we are less than the shining examples of our species we were intended to be. From this lowly position we are then, however, supposed to turn to the very person who made us bad, who told us we weren't good enough, in order to be helped. So the Maker who has caused us so much pain is our only hope for assistance in relieving our plight. Put this way, it sounds sadistic.

It also sounds not unlike the inconsolable position of the child of abusing parents. Any infant is born to a parent or parents on whom he or she depends totally for food and well-being. In the case of the parentally abused child the very person who has given life and who is necessary to the child's sense of hope and confidence is the person who crushes that child. Part of the tragedy of the child abused by a parent – as distinct from a stranger or neighbour – is that the child has been damaged by the person he or she most needs. This is also, of course, the parent's tragedy, for the parent in this situation has committed not only one of the most offensive acts in the eyes of society, but also one that is practically beyond personal repair or consolation.

Realizing that the parent too needs consolation, and that the subject of punishment and authority is such a confused and complex one, in 1982 I wrote a piece entitled 'The Inconsolables'. It opened with these sentences:

> The child who is inconsolable burns down the house; the adult who is inconsolable burns the child; the self-righteous public meddler who is inconsolable burns the adult; the political figure who is inconsolable burns us all. The need to be punitive is a tragic feature of people who are inconsolable.
>
> They are inconsolable in being so far removed from self-possession or the prospect of it that they need to be possessed by, or to possess, others. Since they are not authoritative themselves, they seek authority over others, or others' authority over them . . .[1]

In this scheme of things the God-figure invented by inconsolable man for the purpose of consolation has proved to be Himself inconsolable – as He had to be, since He was the invention of an inconsolable mind. It leaves us, if we are not careful, between the Devil and the Deep. For the Maker who invented an inquisitive Eve and then punished all of us because of her curiosity has a problem with authority.

In *Thou Shalt Not Be Aware* Alice Miller writes: 'Who was this contradictory God/Father who had the need to create a curious Eve and at the same time forbid her to live according to her true nature?'[2] The deep biblical message as it has been practised is that it is impossible for man to attain completeness of form, and therefore his own beauty, without accepting his dependency on an invisible Maker called God. When coupled with dependency on a visible woman called mother, this ties the ascetic knot which is one of the Old Testament's curses. When woman is both visible temptress and keeper of beauty (at least in its human form), as Susan Griffin wrote, beauty itself then becomes temptress, for through eye domination man knows he is vulnerable to a beautiful woman. Were the rest of his senses as susceptible as his eyes this would not be the case, but the eye-junkie is just that – an addict of what his eye informs him, even if the rest of his senses inform him differently.

Man is very afraid of the power of beauty, which he has sought to control: so much so that boys are brought up to imagine it will take away their manhood if they have anything to do with it. Therefore boys are called weedy if they are responsive to beauty. It is seen as the melter of manly spines and therefore as castrator, for if it turns a man to jelly where is his manliness? As if to collude in the awful growth of Beast and the gradual death of Beauty, little boys are brought up to harden their hearts to beauty. They do not make daisy chains, for that is girls' work, and it is cissy for a boy to stand in awe of a sunset. In fact it is so frighteningly cissy that he will make bold plans to fly into that sunset, to land on the moon, to ravage birds' nests, lest in stopping to see, rather than to control, his maleness will drain away from him. There would have been nothing necessarily wrong with boys finding birds' nests if they had found them just to look: it was stealing the eggs that was the problem. In order not to be made weak at the knees by beauty, man destroys her. Continuing with her theme of Eve not being allowed to live out her true nature, Miller writes of this 'destroying the nest' syndrome: 'It is conceivable that the alienated, perverse and destructive side of present-day scientific investigation is a delayed consequence of this prohibition. If Adam is not allowed to be aware of what is before his very eyes, he will direct his curiosity to goals as far removed from himself as possible. He will conduct experiments in outer space . . .'[3]

It is also, of course, impossible for woman to attain completeness of form, for in an eye-dominated culture she will be coerced into being conventionally beautiful and will be cursed and despised for not being so. Even if she is so, she will still not be free to be herself, for culture has organized it so that Beauty will always be in danger from the Beast – whether by theft, rage, envy or need. In his book *Timebends: A Life* Arthur Miller writes of how Marilyn Monroe's beauty prompted in him 'a wish to defend it'. As with Eve, beauty may not be free or inquisitive. Beauty needs a minder, and then the situation comes full circle: man is frightened of beauty, so he makes beauty live in fear of him. Beauty must be guarded. She is guarded in vaults and behind bullet-proof glass. In woman she must be guarded by an individual man.

This brings us back to the idea that a woman cannot live without a man. If a woman gets up and walks away from her minder, then she has to take what's coming to her, whether it consists of whistles and orders to 'Give us a smile' or physical attacks. These problems don't occur if a woman is with a man to protect her or to put an invisible label on her marked 'Owned'. A man will respect the property of another man; he doesn't have to respect something that is 'free game'. The 'free game' is in a terrible bind here, because all her problems would disappear if she would only get herself a man – so she does, but for a symbolic rather than a personal reason.

And so the game of charades goes on. If a woman is with a man she may also use her eyes – she may attain her full power. When she is already with a man she may gaze at other men: she is safe from possible threat because she is with her minder. This gives fuel to the argument that a normal woman should be with a man in any case, and that there's something wrong with one who isn't. Nearly every man can therefore be certain of securing a woman: the appalling nature of other men's behaviour will ensure that a woman needs a male to protect her from other men. This is what is really meant by the boys' club: it is a way of making sure that the male gets himself a female. If he wants a beautiful female he will also take on the added kudos of being the minder of something that other men want. In the end, whether a minder is a slave or a controller, a servant or a master is a moot point.

This is shown in the case of a man who appeared to be the controller of a relationship, but ended up as a slave within it. The man drives a mini-cab. He is tall, attractive and rather shy, but his shyness is offset by a marked ability to get his own way. It's a strange and rather appealing mixture – not quite the strong, silent type, but a gentler version of it.

Even before he married the Canadian woman whom he met when she was on holiday in Britain, he was a pornographer in the sense in which Susan Griffin uses the term. In the way in which these things are known to happen, it all began in his childhood. This man shared his mother's bed as her lover as soon as he reached puberty. His mother, who is now dead, he describes as 'one of the ugliest old bags you ever saw'. His father he never knew. His mother was forty when she gave birth to the child who turned out to be a pornographic man, and he was her only child.

The woman he married is startlingly good-looking: five feet ten inches tall with a tanned, perfect body; wide cheekbones; even, white teeth; large, green eyes; and long, blonde hair. She is so beautiful that it is difficult when talking with her not to be mesmerized by it. At the time of her marriage she was young – twenty, to be precise.

After they had been married for a few years her lack of spontaneity and what can only be described as her blandness palled with her husband. Or perhaps it was something else. He began to require her to dress up in sexy underwear, and after a while he wanted her to do this while other people were around. Like some kind of walkie-talkie doll she went along with these demands – happily, so she proclaims, since these novelties sharpened life up a bit and they had some good laughs.

Gradually the situation developed into him wanting them to have group sex, and passively she once more agreed. While this was going on his own sexual performance was secure because he found it a big turn-on. But he was thirty-five when they married, and by about five years later he was having difficulty in both getting and maintaining erections.

Then the tables turned. While he had been potent she had been quiescent. As he lost his potency she became contemptuous of him, and took over. She had by now obtained a good job, and had ambitions to be wealthy. She began to conduct the financial management of their affairs and put in the extra work needed in order to achieve the long haul up.

They now live in a detached house with acres of garden, a sauna and a jacuzzi, and they run two new cars. He is fat and bald and looks like a somnambulist. She still looks exquisite, although her physical beauty possesses a deadening quality which is quite noticeable after a while: she resembles a plaster cast. He has a bad drink problem. She spends most of her free time keeping fit and making contacts.

Unfortunately this couple also have two children. The paternity of the first child was in dispute, although as he has grown up it is obvious from his features that he is indeed his father's son. However, he has suffered from being treated coldly by a father who for some years was not prepared to accept the child as his own. By the time the child was born the loss of the father's ego had made this blood or ownership tie essential to his ability to care. The father has been quite different with his second son, so the older boy also bears the pain of a father who has been kind to a sibling but not to him.

It is obvious that children are always the victims if parents are unhappy, unstable or unwise. They suffer in all kinds of ways and are marked for life by poor childhood experiences. They may, with hard work or good fortune, learn to live with these marks – but the harm is not, as some people would prefer to believe, rinsed out in the wash of growing up. Since the work of being a parent is so incredibly demanding it clearly needs all the assistance possible. Oddly enough, taking a child's needs seriously, and accepting therefore that mistakes not only occur but should be rectified rather than ignored, makes the job of being a parent easier. Psychoanalyst Dr D. W. Winnicott wrote of this in his books about the child and the family, and came up with the idea of what he called the 'good enough' parent. He used the notion of 'good enough' to show how parents should not hope to be perfect, since that is impossible, but might instead view mistakes as normal, to be noticed and adjusted where possible and where necessary.

However, the mistakes made by the couple in the story above were not small ones. In fact on one level this particular example of modern suburban living could be considered as an update of the ongoing story of Beauty and the Beast, especially since it shows the complexity of this union of opposites. In this case the bad fairy of the story was the Beast's mother – although these days we would recognize his absent, invisible father as culprit too. This couple must inevitably pass on many of their unresolved problems to their offspring, in the same way that they 'inherited' theirs.

One of these unresolved problems is a craving for beauty. This pornographic man now hates beauty, because he thinks he knows the ugliness behind her tempting façade and he believes he was fooled and trapped by it. He believed he could capture beauty for himself, and carry her head under his arm like a trophy to his success in 'pulling a stunning-looking bird' and keeping her. The perversion of the craving for beauty actually comes about because man has thrown beauty away, or to be precise deposited her in woman. However, this does not stop him feeling victimized and believing that it is woman who fools him, not culture. This feeling of being victim the pornographic man is passing on to his eight-year-old son.

In *Thou Shalt Not Be Aware* Alice Miller confirms that children have been sexually abused by adults in the past, and that this is certainly not a new aberration. Although critical of Freud in some respects, she also credits him fully with the achievement of making us aware that infant and childhood traumas mark and affect us for life, and that what happens to young children is extremely important. While this might seem obvious now it certainly wasn't to the Victorians, some of whom treated their young children as pets and playthings.

One of the ways in which Miller differs from Freud is in describing 'infantile sexuality'. She writes of it as belonging not to the child but to adults' projection of their own sexual whims and needs. It is not the child who seduces the adult through his or her indiscriminate and undiscerning sexual needs, but the adult who puts this label on the child in order to allow child molestation. The young child's 'collusion' with this interference Miller describes as necessary to his or her survival in a world in which parents are essential – so the child, instinctively knowing this, complies with adult demands. Miller writes: 'Children will produce pseudo-sexual feelings in order to be a satisfactory partner for the frustrated parent and not to be deprived of the parent's attention . . .'[4]

Taking Alice Miller's viewpoint, the one aspect of child abuse I haven't heard discussed publicly is the fact that to the pornographic mind the child is beautiful in a way that the adult isn't. The child is unlined and supple, and still has soft skin and soft hair. That is the way it *should* be, so that despite the difficulties and sacrifices of being parents we will still want to go on with the task; for in part the child rewards us not only by growing but by smiling, being appealing and making us feel good.

Much of child sexual abuse is undoubtedly about power and the still prevalent feeling that the child is owned, an object rather than a subject – and furthermore an object you can order not to 'tell on you', in the way that you can't order an adult. But we still think of child abuse as being about seduction as well. This seduction, using Miller's analysis, is the adult's need to recapture some kind of beauty, not the child's wish to experiment with sex; which is why it is still mainly men who are involved in child sexual abuse, although it is still mainly women who look after children.

Germaine Greer touched on this problem in *The Female Eunuch*:

> The permissive society has done much to neutralise sexual drives by containing them. Sex for many has become a sorry business, a mechanical release involving neither discovery nor triumph, stressing human isolation more dishearteningly than ever before. The orgies feared by the Puritans have not materialised on every street corner, although more girls permit more (joyless) liberties than they might have done before . . . any kind of sex which can escape the dead hand of the institution – group sex, criminal sex, child-violation, bondage and discipline – has flourished, while simple sexual energy seems to be steadily diffusing and dissipating. This is not because enlightenment is harmful, or because repression is a necessary goad to human impotence, but because sexual enlightenment happened under government subsidy, so that its discoveries were released in bad prose and clinical jargon upon the world.[5]

In order for this statement, which is about control, to be placed in context it is necessary to understand the concept of image. The technology of the camera made it possible for that particular eye to pin, fix and experiment to an unlimited degree.

Beauty has ultimately been controlled through the mass communication of fashion and image, which has brought about an increase in the value placed on stereotype and a decrease in the acceptance of individuality. This makes an army recruit out of beauty. Instead of having the power to startle, surprise and literally un-man, she is rendered uniform, one-voiced and a 'weapon' not of herself, but at the command of others. It is a way of desensitizing the eye of the beholder so that it cannot be shocked.

If most women at any given time are wearing the same haircut, same skirt-length and same colour, a man can mentally adjust to the situation and control it. For a start, he may dismiss any woman who is not 'playing the game' by regarding her as not intelligent/with it/ modern. If she doesn't know that mango is this year's colour, then she is either not very alert or she is ignoring the fact and has possible anarchic tendencies. Either way she can be dismissed as not the 'kind of thing' a decent, law-abiding chap is looking for.

On the other hand, if she does enter the fashion merry-go-round then she will be too busy to get up to any serious mischief. For centuries bosoms, hips, waists and legs have been in one season, out the next. In such a way does fashion not only bedeck, but rule. It seems that if God had been really just he would have given women bodies that changed shape every year; and since He didn't, man has done it for Him. The fact that fashion changes as rapidly and dramatically as it does keeps women safely in the bunkers of acceptable types and men in funk-holes from where their eye-rule of the world is relatively undisturbed.

Since concern about image in advertising and politics has become so pronounced, it is easier to see how much image is about concealment rather than disclosure. It is a way of dressing up unpleasant attributes in pleasant packages so that people will accept them more readily. For the sake of image politicians kiss babies, have voice training and learn how to come across more sincerely when they're actually lying through their front teeth. Image has the long-term effect of confusing and eventually eroding judgement, because in one sense seeing *is* believing and the eye is man's main informant.

It is well known, for example, that until relatively recently many people would not buy 'dirty' or irregularly shaped vegetables; they preferred clean, uniform ones wrapped in clingfilm. While education about nutrition has had some effect, many people still want to buy what *looks* perfect. Such is the extent of eye domination. The eye of the camera has obviously played its part here. The basket of vegetables in the photographer's studio, clean and glistening, informs the human eye that cleanliness is next to godliness.

7

Imperfection Is the Summit

The camera's power dramatically escalated during the twentieth century, when first the cinema and later television became facts of everyday life. The Hollywood Nightmare arrived, and achieved a division between mass fantasy and ordinary reality that had never before been possible. What Hollywood actually did was to make the camera lie on an unprecedented scale. By filming and editing her carefully from particular angles and in short sequences, it made woman seem beautiful and perfect all the time. It made her look a million dollars when her hero woke her at six in the morning and after she had walked for days through the mountains of China.

It also made of her a pin-up girl; and woman, in the shape of a picture, also went to war. She climbed into lockers, bunks and cockpits and became the image of the girl-next-door whom every chap missed. The image was not of peace, for it was meant to stir up a few far from peaceful feelings including those old warhorses, male sexuality and patriotism. The idea was that man went off and did the dirty deeds of war, accompanied by woman in desirable celluloid form to remind him that life outside war was, ironically, worth fighting for. Whether it was the sultry Rita Hayworth or the pert Debbie Reynolds, the image of woman offering either sex or virginity was there. In this way, in an imperfect world man will be able to make woman do the impossible in his name, by making war bearable. As bombs maim those around him, woman will stay pinned and static in his locker, reminding him that physical perfection, physical wholeness – beauty – still exist. In *Monuments and Maidens* Marina Warner writes:

We all dream, and we may try to capture those dreams in memory, and even make them come true; but we also know we cannot control them or hold them in subjection. Neither in their origin nor their development nor their end, will they do what we will; it is the great seduction of illusionistic art, conveyed by the figure of the

81

dreamed model, muse and living doll, that through art man can become a lord of creation.[1]

The so-called Hollywood Dream seduces because it does not let dreams unfold, but rather pins and fixes them so that we believe man to be indeed a creator of dreams. It has a precedent in Genesis, which tells us that God created man 'in his own image' and that this man might 'fill the earth and subdue it'.

The technological eye of the camera and the omnipotent eye of God have combined to produce in culture a formidable adversary to nature. Whether it was cowboys and Indians, *Ben Hur* or *The Student Prince*, the message was a variation on the theme of opposition. In cowboys and Indians it was light and dark (read for that good against bad). In *Ben Hur* it was man against the odds (God against the evil in man). And in *The Student Prince* it was the high call of kingly duty against the lesser call of domestic love.

Within the system of setting as opposites good and evil, God and the Devil, the Bible has wheeled out against nature another big gun – the obscene search for perfection. I use the word 'obscene' because of the way we view perfection. We think of it as a thing or being beyond our grasp, for we are mortal and therefore imperfect. The obscenity lies in the fact that it makes fools of us if we forever search for the impossible. Through this we practise the further obscenity of denying or ignoring the possible, the ordinary and, to use Winnicott's phrase, the 'good enough'. These ideas are expressed in a poem by Yves Bonnefoy called 'Imperfection Is the Summit':

> There was this:
> You had to destroy, destroy, destroy.
> There was this:
> Salvation is only found at such a price.
>
> You had to
> Ruin the naked face that rises in the marble,
> Hammer at every beauty every form,
>
> Love perfection because it is the threshold
> But deny it once known, once dead forget it.
>
> Imperfection is the summit.[2]

This search for perfection has been handed down in the biblical representation of the man, Jesus Christ. In the story the perfection of Christ transcends the physical through His birth from a virgin, and His Resurrection, which was until recently unquestioned. After six years of research, the Church of England's Doctrine Council published in 1987 a document entitled *We Believe in God*. It contains no mention of the virgin birth. Writing of the Resurrection, its authors note: 'The debate continues to this day. That different views are possible both about the evidence of the New Testament itself, and about the implications of a Christian doctrine of God and of Christ, is a reminder of the inevitable imperfections and corrigibility of the models which we use for our understanding of God.'[3] This is the first major report sanctioned by the Church of England hierarchy which allows such a liberal interpretation of the scriptures.

One of the many nuances attached to the story of the birth of Christ is that the visible, physical mother, Mary, was dominated by the invisible, spiritual Father, God, to produce the impossibility of a virgin birth. This represents a triumph of the spiritual over the physical – and, in the way the sexes have come to be delineated and opposed, of man over woman. But the biblical message is more than one of simple domination. It makes a much more complicated statement: that, unlike Christ, the rest of us are born into original sin, and our destiny, if we are true believers, is to spend our lives trying to achieve the impossible – a likeness of Christ himself. The Maker of the universe ordained things so that man would spend a lifetime striving for the impossible (perfection) in order to achieve the unimaginable (eternal bliss).

In creating this kind of God it could be construed that the Jewish chroniclers of the Old Testament had problems with authority. In *Thou Shalt Not Be Aware* Alice Miller describes these problems through the words of a patient:

> The Bible speaks of God's omnipotence, but the Divine deeds it describes contradict this attribute; for someone who possessed omnipotence would not need to demand obedience from his child, would not feel his security threatened by false gods, and would not persecute his people for having them. Perhaps the theologians are not in a position to create an ideal image of true goodness and omnipotence differing from the character of their real fathers until they have seen through this character. And so they create an image of God based on the model they are already familiar with. Their God is like their father: insecure, authoritarian, power-hungry, vengeful, egocentric.[4]

She goes on to describe the consequences of these problems:

> But who is it actually who is so eager to see that society's norms are observed, who persecutes and crucifies those with the temerity to think differently – if not people who have had a 'proper upbringing'? They are the ones who learned as children to accept the deaths of their souls and do not notice it until they are confronted with the vitality of their young or adolescent children. Then they must try to stamp out this vitality, so they will not be reminded of their own loss . . .
>
> The Church's struggle (supposedly an expression of God's will) against children's vitality is renewed daily by training them to be blindly obedient to those in authority and to think of themselves as wicked; this approach is more reminiscent of Herod, with his fear of the resurrection of the truth in the child, than it is of Jesus, with His demonstrated confidence in human potentiality. The hatred rooted in the small child's reaction to this training swells to immense proportions, and the Church (in part unconsciously) abets the proliferation of evil, which, on a conscious level, it professes to oppose.[5]

To use Dr Miller's phrase, the 'struggle against vitality', which is part of Old Testament doctrine, is also part of something as seemingly harmless and fun-laden as the Hollywood Dream. At first glance the link between the Old Testament and Hollywood might seem obscure, except for films like *Ben Hur*, *The Ten Commandments* and so on. But what Hollywood initially did was to employ a fixed set of rules about authority and relationships which were taken from the scriptures. The starring roles were taken by man and man, man and woman, good and evil. Somewhat exceptional were certain kinds of musicals: Fred Astaire's dancing could hardly be called moralistic, but the plot – and there had to be one – was a predictable version of a woman being tamed, or a man seeing the error of his ways. In the end Beauty and the Beast, Tarzan and Jane, cowboys and Indians, Fred Astaire and Ginger Rogers might all have been called the same thing.

It was the sameness of the basic theme that was the problem. It was a theme which presented man as superior to woman and cowboy as superior to Indian. It also contained the fantasy that perfection is a noble rather than a dangerous aim. This perfection is dangerous because it goes against reality – not only in the biblical sense but in the natural world, in which all living things are not fixed images but in a constant state of flux. The eye of the camera and the eye of the God-figure have conspired through culture and scripture to deny this, and have tried instead to assert themselves as undeniable authorities. They try to refute the authority of the individual, which nature prizes above all else for that *is* her gift – uniqueness.

One of the miracles of the natural world is that no two snowflakes are ever completely alike. The gift or prize that the natural world offers is the opportunity for creation at its most essential and irrefutable. It offers the only opportunity of uniqueness – and of uniqueness that is in itself creative, in that all living things can reproduce themselves. It therefore gives man and woman what no one and nothing else to our present knowledge can provide – individual experience. It is this individual experience which gives rise to a sense of personal authority and personal meaning.

If humans were not individual, personal authority would not be necessary. Neither would the singular search for meaning, for if we were reproduced like robots our meaning would have been devised and decided by someone or something else. It is our uniqueness which gives us the possibility and the need for a personal search. Without this there would be no need for a meaning in life.

The search for meaning leads to adventure, the importance of which the philosopher Alfred North Whitehead stresses in his book *Adventures of Ideas*. Without adventure, Whitehead claims, a civilized life is not possible. Meaning and adventure are both linked in the search for beauty and for civilized values.

The spirit of adventure has been raided by culture and scripture so that it has become a mass fantasy rather than an individual reality. Hollywood told us that adventure happened between cowboys and Indians. Scripture told us that we are not in fact totally free to find our own destinies, for there are only two paths in this world: the one which leads up to God, and the other which leads down to the Devil. When systems of opposites are deliberately set up so that you have to choose one of two sides, individual choice is restricted. The system itself becomes fixed into a self-perpetuating, self-limiting, ritual pattern from which there is no escape. This inability to escape, or pinning down of universal issues into stereotypical opposites, is a kind of cross to which the fundamentalist mind has nailed itself. It has done so for fear of suffering eternal death in the form of damnation, but through it manages to bring the quality of deathliness into life itself.

The cross of unattainable, unnatural perfection which funda-mentalist Christians have to carry is a necessary stimulant to that primary source of destruction, self-loathing. It all contributes to its own ideology: that humans are not in themselves capable of peace or balance; that life on earth must therefore always be chaotic; and that one's escape from this rather daunting fate is to hope that life in the hereafter will compensate for present tribulations.

The Indian philosopher and educator Krishnamurti, who died in 1985, once said mischievously in conversation that the Christian religion forfeited any possibility of peace on earth when it invented the idea of Heaven. In his work he tried to express and illustrate the difficult idea that a *radical* change of heart – of awareness – comes about not from years of academic study (although in fact deep thought is crucial) but from, seeing clearly. One of the problems in explaining this 'seeing' is that the eye-junkie which the modern man has become has difficulty in equating the process of seeing with anything other than domination.

When you contrast one of Krishnamurti's phrases, 'seeing *in the moment*', with the concepts which the Old Testament has come to represent, his meaning becomes easier to grasp. The search for perfection and its denial of reality have made biblical man practically unable to live in or experience the present; seeing the present or 'the moment' is therefore impossible for him. This is the cross he bears. He comes from the twin pasts of his original sin and his banishment from bliss, and heads towards the twin futures of success or failure, Heaven or Hell. Through striving for perfection he hopes to succeed rather than fail, but he is always striving after the impossible. He is strung between Eden in his past and Heaven in his future, in this tension called life on earth which is only transitory. Or else he is strung between the black hole of his non-being, his past, and the inferno of Hell which is his future.

This future must necessarily torment him in his present, even though it is not yet actually with him. It may turn him to drink, drugs or whatever else will obliterate both his concrete and his nebulous anxieties. We have come to seek perfection not as a present completeness but as a future goal. We seek it not as a fluidly changing form but as a neurotic, authoritarian need to deny and conquer the change which is its life-blood. By doing this we have almost annihilated our ability to be aware or to succumb to the present. Krishnamurti's life work was devoted to explaining how 'seeing *in the moment*' will bring about a quantum leap in the consciousness of any person who engages in it.

The search for a perfection outside the individual – the search, in other words, for a uniform perfection, so that individuals become negations of themselves and replicas of each other instead – can only ever be a fascist search. The search for perfection embodied in Hitler's preoccupation with a master race doesn't seem to have been adequate warning of the danger that culture presents. When placed in opposition to nature rather than in co-operation, culture can become perverse and destructive.

The problem is that culture wears such a pretty face. The faces on some of today's glossy magazine covers tell another kind of fascist story. The contents of these publications would have us exercise, sexercise, ritualize ourselves away from the ordinary and obtainable towards the extraordinary and unobtainable. The ideal clone woman these days is still slim, although she now has some intellect and social responsibility to bring to the picture. She is likely to be concerned about nuclear weapons or the environment, and may indeed hold a prestigious job. She is alert, bright-eyed, short-haired and open-faced, and follows an invisible manifesto. It states:

> I am modern more than anything else. I am so up to date that by next month I won't be here because they will have found someone even more up to date, and I am always seeking to better myself. I strive without letting the sweat show, I age without letting the lines show, I think without wrinkling my brow, and I am a good person. I jog before breakfast, do aerobics during lunch, and go to jazz dance classes two evenings a week. I am independent-minded enough to be perhaps slightly older than last year's version of me, and even if I am not an executive I have high self-esteem and value myself. I always carry a condom and I never look depressed.

This superficially charming creature came straight off the branch line which leads from God as omnipotent voyeur through to woman as trying to please and be pleasing at all times.

As she stands, hand casually in pocket, striding confidently into the future, she seems harmless enough – but she is an embodiment of the tortuous science that image is all. She has also moved camps, for in the divide of opposites between man and woman, woman has traditionally represented art and man science. There has always been a composite woman who is a denial of any one real woman, in other words a denial of reality; and now that composite woman wears some of man's trappings.

In *Monuments and Maidens* Marina Warner speaks of the habit through the centuries of seeing woman not as individual but as symbol, so that in the eye of man woman is not mortal but metaphor, not an individual but a type, not subject but simile, not flesh but fable, not person but parable. Looked at in this way it is not surprising that she is violated, for offences against women are thought of as generalities rather than particular crimes. Part of man's problem with woman is that he has been encouraged to think of her in the abstract or in symbolic form; and, because her flesh-and-blood reality has been denied, woman has been depersonalized. She has come to have fewer feelings, and the good-girl image of the late eighties' magazines has colluded with this view while at the same time claiming to reject it. Warner writes:

> the [nude's] image assumes all the while the beholder's erotic appetite for a body like hers as if she were a love goddess. She very rarely commands the drama in which she takes part; she is raped or at least arrested, uncovered, done to rather than doing. She is '*a negative imprint of domination*' [my emphasis] . . . The nude lies in architraves, holds up portals, ministers to great achievers in the streets of cities from London to Vienna to New York, and we are rarely asked to care for what she is feeling, rather to feel better because of what she makes us feel.[6]

Warner echoes Edwin Mullins in writing:

> Biological sex cannot be the ring-fence in which the imagination lies wingless. Writers cleared it before painters, but visual representation, sculpted and painted, has continued to reify women in a manner some writers of fiction overcame some time ago, and mass communication of imagery has reinforced its limited code. As Matisse said in 1953, we live in an age 'when a flood of ready-made images . . . are to the eye what prejudices are to the mind'.[7]

The twin needs to make woman stereotype and to make her perfect are part of the modern manufacturing industry. They are also part of the on-going battle between culture and nature: if culture can actually make an object out of woman then it has complete power to use her as it wishes. This is why women who are individuals have exacted such high penalties, for they transgress codes of generalities which inform the way the world is perceived. Whether such a woman is called rampant feminist or witch, the attitudes that inflict this on her are not so much prejudiced as paranoid. In denying individuality or uniqueness, culture goes against nature and tries to arrive at a state of mastery. This mastery exemplifies the idea that it is God, through scripture, who decides and dictates.

Photography and artwork have now reached such heights of sophistication that nature can be completely transcended. It is possible to freeze-frame a plain-looking woman – given the right lighting, camera angles, make-up and background – and make her look stunning. In this way the camera always lies, because it does the impossible – it transfixes a moment both in time and in space. In nature such transfixing only occurs as an individually felt experience – we can be stopped in our tracks by the sudden sight of a sunset or a field of wild flowers.

One of the major differences between photographing a woman and looking at a beautiful sunset is that one is a far more controllable exercise than the other. While it is possible to photograph a sunset, it changes from moment to moment of its own accord. The woman obeys the camera's instruction. She is a movable feast. Nature isn't.

The photographer can stand a woman anywhere, and even alter her 'flavour' sufficiently so that in a dozen different pictures she will look like a dozen different women. The camera has achieved the dream not only of recognizing and capturing a moment in time, but of *deciding* it. In this way a woman – or indeed a man – may be pictured not only to grasp what makes them unique – their essence, if you like – but to fragment them, so that they lose uniqueness and become whoever you want them to. These identikit people exist only for the camera, and are adaptable symbols of an age in which the eye of the lens is a powerful describer of the world of image. Beauty is not a part of this because it is intrinsically unique: image is what is being played with here.

The eye of the God-figure and the eye of modern technology combine to produce sensibilities connected with the idea of perfection, whether it is an image of Heaven as the perfect place to be or of the face that will launch far more than a thousand ships. Perfection is the apotheosis of culture, as it is of scripture, and it denies nature – for nothing in nature is perfect, and certainly not perfectly symmetrical. In manufacturing industries you can repeat successful formulae as often as you like; in the natural world you can't.

The need to achieve the impossible dream, however, made a mass invasion with the era of still photography and then moving films. The Puritan within the chief cameraman would have us believe that the perfect life exists out there, and that Heaven can be attained through consuming the right product or swallowing the right fantasy. In his book *Seeing is Believing* Peter Biskind writes about the films of the fifties and sixties and their obvious and not so obvious meanings:

> In films of the sixties, both right and left, the center's attempts to reconcile contradictions finally broke down. Nature became a value totally oppositional to culture, now experienced as corrupt. Sex, in the hands of both James Bond and Arlo Guthrie, became a weapon against the 'system' . . . patriarchy became an enemy of matriarchy, increasingly experienced as emasculating; vigilante violence became an acceptable alternative to the law, now perceived as ineffectual.[8]

Biskind's words draw attention to a seeming contradiction in arguments about perfection versus imperfection, culture versus nature, or saintliness versus human nature. For he writes that during this period Hollywood was *subversive* of culture. Culture was the baddie and nature the goodie. Culture was portrayed on the screen through nasty, global plots set up by ugly and sometimes invisible businessmen; nature through handsome, sexy heroes like James Bond who saved the world from culture's fiendish plots. So in the films the invisible God or good figure of the Eden myth became an invisible baddie; the female sexual temptress called Eve changed into a clean-as-clean sexy male with a boyish twinkle in his eye.

But the stories sound awfully familiar – still the same old collusion of opposites. Even though the women in the Bond films were sometimes on the side of the baddies they were all beautiful, and James Bond usually got a 'good' beautiful one as a prize at the end. Hollywood was playing around with stereotypes: 'Let's have culture as the villain for a few years, and make nature the hero.' (Hollywood hadn't at that stage thought up a *female* version of Bond.)

This system was, as Biskind points out, oppositional. The 'centre' ground, the ground of reality, was missing. In reality every person contains within themselves opposite qualities, which change and harmonize in a highly complex and intricate way. In oppositional thinking it doesn't matter who wins a battle, because the war goes on – and on.

The seeming contradictions which the mixing up of opposites brings about is diabolically clever, though not *consciously* planned. It is a way of keeping most of the people confused most of the time. It makes counter-argument difficult, for it is almost impossible to explain what is going on in the psychology which works with fundamentalist traditions. One minute this psychology has presented

God as invisible – then it switches, and the Devil, or the baddie, is invisible instead. One minute woman is a temptress through Eve; the next she is on a higher-than-high pedestal and her name is Mary, mother of Christ. When culture is really being tricky it of course sews Eve and Mary together.

I have argued that culture presents females as visible – the Mother Natures to God's Mr Big – but it also makes them morally *invisible* by not allowing them full accountability. Sometimes it does many oppositional things more or less at the same time. Hollywood has often put woman on a pedestal – the ice-cold, unattainable beauty whom men worship. But even within the same film she will be presented as the spiritual inferior, while man goes on to perform deeds for God so as to forget her.

So when one tries to gather solid arguments – for women's rights, for example – the so-called evidence about women is convoluted and often conflicting. When I interviewed women in the early seventies for a series of newspaper and magazine articles on feminism, they reported a bewildering array of contradictory 'plots' used against them to deny them more power. Many women said that men told them they were living in clover by being allowed to stay at home and be protected from the big bad world of politics. Politics was, of course, exactly where the power to change their status lay. So women were being told they were living in clover while they inhabited one small domestic plot and men had the run of the whole field.

The idea that women live pleasanter lives by not having to soil their hands with the muck and dirt of the big bad world is not without foundation. As women who have entered politics know, it is often a tough, dirty business. However, when some men used a 'You are being cosseted and protected by staying at home' argument it made women who wanted to take their share of moral and political decisions seem perverse. Such was the power of that particular piece of trickery. It used the system which falsely says that men and women are opposite to substantiate the argument that women should keep their soft, pretty selves at home while big, macho men do the political shovelling.

The paradox is that in any one day a person may feel superior and inferior, high and low, wonderful and apologetic. This is normal. What is not normal is to institute a system in which all the shades of these and countless other feelings are disregarded. As far as Hollywood goes, it's the old line: 'If you can't tell me the plot in three sentences we haven't got a deal.'

The 'deal' in the poem 'Imperfection Is the Summit' is therefore even more critical. It is a move towards accepting shades and nuances as more legitimate and interesting material for life itself and for its cultural portrayal than fantastical goodies and baddies. The title of the poem might at first seem perverse – again because of the way culture has reinvented reality. For culture has paraded perfection as the acme of human achievement. The Old Testament viewpoint tells us that perfection *is* the acme, and the camera creates it for us at will. Bonnefoy's poem shows us how perverse *this* idea is. It shows that the search for perfection *as a fixed or attainable entity* will perpetuate the notion and practice of war. For fixed perfection opposes nature, because nature is not static or fixed. In fact nature is its own hammer, and 'destroys' its own beauty from moment to moment – so that other, fresh or new beauty can take its place. Within creation, 'good' destruction is present.

Trying to fix the moment, or beauty, so that it can be held on to a little longer is in itself destructive – and impossible in the natural world. For the natural world creates from second to second, and is itself the source of *that* re-creation – time. In nature the sun *will* sink beneath the horizon, it *will* go down, it *will* die – and it does so in order for there to be creation in the form of another day. This is summed up in the Taoist saying that noon is born at midnight.

Therefore Bonnefoy's instruction to 'destroy' and to

> Love perfection because it is the threshold
> But deny it once known, once dead forget it

means that creative destruction in the form of change – and of being alert to that change – is vital. The Old Testament psychology which pervades our thinking and raids our vitality says the opposite. It does not recognize the womb, in which creation and destruction live together in necessity, beauty and hope.

8

A Tale of Two Sexes

The war that goes on and on within a system of separated opposites is the battle of the sexes. This battle is thought of as normal, as an inevitable consequence of there being two opposite sexes in the world. The accepted 'wisdom' is that it is natural for opposites to fight, when in fact it is not. *Culture* has decreed that man and woman, God and nature will do battle. It has said: isn't it a better idea to have Mother Nature at our command, than us at hers? Power-sharing, which seems the only long-term solution, is lost in the either/or situations on which oppositional thinking insists.

What has happened as a result of liberties taken with the natural world and with his own nature is that man has trapped himself. The trap has tightened over the centuries – for, ironically, in setting out to show nature who was boss culture left woman to bring up the children.

Freud talks of the terror that a boy experiences at being banished from his mother's breast and her lap. Is it possible that fundamentalist man's terror of banishment from maternal bountifulness led him to create a *man* who is bountiful (God) and a woman who was both wicked and banishable (Eve)? Is man turning the tables on mother, so that instead of *her* having the power to sling *him* out he reverses this situation? He creates a father (God), who has the ability to sling out Eve, who was the mother of the human race. If we take Eden as symbolizing babyhood or innocence, fundamentalist man has made a mother out of God. This mother sent children from the garden because the female child, Eve, was a naughty girl. Although this same mind has given God a male gender, His role changes when this mind wants to get round the pain of separation from its mother and its own emotional stock.

A redraft of the Adam and Eve story is found in the legend of Sleeping Beauty, in which a curious Beauty is punished for her prying. The prick of knowledge (a needle) sent Beauty to sleep for a whole century. Only a handsome prince – in other words something entirely outside her influence, especially since she was in a deep swoon – could wake her from this living 'death'. One interpretation is that for woman beauty should be enough, and the wish to lead a normal life too is being greedy. Curiosity is seen as a punishable offence. Another interpretation is that it takes a good man to wake up a woman and remove from her the curse of living in a twilight world. A handsome prince can take a woman from obscurity into the full light of a life which is complete.

These kind of moral tales have had their effect on man as much as on woman, and particularly on man and woman as young people. As long as girls are still brought up to wait for their princes and boys are still brought up to think of emotions as accidents or sensations, like unwanted erections, men and women will continue to be formed in the old moral codes. To the average modern teenage boy Eve is the woman who copped Adam with a Cox's Orange Pippin, and Sleeping Beauty and Cinderella are raging goodie-goodies. Boys sneer at fairy stories because they think they are weedy, but there is another possible reason for their attitude. Fairy stories cruelly face boys with what they are not – princes – and may set up in them the fear that, whatever women want of them, they will not come up to scratch. Of such emotional elitism are these tales concocted.

In fact man set himself many traps, not just one. His own fairy stories carry the message that his heroic days are over. Were they ever with him at all? he wonders. And by seeking fixed images which must have seemed at first to be at his behest, man has found himself cornered again. For the fixed image lends itself so readily to pornographic use.

I was once asked to speak at a conference on pornography, and, like the other speakers, had to find a working definition of what I meant by the word. I came up with the reasoning that pornography is something which discourages an individual's full knowledge of him or herself, while pretending to do the opposite. In *Friday's Child* I wrote:

> Pornography . . . appears to be sexually explicit and adventurous. But . . . [it] militates against sexual excitement because it is a drug . . . It is like a fix in that looking at a particular pornographic picture initially excites, but . . . soon . . . you cannot get aroused without this picture or a substitution for it . . . that is why [pornography] brings about a loss of personal freedom and a loss of genuine sexual feeling in the long term.[1]

Pornography is concerned with image rather than reality and, like alcohol, might not be harmful if taken in small doses and kept away from young or immature people. In concerning itself not with reality, but with its opposite, pornography has the power to limit imagination and exploration – and therefore to limit individual discovery or behaviour on the part of either the voyeur or the object being looked at. So in trying to trap nature in the form of woman, man traps himself. This is one of the ways in which pornography and violence go together, for a person who has trapped himself is going to be enraged.

The need to have the image fixed or the woman pinned down sets a further trap for man: gratification eventually becomes more difficult. The pornographic mind is one that cannot bear reality, so it cannot grow. This is its own result and its own punishment, which it ultimately visits on others. The pornographic mind is hampered, indeed crucified, by its own need to have an image that is fixed and controllable. Such a mind is, of course, excruciatingly vulnerable and lives in a state of fluctuating short-lived triumph and constantly returning terror.

Man's diktat to woman to look good at all times is not only intended to placate loss of beauty in himself. In the pornographic psychology a woman who does not make the best of herself is viewed as perverse and aggressive. Women are supposed to fit into the image of the world that suits men. Women who don't do this are not so much ball-breakers as image-shatterers. They wreck the way the world has been ordered. They are iconoclasts who dare to rake up the sacred ground of woman's image in man's eyes.

The system is clearly concerned about form, and about fixing form so that it becomes governable, manageable and therefore safe. It contradicts the image of man as adventurer, no doubt an image that had substance while it was the world *outside* himself that was being explored. With the world *inside* himself, his own psychology, man has been considerably less enterprising.

So has he been with his constructions of woman. Rather than have her roaming free and possibly startling, he has designed a system of polarized outfits into which she may slip. Guises like virgin or whore, mother or temptress, ice-maiden or sultry sex-pot are part of the collection. Man sticks to these stereotypes, but because his own unrecognized needs are complex he sometimes sews up a number of them in one costume. What isn't on is for a woman to wear several of these dresses at the same time other than at man's behest – for *he* is Master of the Wardrobe. Modern woman gives man a terrible jolt when she walks around in shades and colours of her own, which defy his stereotypes and his conflation of them.

One of the biggest traps that man set woman – and himself – was the form of the virgin. Man thought he would be really safe by foisting on to woman the idea that her worth and status would depend on a thin membrane called a hymen. He didn't realize that his own sexuality would then become virgin-fixated and that he would risk losing his ability freely to enjoy a lively, inquisitive woman.

The cultural virgin is a complex construct, and relates to man's need for a fixed object that he can pin down. The form of the virgin is particularly interesting for what it says about man's need. The virgin is intact – that is her definition: she is an unbroken or unsealed unit. When this state of virginity is 'lost' – which is still the way we describe it, even when it is 'lost' to the man who loves her – the virgin has relinquished something. In being no longer intact she has lost not so much face as formula, not so much hymen as system. Man has given the virgin an impossible conundrum. If she remains virgin she remains without benefit of male touch, and is therefore not fully woman. If she is touched, she drops from the pedestal of virgin and becomes only wife instead of acclaimed being. Either way she is trapped. She contributes to the myth of man being a lord of creation and master of destruction. The paradox is that, through penetrating her, man creates a full woman and simultaneously destroys a virgin.

This is the pinnacle of creation – to have life and death, creation and destruction in a single myth. Its power lies in the fact that it is so close to the real world: every moment of life is a moment closer to death, and in the natural world life and death are inextricable. It is in the virgin that man has come closest to controlling this natural law, which is why the virgin is so worrying. In her touching there is loss and gain, both for him and for herself. But since her elevation to high importance is a man-made myth, she cannot escape decline in his eyes. For when she loses her virginity man decrees that she becomes not more of a woman, but less of an ideal entity. He therefore places great store on the ritual of this happening. In some cultures bloodstained sheets from the marriage bed are displayed, not only to prove the man's virility but also to prove that the woman was a virgin. Man builds his own sorrow, and hers, by viewing this as the pinnacle rather than the beginning of sexual experience. Nor can fundamentalist man understand that the *quality* of virgin or innocence, rather than the form of it, may occasionally be present in a woman even when she is a mother and a grandmother.

The virgin represents in human form part of the disposable culture that has been created in disregard of natural laws – the 'use once and throw away' attitude. In nature – and in human beings – there are cycles. The emotional cycles in both woman and man mean that the *quality* of virginity may be present throughout a woman's life. This is not to say that, in the case of woman, she returns to copy her younger self. It means rather that, as the layers of life build up in her, so should her understanding of herself and her qualities. She may well have 'thrown away' her actual physical virginity; culture would then throw her on the virginity scrap-heap. But she will often understand the meaning of virginity more deeply as she grows older than she did as a young woman; nature says that all seasons return time and time again, as do human qualities.

In both woman and in man, an understanding of the nature of childhood, innocence, individuality and shyness may, with permission, increase during the years. For understanding deepens as time goes on – or at least it *may* do so if it is sought and worked for. Culture says otherwise, which is why pornography has such a hold on man as well as woman. The pornographic mind is addicted to youth and perfection and is petrified of age, experience, and in particular of knowledge and compassion.

The idea that 'wholeness', in the form of the idealized virgin, is in the past and possibly in the future, in the form of Heaven, is a biblical one. It was created by the loss of Eden and the promise of life after this Hell on earth. The Eden myth says that bliss is behind us, Heaven in front of us, and that the present is concerned with making up for losing one and looking forward to gaining the other. The cultural virgin is in a similar position. She has irretrievably lost her hymen, but Heaven may await her in the next life if she is a good, quiet woman.

The 'death' of the virgin – or, to be precise, the ending of the state of virginity which culture imposes on woman – has its macrocosmic counterpart in fundamentalist end-of-the-world theories. As virgin ends in woman, so shall life on earth. In the Old Testament mind there was a beginning, which was Eden, and there will be an end, which is God's wrath at Armageddon. At the end God will appear and rescue the 'goodies', leaving the rest of us to get on with our Hell and torment.

This is a really nasty thought. It vindicates evil by supporting the violent notion that the earth will end in a blaze of destruction – and that this is inevitable. If you think this way evil becomes a necessity, for if we were all good the fire and wrath would not be needed. It also introduces the smug notion that if people down here behave in a thuggish way they will get their come-uppance at the Day of Judgement. This is one of the biggest traps that man set himself, for it meant that he transferred his sense of moral responsibility on to the

God-figure. In order to fulfil his own invented apocalypse myth it was also inevitable that he would invent weapons of mass destruction. There are decent Christians who do not concern themselves with the complex issues of world peace and the balance of the environment because they believe in the apocalypse. After the apocalypse, culture will presumably be given a new world to start all over again.

It is belief in an invisible, omnipotent God-figure which makes these thoughts possible and therefore more likely. His ascendancy over the natural laws of cause and effect, birth and death, summer and winter means that in His followers' system of belief man can always conquer nature. In particular it gives man the idea that he can conquer nature's most final judgement, death. Death is rather difficult to get round, but man did it. He said, through God, that death wasn't death after all because his Maker would bring life after death – and a far better life than the here and now. In this way man, as the lord of creation, outwits dumb, stupid nature. If culture does blow us all up with nuclear weapons it will have fulfilled its God-wish. As with the virgin, this is a rather final judgement: the ultimate trap.

Because nature changes, man has wanted to create static perfection, whether it be in the ultimate computer system, in weapons, or in the castle to end all castles, the totally impregnable fortress. In his chapter called 'The Castle of the Self' in *What a Man's Gotta Do* Antony Easthope writes: 'The ego must maintain that it is always the same. In the middle of change it must find repetition and establish itself as a fixture' and 'At present in the dominant myth the masculine ego is imagined as closing itself off completely, *maintaining total defence* [my emphasis].[2]

Will we allow intelligent life to succeed us? Will we leave our progeny sufficiently free of radiation, chemical interference and other causes of deformity to survive? If we do, writers and historians of the future may well characterize late twentieth-century Britain something like this:

In this technological age it was apparent that inventions were quickly superseded, and that with increased knowledge and skill this must be the case. But people continued to work as if it wasn't so. They continued to believe that individuals could find a way which over-rode all others of making their new inventions impervious. This attitude may well have stemmed from the fact that the people of Britain, in common with those of North America and parts of Europe, had already accepted the invention of a perfect God-figure who was invisible and not subject to natural laws, to any ageing process, or indeed to any process of time or change. It resulted in an ultimately crippling perfection complex.

This perfection complex has given man a strange attitude to his own body. As Easthope writes:

A hard body will ensure that there are no leakages across the edges between inner and outer worlds. Nature, it seems, has betrayed the perimeter of the male body. It has opened up there a number of gaps and orifices, though mercifully fewer than for the female body. What holes remain must be firmly shut, for as Norman Mailer makes clear in his war book, *The Naked and the Dead*, the first worry for men in combat is 'keeping a tight arsehole'. Tensed, the whole frontier can be kept on red alert.[3]

The crisis of being on red alert, with beauty, Heaven and paradise all 'out there' somewhere, is acute, and means that man has a powerful sense of being cornered. It means that man sees himself as a victim of nature, not culture, particularly through what a beautiful woman can possibly do to him. He sees woman rather than man as having the upper hand, the hand that is hidden from view and therefore all the more powerful. He sees himself as potential victim, not woman as actual one, even when she has been sacrificed as the young and beautiful have throughout the ages.

By taking control of the eye, of the seeing; by hi-jacking beauty and deciding who and how she should be; by equating her with perfection rather than adventure; by honing her so that she did not frighten him but still excited him; by making her symmetrical and not rapturous; by all these means man thought he would keep himself from danger. When women like Marilyn Monroe became his idea of too wild because too beautiful – when beauty, in other words, occasionally went on the rampage – he made her dumb. He called her dumb blonde or used the symbol 'blonde bombshell' to describe her possible effect on him. When she filled his eye, he made her shut her mouth.

But feminist woman didn't shut her mouth. Instead she started thinking about some of man's myths. The Book of Genesis offered a particularly interesting one:

And the serpent said unto the woman, Ye shall not surely die.
   For God doth know that in the day ye eat thereof, then your eyes shall be opened, and ye shall be as God, knowing good and evil.
   And when the woman saw that the tree was good for food, and

that it was pleasant to the eyes, and a tree to be desired to make one wise, she took of the fruit thereof and did eat, and gave also unto her husband with her; and he did eat.

And the eyes of them both were opened, and they knew that they were naked; and they sewed fig leaves together, and made themselves aprons.

A possible interpretation of this story is that Eve was responsible for ending the moral vacuum in which she and Adam had been placed. She could therefore be seen as the beginner or mother of morality. Previously she and Adam had not known good from evil. Surely this is ignorance rather than bliss, for, as the philosopher's question goes, if you are ignorant of 'bad' how can you possibly know and therefore enjoy – let alone *be* – 'good'?

The picture of Adam and Eve as 'not knowing' makes them like God's toys: for knowledge is equated with morality, and morality with the decision-making processes which distinguish humans from animals. The question that raises its reasonable head over the morality of the Eden myth is this: is there any value in being in Eden if you don't know that's where you are?

In the contorted thinking around the invention and traditional interpretation of this myth it is Eve who is held responsible, not for morality but for banishment. Following on from that, man made and dictated moral codes. When modern woman became moral – when she became accountable in the world – she discovered many traps. She was furious with the way that man had ensnared her, yet if she was heterosexual what was she to do about it? How does a marriage of the personal and the political square with going to bed with the bad guy? Should she be celibate? Should she be a political lesbian?

There was a time in the seventies when feelings were running so high that women's interest in heterosexuality and in men became depleted. It was all too difficult to cope with. Some women decided to use their energies in getting on with a career, and others decided to 'cool things with men' until the anti had died down a little. For the first time in history, it was men who were marginalized.

Another trap then emerged. It became far too tempting to reverse the system of opposites that man had set up – just to turn the tables. If women had been kept down before, let men be kept down now. If women had been kept from speaking at meetings, let them now have their say and let men shut up. It was all too easy to blame man for everything that had gone wrong in the world, and in particular to blame him for war.

100

A TALE OF TWO SEXES

The idea of men as war-mongering and women as peace-loving is a false one, as was pointed out by Meg Beresford when I interviewed her in the autumn of 1985 while she was General Secretary of CND.

I don't agree with the argument that peace is a woman's issue. It's far more complicated than that. Many of the major movements in the past two hundred years have had women in common. Women were remarkably important in the abolition of slavery and in the Civil Rights movements, and of course in the Suffragette movement. There are connections to do with human liberties.

The reason why the issue of disarmament would engage a great many women is that it is about liberty, and is a progression from women wanting the right to control their lives to wanting the right to *have* lives – to live. It's not because women are 'better at peace' that disarmament concerns them, but because they have been emerging in the last couple of centuries as people who have a strong drive towards improving the quality of lives. Life is the issue. In this context it is not an accident that the Greenham Women, Women for Life on Earth should be so important. They are part of a pattern of women's participation in important events.

The trap was to be blind to woman's complicity or to refuse to accept it – to consider woman as the historical sleeper and as history's victim through the deeds and pens of man. The blind side of woman, the side that would not see, was both instrumental in her continuing defeat and complicit in it. The myth of Sleeping Beauty would have her believe that the prick of knowledge will send her into a sleep from which she will not awaken. It would also have her believe that what went on in the world during the time she was slumbering was not of her making. What greater alibi can one have against the deed than to have been asleep while it was all going on? What better defence than to have slept through the troubles?

The awareness that began to change this situation came about slowly. It happened through a deeper appreciation of the impossibility of making divides between male and female, political and personal, without tearing yourself apart. Through a wider understanding of the work of people like Jung it became clear that in both the external and internal worlds male and female are intermingled. Their separation or division always causes pain and conflict.

There is one separation which early feminists made – from moral outrage about what patriarchy had done to women. For a while feminists reseparated man and woman, but in a different way, this time calling woman goddess and man evil. Jill Tweedie discussed this when, following the theme of Teresa Stangl's admission, she wrote of how a definition of 'bad man' and 'good woman' just won't do:

> Behind every great man is a woman, we say, but behind every monster there is a woman too . . . there she is in the shadows, a vague, female silhouette, tenderly wiping blood from [her] hands . . . such women have deliberately blinded and deafened themselves to the agony of anyone but their lovers. That marks them as accomplice . . . people who love and service a monster . . . bear some of the responsibility for the monster's deeds.[4]

Modern woman's moral accountability was wryly recounted by Jenny Lecoat in a *Cosmopolitan* article in 1987. Ms Lecoat made the point that a woman should be very responsible about whom she sleeps with. Headlined: 'No Conservative sex for me. Sex with Tories is out', her article stated:

> I am a reasonable woman . . . [but] I will not screw Tories . . . I don't want anybody who spouts nonsense about the unemployed getting off their arses, getting anywhere near mine; nor do I want any man professing respect for me when he has, at base, no respect for the rest of the human population . . . Maybe I'm limiting my experience. Fine. Sex with Tories, condommed or not, is an experience I can do without.

The possible trap for woman in the search for her own moral identity was that she would take revenge on man. While Ms Lecoat would welcome this if the man was a Tory, there was a danger that all men would be called bad.

In her book *The Wild Girl*, a first-person fictional account of Mary Magdalene's relationship with Christ before and after His death, Michelle Roberts writes eloquently of the possibility of this revenge. In a sequence of dreams which Mary has after the Crucifixion, Christ is in effect crucified a second time. In the following sequence a token man is being tried for the crimes of all men against women.

> I stood in a hall of judgement . . . I was dressed in scarlet, and so were all the women in the hall. All of them were judges, and all of them were advocates, and so took turns to read out the charges . . . the litany of crimes was long, and terrible, and the chanted indictments repeated certain words over and over again.

— You have raped us, countless times. You have raped strangers, in peacetime and in war, to establish conquest of a territory whose nature you fear, to continue your separation from the woman in yourself whom you have lost and whom you hate . . . Your fear of difference, of the dangerous Other you have invented, is so great that you mutilate us to fit us to your pattern . . . cutting out our desire and our intelligence because you think those things are male.

— You have created God in your image alone, and you have spoken in the name of God to name us as Babylon, the harlot city who must be trampled and overthrown . . .

— We *are* the scarlet women, oh Man, of your deepest nightmares, and we have risen at last, and we shall oversee your downfall, for this is the last reckoning, and this is the judgement place . . .

I called out: what shall we do with the Man?

There were as many answers as there were women in the hall. I could hear only a few voices above the tumult.

— Let us kill all the male children.

— Let us kill all the men.

— Let us withdraw our love from them forever.

— Let us burn all their libraries and burn their books. Let us destroy their lies and begin to tell our own truth.

— *Yes*, went up the mass cry: let us burn their books.

And so the contents of all the libraries in the world, from the whole of history, were brought in and thrown on to a great pyre . . . Then I saw that my book was among those about to be consumed by the flames, and also the books of many other women. And the Man in the dock uncovered his face and raised his head and looked at us all, and I saw that it was Jesus . . . He was naked, and vulnerable, and he stretched his arms out towards us.

— I have lost my bride, he called out: and I am seeking her. Is she here? Can I come to her?

— You burned your bride, one of the women shouted back: many times over. It is too late now.

— Wait, I whispered: I think I have changed my mind.[5]

Michelle Roberts's message here is poignantly clear, as is that in another imagined dream:

This time I saw Jerusalem . . . Seen from a distance, the holy city was . . . lovelier by far than her image in all the words and songs of the sacred books.

She was single, meaning whole, as Jesus had said, and when I saw her gleaming before me I knew that if only I could enter her I too would become complete. Now I carried the knowledge of my own capacity for evil in my heart; now I knew what separation and hatred meant; and now I needed to go into the knowledge of good. Here she was, the new Jerusalem, the bride with full knowledge of her husband.[6]

The 'bride with full knowledge of her husband' is a beautiful concept. A husband with full knowledge of his bride is equally beautiful. This is what the figure of Christ may represent, and this is why, almost two thousand years after His death, He is still celebrated. The Christ of the New Testament is fully heterosexual in that He encompasses His bride within Himself. But Old Testament values are not so much heterosexual as hierarchical. Man's moral code, based firmly and perilously on the invisible God-figure, has made the relationship between men and women structured, so that men and women relate through ideas and instructions about each other. The process is one of idealization, not reality. Man is supposed to be pure and strong and near to God; woman is supposed to be perfect, unreal and near to home.

The idea that woman should be perfect, like an image or a dream, is an offence against what is natural, against what is changing and ageing in her. But it is nature which frightens man, and which he must in turn present as frightening. In setting out to trap nature and woman, and nature *in* woman, man has of course trapped nature in himself. His own vital, vibrant self has been pitilessly abused and denied.

This self has become afraid for another reason, too. For in the process of downgrading woman man has found to his horror that he has used her as a dumping ground for things he considered a nuisance – like beauty – and that she now holds what he most needs. By both idealizing and rubbishing woman, she has become in one awesome creation the receptacle for the hopes he has of reaching Heaven and the fears he has of descending into Hell. She is both virgin and whore – a diabolical trap.

When he has intercourse with her she is his receptacle in receiving his sperm. But will this intercourse lead him to the bliss he seeks through union, or will it lead him to Hell for giving in to temptation? In the psychology that the fundamentalist mind has brought about, woman has become such a complicated structure that man lives in terror of the creature he has supposedly caught in his own snare.

Woman has become man's bank, but in a strange situation which makes him both depositor and manager – he has to be, in an attempt to make his bank safe. This explains why a certain kind of man becomes 'inconsolable' if he doesn't know where his wife is. It is called possessiveness – which it is – but that doesn't explain why it happens. Woman scares the hell out of a certain kind of man if she wanders off on her own, for she is taking so much of him with her.

It sometimes seems that man gave so much of himself away – deposited, dumped so much of himself in woman – that he will always trouble her. He will rummage through her and sometimes crack her open like some grotesque human piggy-bank in order to count the remains of himself, to confirm what he has stored and to reassure himself that it is still his. Woman has certainly been field hospital to man. She has also been the bank of his emotional world, which is the reason why men still go to women to discuss emotional problems: that's where the emotions *are*. If woman now decided to wreak her revenge on him for this, it would be tragic.

Fay Weldon created a scenario for such a situation in her novel *The Life and Loves of a She-Devil*. She describes a spurned wife (read for this symbolic good woman) who, when her husband runs off with a rich and glamorous author, decides to exact a long, painful revenge on them. In the process she hurts not only her husband and his mistress but various other stray parties like her own children. The pain she herself endures is arguably the worst of all: as her ultimate revenge she chooses to undergo extensive plastic surgery that will render her a physical copy of the mistress whom she has meanwhile driven to her death. The mistress, however, was five foot tall; the wife was six. But she goes through with her metamorphosis. Chopped about, our originally Junoesque heroine becomes like the Little Mermaid in Hans Christian Andersen's story and suffers knives through her body whenever she takes a step on her size-eight-sliced-in-half-feet. However, she grits her teeth; it is all worthwhile for the satisfaction of revenge – which of course turns out to be bitter.

This yarn, crackingly and amusingly told, seems to be a modern parable. You take a big, strong, capable woman (which is what today's woman has supposedly become), get a man to thwart her (as he has always done), and see how she destroys practically everyone in the plot by seeking revenge on him. Note particularly how she herself ends up empty-handed, empty-hearted and brooding painfully over the domain she has conquered, and now no longer wants.

Because of Eve and because of the retention of Old Testament values the morally accountable woman has not been a part of history.

Certainly woman has had morals imposed on her, and she has suffered from the double standard that insists on her being good and virginal while man may be whatever he likes – but this is not the same as being accountable. The woman who sees things in her own moral light, and who makes up her mind about what constitutes good and bad, is a new phenomenon. Obviously man had much to lose through her initially, for she has discovered things that he wished to hide.

One of these discoveries is that, while man has been a moral schizophrenic, woman in the past has had to be morally stitched up – in a system long predating Hollywood – and has needed to play good woman to his bad boy, and bad girl (Eve) to his God-man. This system says that man is not only a bad boy, prone to unasked for sexual urges about which he needs to do something, but also judge and chief administrator, who constructs and enforces a moral code by which the bad boy is whipped into line. In other words, male sexuality and its link with aggression has been accepted as man's lot, and to this unfortunate destiny (for who would wish to be thought of as being prey to a penis?) is added the job of being the person who decides what morals are and should be.

Woman has now entered this arena, and has brought with her the possibility of a relationship between the sexes in which neither has to trap or disadvantage the other. Needless to say, her appearance was not greeted with roars of delight, for to fundamentalist man she looked like an apparition. She resembled a genie who had risen from the trap he had set her and now towered over him. It has become clear that, in trying to rule woman, man had become her slave. When he excised beauty from himself, like an unwanted limb, he guaranteed that woman would be troubled by his demands for it back – in other words, his own dependency. He also guaranteed that he would be the eye's potential lackey, and that this figurative 'window of the soul' would be clouded with envy.

In order to accept woman in her own moral right, man has to escape from more of his own traps. The phrase 'in her own right' is the problem, because man had depended on woman to act out his moral 'rights'. He might be morally riven with contradictions of the most fundamental kind, but in the past his creature, woman, has saved the day for him. She has never in the past taken personal credit for doing so because she was man's moral invention, not her own. Man orchestrated the virgin/whore theme so that if woman did well it was his triumph, and if she did badly it was her problem.

This was a dirty trick.

9

Department of Dirty Tricks

It is 1988. A young American woman is visiting London. She is nineteen and has long golden-blonde hair. She is tall and slim, with a small waist that accentuates her curved hips. She is street-wise, having worked with disenchanted teenagers in New York. London feels safe to her by comparison, so she does it. She goes out one night without her 'disguise'. She is assaulted by two young men but manages to break free, possibly because her fitness, fury and American accent disconcert them. For the rest of her time in London, however, she plays safe.

Her disguise looks like this. She winds her hair round a finger, and bandages it to her head. She has a peaked black cap, the kind that rastafarians sometimes wear, which she bungs on top. Then she puts on old running shoes, dark grey trousers and a scruffy black jacket.

She says the disguise works because it makes her look like a man. She's wrong. It works because it makes her look like a dowdy woman. She looks at least ten years older dressed this way and, as often happens, her mannerisms change subtly to fit her new image. She loses some of her delicacy, which, blended with her obvious strength, makes her an attractive person both to be with and to look at. The person wearing these clothes is a 'tough cookie', not a young woman still in her teens, and watching her watch herself in a mirror you see her practising the change.

Her jaw juts, she hunches her shoulders a few times like a boxer squaring up, and even her voice takes on a rougher aspect. Then she sits down again and forgets the mirror. Now some of her 'open-ness' and delicacy returns, and you are confronted with a paradox. You want to close your eyes, shake your head and look again.

'I guess it used to be corsets,' she says, philosophically. 'It's got tougher out there. These days the bandages show.'

The bandages show because of the casualties of war – both male and female. On a woman they show because inconsolable men are attacking her on the street. On a man they show because feminism has badly damaged the male ego. The battle of the sexes is, like all wars, dirty, but it does not have the mitigation of being just. There was no justice in man having the upper hand over woman in post-Christian history. There would be no justice in that system being reversed. What would be fair is to say that man did not bother to dig up either the map of womanhood or the map of manhood from the trenches of pre-Christian life. Having buried the male perspective under a ton of myths, he set about designing and contouring woman so that instead of looking like herself she was patterned to fit his dreams.

Meanwhile, he had set himself up as the manager of beauty; and beauty, as she spun and clawed her way out of her wrapping, turned snarling at her now confounded watchdog. She called him rapist, oppressor, warmonger, liar and much else besides. He retaliated and called her strident, frustrated, ugly, mannish (interesting one, that) and whore.

It rolled on from there, as feminism gathered pace and the Department of Dirty Tricks with it. The DDT has man call woman a ball-breaker for presuming to have an independent thought, and woman call man a chauvinist bastard for being genuinely courteous. It has woman morally seamless, and man morally divided between bad boy and chief executioner. To children it gave this heritage.

Man tried to make woman Heaven on earth by clothing her in beauty and leaving her safely at home where outside influences, and particularly other men, could not tarnish her. He declared that by doing this he was being kind, generous and protective, which of course he wasn't; he was trying to create for himself an oasis where he could be soothed and – yes – civilized. In man's complex, divided morality he has presented himself both as beast and as knight, and woman-at-home fulfilled both these aspects of him. She tamed and soothed the beast, who went snarling and crashing out into the world to kill and plunder, and she worshipped and respected the knight or lord who was her protector.

One of the dirtiest tricks doing the rounds at the moment is man's revenge on woman for biting the hand that had hitherto clothed her – withdrawing his public concern or care for woman, leaving her prey to a system which he knows bears her violence. The comment: 'If she wants to be liberated let her start her own bloody car in the morning' carries some justice. But the one which goes: 'If other men wreak havoc on her it's her fault for spurning my protection' doesn't.

This Mafia-type approach was demonstrated in the behaviour of a group of men who fell about laughing when a youth sexually assaulted a woman in the street near her home. He grabbed her breasts, forced her against a wall and tried to push his hand down her trousers. The woman managed to fend him off, but when she reluctantly went over to the group of laughing men to ask for help in chasing or identifying him one of them said: 'Nothing to do with us, luv.'

There are two aspects to man's withdrawal from woman of his protection which can make the issue confusing. (The story above obviously isn't; it's a straightforward example of: 'If you want to be liberated, get on with it and see if I care.') The vindictive withdrawing of protection has clearly had the desired effect of making woman more vulnerable on the streets. Attempts are now being made to push her back into her box, so that man may once more take control of her.

At the same time as the un-decent man is trying to do this, the decent man is struggling with a different problem. *He* would indeed help any woman in distress of any kind, but his problem is that he doesn't want to be seen to be perpetuating a traditional paternalistic pattern. So he has to keep a watchful eye out for the woman who is victimized by un-decent men, but without seeming to be doing so. He wants to see woman achieve the dignity of being a person who can go out without permission – in other words, unescorted by a man. He understands the dangers both of her going out alone and of his too-watchful gaze making the enterprise even more difficult for her.

Most decent men find they are confronted by a further barrier. Since they are not women, it really is hard fully to understand the extent to which women are pursued by bad men. Women are thought to be exaggerating – indeed, some are – when they talk of the number of times they are accosted, assaulted or badly frightened. In fact the effect on women's lives of losing general male protection has been awful, and has fuelled their anger into thinking of men not just as wrong, but as downright perverse.

Typical daily incidents go along these lines. While walking to the bus-stop every morning a woman I interviewed had to pass some workmen doing up a block of council flats. For quite a while the woman had been bothered by their comments. She treated them in a variety of ways, ranging from ignoring them to being jocular, but she wasn't in fact keen to talk with these men or even to be noticed by them because of an experience she had had a few years earlier. She said:

> I knew from police reports that the majority of women are said to
> know their male attackers, and having been raped by a man I knew

I wasn't keen to 'know' any more men than I had to. The workmen who said straightforwardly 'Hello' I didn't have a problem with. The ones who were difficult were the ones who shouted: 'I bet she's a slow burner' and stuff like that. The ones who said: 'Stuck-up bitch' just loud enough for me to hear were the ones that really bothered me.

So one day, quaking in my shoes, I stopped. I went up to one of them and said: 'I'd like to have a few words with you and your mates.' I said I was happy to say hello and have the occasional joke, but that offensive remarks weren't on.

It went quiet for a bit. Then, going to work one day, I got a clod of wet cement thrown at me. I decided to ring up the council and complain, and I was never troubled after that. However, I still felt nervous passing that place – and while the council suggested I might try using a different bus-stop there isn't one, short of flying, that isn't a long way round.

At a special meeting called to discuss attacks on women in a London neighbourhood one woman got very angry. She had just heard another woman, who lived in a cul-de-sac, express a bitter wish to be able to fly because of harassment by men who used the café on the corner. The angry woman said:

It's the men who are causing the problems and the women who are supposed to sort it out. Men verbally assault women, and women have to worry about whether they're handling it properly. Men rape women, and women are supposed to take lessons in how to lie still rather than get killed.

Men rape, men assault and men cause the problem – yet every one of us in this room is discussing what women can do about it. No, I don't want to spend my evenings learning self-defence – and then find out that by the time I have to use it I've forgotten what to do because I haven't been on the latest refresher course. The police offer us these courses and it makes them look as if they're doing something, but all it's doing is placing the onus on women again.

Why do I have to worry all the time whether my presence in any one place at any one time is going to provoke a man to attack me? No, don't teach women to fly out of cul-de-sacs. Treat the problem at source. Teach men to be human.

But it isn't as straightforward as this woman might have wished to believe, particularly on the basis of traditional assumptions. Those assumptions are that man is morally schizophrenic and that, while the 'bad boy' in him must be punished, this must happen at his behest, not woman's. Even if it is woman who is damaged by the 'bad boy', man has claimed it is his business to decide what should be done about it, not hers. Man believes that woman has no right to interfere in his scheme of justice, in which she is a member of the 'other' side. Man has accepted the idea of killing other men and meting out justice through a legal system which he devised and enforces. That way it's still all boys together, and when a really atrocious crime is committed – like the murder of a woman – the legal man is at his most protective and wrathful.

In declaring herself a person, however, woman has deposed this neat order by which man locked the unacceptable face of himself behind prison bars and then carried on regardless. Woman asked him to accept something far more complex – the bad man within himself, and the bad man who is his drinking companion/business associate/squash partner and so on. Woman asked man to accept the daily bad man – not the 'enemy' who is a different class, nationality or colour and therefore 'other' in any case, but the enemy within. Man has condemned other men in the name of justice, religion and war, but not in the name of woman.

Now the combination of his need for a seamless psychology and his actual moral schizophrenia are causing havoc with the old order. He doesn't want to look at sexual attitudes and moral dilemmas because he knows that doing so will upset the carefully balanced equations: I the good man, you the bad safely outside me; I the strong man, you the weak woman; I the righteous cause, you the evil which must be destroyed. These lofty divisions have to collapse, and man, who has no pity for himself, fears that the rampaging zealot within him will not tolerate or contain his daily offences.

This is why some of the men's groups which were set up in the early days of feminism didn't work: a combination of zealotry and guilt did them in. As a man then in his mid-thirties, who left two such groups, said:

I couldn't bear the chest-beating. I wanted to learn about the joy of being a man as women had learned how to get their own buzz from other women. In the groups I went to it's as if they wanted you to feel guilty for all the bad that man had ever done, right from the beginning of time. They didn't help feminists organize creches because it was fun, and because it was fun working with children and looking after them – they did it as a penance. It was so serious, and so painful. It was an awful experience. I felt really down after it.

The guilt makes it far more difficult to deal with what is happening to women. For men who feel guilty will not want their burden added to by learning even more about men's violence. But men have to know the ferocity which women suffer, particularly through rape. One woman said:

I couldn't believe such hatred existed. He made me do the most terrible things and he was threatening me with a knife if I didn't. I kept on praying I would lose consciousness, but I didn't. He was saying things like: 'Take that, you bitch! . . . You're nothing but a tart . . . You women think you can do what you like. Well, see how you like this.'

Most men find this kind of description difficult to take, even to the extent of not being able to take it at all.

Another disturbing aspect of rape is that some women are doubly punished by their partner's reaction to it. A woman who was viciously raped described her husband's reaction to her in these words:

I know I looked a mess because I suppose I acted stupidly. There were two of them [rapists], and in the end what happened between my legs was nothing compared with what happened to the rest of me. I was badly beaten up because I wouldn't take it. Rick [her husband] took one look at me and said: 'Christ, what a mess!' I'd survived till then, but that did me in.

Eventually she divorced her husband. She added:

I've always looked men straight in the eye ever since – and they don't like it. I have nothing more to look for in a man: two raped me, and the one I was married to put the final boot in. I've called their bluff ever since. Men only want to know women when women look like men want them to. When you're bleeding on the ground they can't take it. It's too much for them, they haven't the guts. They'd pick up another man if he was knocked about, but they can't look a woman in the face if it's not the face they want. That says everything I need to know about men.

A female office worker in her mid-twenties described this syndrome in a different way:

> There was a man who had a shop round the corner from where I lived, and every morning as I went to the bus-stop he would come out and leer at me and make suggestive comments. It got so bad that I started walking a long way round to another bus-stop further on. This meant that I got wet if it was raining and was sometimes late for work because the bus was full by that stop.
>
> Some of the men in the office started passing remarks about this, so I told them what was happening. You try telling an office full of men that you're late for work or soaking wet because a creep round the corner is harassing you – and watch them get their heads down fast. They don't know what to do with themselves.

The problem is that, as long as some men don't know where to put themselves when women start talking about assault of any kind, those men who are committing the assaults are given an even freer hand. They don't fear women, and while they have nothing to fear from their own kind either there is nothing to stop them, for the law seems little able to.

I have spoken with hundreds of women who have been raped, yet not one of them has reported an attempted or actual rape to the police. The reasons are complex and include the woman's fear of humiliation and a sense of futility because she may not be able to give a clear description of her attacker. She might also wish to put the incident behind her. One eighteen-year-old denied the experience to such an extent that she refused all emotional assistance when she came one evening to a youth agency where I was doing some work. She only wanted advice on where to check on whether she had caught AIDS, and just said that she wanted to forget the whole thing. There is something unreal about hearing an eighteen-year-old say in a quiet, composed voice that her only concern is to find out whether or not she has caught a killer disease from two football supporters who repeatedly raped her at knife-point.

The real dirty trick here is to be told that there is nothing that can be done about the crime of rape except to tell women to keep indoors or to get themselves minders. The idea of a society geared to encouraging healthy adults to stay in – while the sick child, the child who needs to attack women, is not given the 'hospital' treatment he needs – is very odd. It is ironic that the potential victim is asked to reduce her circumstances, to become somehow invisible on the streets or else risk showing up as a crime statistic, while the potential attacker wanders round freely. It is the kind of muddled thinking that led the police to advise women – not men – to stay off the streets of Leeds while Peter Sutcliffe, the man the press called the Yorkshire Ripper, was still at large.

From there it is only a short step to saying that, if a woman does go out and gets attacked, it is her own fault. It does not need a change in the law to alter this, but it does require a change in attitude. It means appointing a Home Secretary who does not view his or her job as giving a licence to lock up women in their homes after dark, while their menfolk buy rounds at the pub as consolation for being deprived of 'spare' female company. It means employing someone to set up an educational programme for the benefit of police forces and politicians. This would avoid discrepancies in thinking of the sort that enabled the Metropolitan Police to open special units for rape victims and in the same year to publish a document like *Positive Steps*, which advised women to stay indoors at night. It particularly means taking violent crime – which sexual assault is – seriously enough, so that efforts will be made where they can be most effective: in schools.

In *Friday's Child* I wrote that if we want to see any improvement in rape statistics we need to work with boys now. Having done so myself for more than a decade, I realize how difficult adolescence is for them. Punitive attitudes towards themselves and towards women begin in the no man's land which is most boys' 'unattended' puberty.

Puberty is unattended for boys because they are, in the main, banished from good adult help. There are a number of prevalent but obscured ideas which bring this about. One is the old-fashioned notion that in order for a boy to become a man he needs to 'go it alone' – so helping a boy during his teenage years is seen as possibly emasculating him. Many mothers fear doing this to their sons through giving them too much love and attention.

Other mothers fear that their teenage sons' developing sexuality means that it would now be inappropriate for them, as females, to relate closely to a *sexual* person of the opposite gender. Mothers do not have this fear with girls. Fathers are, in the main, emotionally absent. They might take the boy fishing, but they are unlikely to discuss with him how complex and frightening becoming a man can be. Another ingredient in the make-up of the emotionally abandoned teenage boy is that, while a girl's developing sexuality makes her a potential mother or nurturer, the boy's is viewed as something far less benign. I wrote:

It's as if we view a boy's erections as making him not a possible father but a possible aggressor. So the boy has now become potentially dangerous. And far too many boys go right on out and fulfil this prophecy . . .

If we are asking young girls not to get pregnant we must also be asking boys to co-operate. If we think asking for this co-operation is a waste of time then we really do believe that they are incapable of considerate or moral behaviour. This is not only insulting to teenage boys but also serves to continue making boys and men outcasts from moral codes we would like to see practised . . .

It leaves boys in a moral wilderness from which they are far more likely to attack, for if you presume a teenage boy is beyond the pale he will do you the grave dis-service of proving you correct.[1]

I then went on to explain that boys tried to dupe us, with their sometimes surly and aggressive postures, into believing that somehow they would muddle through on their own. This is hardly surprising when that is what we expect of them anyway. But if we go along with this charade we achieve the extraordinary feat of being sexist to both young women and young men. For suggesting that boys will muddle through without careful guidance is denying them care, and puts a double onus of being careful on to girls. It denies boys their share in moral responsibility, which most girls are encouraged to have if they want to avoid pregnancy or being called foul names for behaving promiscuously.

The division of the sexes is present here in the age-old idea that boys are sexual animals and that girls have to be taught to fend them off. Because of this existing division one of the subjects which I discuss time and time again with boys is rape. I wrote:

To talk about rape and the education of teenage schoolboys in the same breath sounds harsh, unpalatable and possibly damaging. It sounds as if . . . I want the riot act read to a group of young people, many of whom are extremely vulnerable. But this is far from the truth. By discussing rape with boys I do not treat them as a pack of potential criminals, but as people who have been, in the main, denied the moral education due to them . . .

The lack of easy, open discussion means that boys are prey to their developing sexuality rather than its host. It means that they are themselves easy meat for rumour, pornography and for gang warfare, for at least the latter gives them a collective sense of

115

identity while their individual one has been taken over by a nightmare called uninformed adolescence.[2]

A major part of this nightmare is that object of ridicule, reverence, fear and fantasy, the penis:

> The progress of the penis from a relatively harmless water pistol into a fully-fledged 'weapon' with a mind of its own can be initially disconcerting to boys, but it needn't be a major disaster for any of us unless by a conspiracy of silence we make it so. And we do. By leaving boys to the feeling that they *are* prey, and that they are outcasts, we make sure that some of them will eventually want to visit these misfortunes on to someone else. And by not introducing them to the 'female perspective' at a young age we make sure that there are certain things they really don't understand.[3]

One of the things many boys genuinely don't comprehend is that sex can be unwanted. They are so used to the idea of 'going out and getting it', and are so buffeted by the voices of peers claiming their own prowess, that the female perspective is missing.

If boys haven't been brought up to see through male myths they won't understand that sex is not about going out and scoring. If they haven't been brought up to understand that most women want more from sex than a bit of physical release they have problems in understanding what young women are 'on about'. They think girls refuse to have sex with them (and despite shock-horror statistics, most girls still do refuse) because they are being stuck-up and perverse. The boys think the girls are holding out on them deliberately. Because of this they think the girls have the upper hand, and so they set about bringing the girls down.

My experience of working with young people has shown me that a small amount of work achieved at this age literally saves lives. However, it is not in the main undertaken, so bad attitudes within and between both sexes are perpetuated. Although some improvements have been made through social studies courses and the kind of work I have just described, far too many boys still feel that it is a man's *duty* to dominate a woman. The feeling is still prevalent that women are sexual trouble-makers. In other words, the potential for boys to form strange ideas about women, and therefore the potential for future rape, is not being tackled at source. Notions of domination, and fear of women, are still present in the next generation of adults. Many attitudes and resentments harden up from this age and are carried through indelibly into adult life.

DEPARTMENT OF DIRTY TRICKS

Rape disturbs man because it sunders the moral uniformity of woman and brings up all the questions about protection and why the hell woman had to disturb the status quo in any case. If woman hadn't wanted to alter things this wouldn't be happening, so there is a sneaking feeling that it is all woman's fault. If it is her fault, man does not have to look either to himself or his own kind to sort it out. By taking up a public profile woman has suffered herself, and in man's terms she has suffered him to do what he would rather not – to take issue with his own kind.

Man has given up his role as village policeman who would clip an errant child round the ear. As villages and towns became more crowded, he was faced too often by children whom he did not recognize and could not name. Since then there has been a big hiatus in the bringing up of boys. Woman has been blamed for going out to work; but man hasn't been for not giving his sons role models which are healthy for society. When a deeply paternalistic society which is geared to protecting women fails – as it must – it is no reason for man to stop being a minder at all, of sons or of women. The protection racket as it operated was a dirty game, for like all rackets it was run to benefit the person who collected the money.

10
The Child Who Says No

Against this recently discovered background of exploitation it is hardly surprising that, as a woman in her late thirties told me sadly: 'Something's missing these days between men and women. There's something urgent and exciting that isn't there any more. It's as if we don't have the hots for each other any more.' It's only to be expected that having the hots for each other is absent, for sexual excitement doesn't happen in a vacuum. These days it isn't only a man and a woman who get under the duvet, but a whole hot-bed of politics and sexual attitudes. As Angela Carter writes in *The Sadeian Woman*:

> We may believe we fuck stripped of artifice; in bed, we even feel we touch the bedrock of human nature itself. But we are deceived . . . Although the erotic relationship may seem to exist freely, on its own terms, among the distorted social relationships of a bourgeois society it is, in fact, the most self-conscious of all human relationships, a direct confrontation of two beings whose actions in the bed are . . . determined by their acts when they are out of it.[1]

The acts are sometimes treacherous ones, as both man and woman struggle with need, anger and the tendency to be vengeful. The need is for identity at a time when gender roles are in a state of unprecedented flux. While this is taking place men and women are looking for the security of hanging on to someone or something. The fact that male and female roles are in such disarray brings about a lurching kind of terror, as within themselves and in relation to each other man and woman lunge between one crisis and the next.

Sometimes they do this for the dubious privilege of establishing the 'boss position' – like the man who, packing to go away for a month, lets the woman he lives with see him put a large supply of condoms in his suitcase. Or the woman who lets the man she is living with know that, if his penis isn't up to the job, then her vibrator is. It is the man who seeks anal intercourse with a woman and calls it a 'vaginal bypass', and the woman who says man is a nuisance made tolerable by 'regular despunking'. Or the man who sets a mental timer by women – now that they have declared UDI – doing exactly fifty per cent of the sexual work. Or the woman who decides that, because 'men have had it their way for so long', she will now have it all hers.

The last woman does not so much want man to change, as to change according to her design. In retaliation for man designing the shape of woman, she now wants woman to design the shape of man. She issues imperatives and instructions, and one man who was prepared to listen found himself out in the cold again: 'She told me to look at my emotions, so I did. She told me to be considerate about her sexuality and her orgasms, so I was. I enjoyed it. And you've guessed it – the next thing I know she's left me for a bronzed, macho hero who knows how to be assertive.' With such confusing and mixed emotions do man and woman get into bed with each other.

I discussed one form of sexual revenge in an article written for *Cosmopolitan* magazine in 1985: 'In the sixties there was a phrase used by certain men to describe sexual intercourse – it was called "having your revenge",' I began. I assume that this was man's revenge against what he called 'domestic drudgery' in the form of woman. When man was considered a slave to his penis, and – ironically – a free rather than a domestic animal, he married in order to have sex. It was a way of getting the woman to say yes. However, he paid heavily, for as well as this he got the much reviled nagging/small talk/babies/nappies/hair rollers business. Sex, I assume, was what man regarded as his reward for all the terrible domestic things he put up with. The fact that it was called 'revenge' came from the still prevalent notion that man needed sex more, and it was still something you thrust on a woman rather than engaged in with her. I went on: 'You wouldn't hear the phrase used now – or would you? Because women now admit they enjoy sex, any idea of intercourse being a vengeance upon women (except of course in the case of rape) is ridiculous. However, in the wake of the sexually experienced woman there is a new kind of revenge – the *man* who says no.'

I described this as 'downing tools' and quoted a man who was doing it – or more accurately suffering from it, for while he admitted that it was revenge which prompted him he said it was caused by terror and egomania. I called him Robert and his wife Maureen:

He ended up by refusing to have sex with Maureen. Instead he had sex with other women who lived out his control fantasies. He said: 'I don't experience a proper sexual relationship. This is the tragedy of most men. When I make love with – sorry, screw – a woman who has put on stockings and suspenders for me I'm in control . . . It's not sex I'm into. It's egomania . . .'

119

There are two ways a man can revenge himself on a woman. He either takes control of her as he has always done, or he walks away from her. Either way he's in charge, and that's what men want.

Dr Fay Hutchinson, national medical spokesperson for the Brook Advisory Centres and a member of the Institute of Psychosexual Medicine, describes the 'we won't play' syndrome in the following way: 'The sense of failure that some men have these days is very powerful . . . You may call it [saying no] revenge if you like, but . . . I'm very struck by the terror . . .'

Robert said: 'I'm glad someone understands the terror because for me it's not about performance – it's about ego. And I'm never going to be able to trust myself to a woman while I basically have the need to dominate her. What does terrify me is that I've actually looked at all this, and I'm still in a mess. What about the millions of men who haven't even given it a second thought?'

Near the end of her book *Fear of Flying* Erica Jong describes the heroine's relationship with a younger man who is able to accommodate her as a complete woman rather than as a spare geometry set. However, one night he is sulking while she wants to make love, and she suddenly realizes what absolute power is given to the partner who owns the penis. Try as she may to persuade him he will have none of her, and tells her she can go masturbate in the shower. The cock is his, and without his permission she can't have it.

The ownership of a penis has resulted over the centuries in man assuming sexual and many other kinds of superiority. But this is in fact an extraordinary piece of duplicity, for the penis and testicles make man excruciatingly vulnerable. His genitalia are in a far more exposed position than woman's. As well as being immobilized by a blow to the testicles he is also vulnerable to attack when his penis is erect, for bending it backwards at this time would be painful.

By comparison, woman is relatively unexposed. She is also unexposed in a different way, because in order for sexual intercourse itself to take place the penis has to perform the miracle of rising. The vagina has a corresponding 'duty' to be wet, but this is not a visible chore and can be easily substituted for with saliva or a lubricant. There is no substitute for the penis being erect, and although 'soft entry' is possible it can be difficult and incorporates the potential vulnerability that the penis has been *seen* not to rise. Man is sexually exposed from the day he is born. Woman is not.

A man in his late thirties, who writes children's plays, said:

Men are brought up to be penis-orientated, and it's definitely because the penis has to *do* things. That's where men start getting performance hang-ups from. It would be very interesting if in order to have sex you needed to have an erect penis *and* the vagina had to perhaps puff up as well. Then the difference between men and women might lessen because they'd be more sexually equal. Feminism has taken the heat off men in one way by saying that it's not just about fucking but about exploration. But a man still thinks he's less of a man if his penis doesn't show willing.

So far the balance in sexual equality has been weighted *against* man, for woman has been able to hide both her sexual arousal and the lack of it. This looks to an envious eye suspiciously like having the best of both worlds. She can also still have sexual intercourse if she is bored, tense, tired, preoccupied or under stress. Any of these circumstances may mean that a man cannot get an erection, and while other forms of love-making are possible intromission is more difficult.

This is not to suggest that penetration is the only or even the main part of love-making, but rather to see what has been involved in falsely and dangerously establishing it as so. It is dangerous, first because the need for chemical contraception would not be anywhere near so pronounced if intromission was a small rather than a large part of love-making, and second because dependency on penetration feeds a performance ethic. When you add to the fear of not getting an erection when he wants one the risk of getting one when he *doesn't*, man's sexual vulnerability is further increased. It is exacerbated still more by the knowledge that woman is capable of being multi-orgasmic.

This facility can give rise to dismissiveness on the part of women, who may say of the penis: 'I wouldn't want to walk around with anything as unpredictable as that between my legs', and envy on the part of men. A male teacher once said in conversation that woman had 'an infinite number and variety of orgasms tucked up her fanny'. He said that he had only experienced four or five different *kinds* of orgasms, and never more than that number in any given day or night. 'When you add it all up,' he concludes, 'there doesn't seem to be a single sexual advantage that women don't have.' It might be argued that she lacks one advantage in that she is 'slower to arousal' – but if sexual activity is meant to be pleasurable, then taking longer would seem to be having more of a good thing, not less.

In view of all this it was a hefty plot which could turn the vulnerable male into the sexually superior partner. I say 'sexually superior' because part of Freud's castration theory depends on the notion of the female as castrate because penisless. It is the possession of a penis which is viewed as the 'normal' state of ownership. It could be just as valid to argue that to be without a vagina is to be without a vital inner chamber and therefore roomless. Man's inability to make a home for himself, to be at home in his own body, is certainly one of his traditional traits. Maybe all those early surgeons who hoped to find the human soul when they cut open bodies were looking in the wrong place!

The difference in attitude towards the penis and its enveloping counterpart, the vagina, must come from the visual dominance that has played such a large part in man's culture. It must also *decide* whether or not the little girl is castrate, for when she asks the question, 'Why haven't *I* got one?' the answer she is given depends on and determines how she is viewed. If the answer comes from the notion of her as castrate, she may indeed feel cheated. If, however, it comes from the idea of her as equal counterpart to the little boy the answer will be given and interpreted differently. She will be told that he has something, that she has something else, and that this is fine.

There is, of course, no reason why a boy child should question why he doesn't have either a womb or a vagina, since these are not readily visible. But a culture which rests its case in an invisible God is hardly in a good position to argue that what is not visible is of no account. In any case, it is not as if the vagina and womb are actually invisible; they are just not external.

However, the dirty trick which turned the sexually vulnerable male into the blueprint for all sexuality happened long before Freud (who was himself the product of it) wrote of woman as castrate. It began with man's need to make cultural order out of the potential chaos and anarchy which is what woman's sexual diversity allows. To be precise, it began with man's cultural need to name his own children and to create his own line. Without enclosing woman – or marrying – he had no way of passing on his name. Without her monogamy he had no absolute way of knowing his child from any other man's. Woman knows her own children, because she produces them and recognizes them as hers from a very early age. Man doesn't.

In *What a Man's Gotta Do* Antony Easthope writes:

> If nature cannot provide proof of who a baby's father is, then in the name of the father law can step in and decide paternity . . . The masculine myth keeps coming back to the idea that the father is

absolutely *all there*, that sons are perfect copies of him, that they are masculine all the way through, and that fathers and only fathers are really responsible for making babies.[2]

This was arranged through a marriage contract which, until recently, a woman had to enter in order to be anybody or to have a reasonable life. Marriage, it was put about, 'made' a woman – which was a colossal dirty trick, for the truth was the other way round. Through marriage man got to name his children, to have his home kept, and to exact the obedience and respect he so much missed within himself. Yet in all this man was presented as giving woman the security of a home, of *offering* her marriage – which she could not offer him – and of sacrificing himself to her when he could have been having a good time gadding around. The mythically rampant and sexually ever-ready man was of course a cover-up for the fact that woman was really the 'ever-ready' partner in the biological sense. Being multi-partnered might have suited *her* very well.

However, marriage need not have been a dirty trick in itself had it been honestly approached as a way of giving the disadvantaged male knowledge of his children, and security. What *is* unscrupulous is to suggest that something you have imposed on someone else for your own benefit is actually for theirs. Phillip Hodson verifies the point made by the journalist in Chapter 2:

> Practically all adult males who can be married *are* married. They actually have every incentive to be so since research shows that men *without* women have higher rates of suicides, insanity, cancer and coronary thrombosis than those who enjoy lasting relationships . . . About 93 per cent of people get married in Britain. Of the men who remain single, twice as many are likely to kill themselves as married males of the same age, four times as many are likely to enter a mental hospital, one and a half times as many may suffer a coronary and twice as many are likely to die of cancer of the throat or mouth.[3]

Western culture's perverse notion of masculinity was something Clancy Sigal wrote about in the *Guardian* on 7 May 1986. In discussing the child within the man, who is not only left behind but obliterated by this culture, he wrote about his own heart attack:

> When that special landscape of a child's heart misted over, when I grew tough and 'realistic', I'm sure I began the process that landed me in intensive care . . .

I wonder how many of us keel over with heart attacks as an inner protest against all this adult male stuff that nobody exactly forced on us, indeed seemed at the time a positive and necessary good in our lives? . . . We cannot abolish manhood as we know it. (Why? a child's voice within wants to know.) And I'm not even sure that, if we cancelled most of the obnoxious macho aspects, it would still erase the terrible rush to self-judgement that becoming a man, at least in America, entails. We leave behind too much in the scramble to sit at the adults' table.

By wiping themselves out with 'cardiac events' in such massive numbers, men may be voting with their hearts to get out of the trap at whatever cost. If untended, the child within us becomes a terrible and terribly powerful enemy.

It is obvious that dirty tricks eventually rebound, like boomerangs, on their perpetrators, and if the emotional heart has a fortress round it then the organic one becomes the sufferer.

In my mind's eye I can see a vivid, Alice-in-Wonderland-type picture of the inside of the body, where a large, thunderous infant is stamping on arteries and tugging on the plugs of the system. This ferocious child, who wants to attack the core of the adult, was recently challenged by the arrival of heart transplants – which are carried out predominantly on men. Such skills whack the infant into place with the insistence that even this organ is replaceable – but at a cost. Dozens of hip replacements – predominantly a woman's operation – can be performed for the cost of a single heart transplant. However, culture prefers the spectacular miracle to daily hope. That is its arrogance and its need. And the child as man's enemy is what culture is based on, for the child has the potential for self-volition until he or she is whipped into line.

The child is therefore beaten, ritually caned, wilfully and desperately walked away from – and still she will not go away. She is indeed a terrible and terribly powerful enemy, this tyrant infant, for her energies are indefatigable. They have to be, for she is alive and therefore must demand recognition in whatever way she can. The child as symbolizing the world of the imagination and the emotions will insinuate herself into every crack she can find in the carefully constructed but brittle adult armour.

Actually the child does not want so very much from the adult. She wants to be known and accepted and, in a sense, named. The problem is that, since man cannot name the child *outside* himself without woman, so he cannot name the child *inside* himself without woman

124

either. He establishes property rights to the vessel through which the child comes into the world – woman's body.

Man speaks with *woman* about his emotional life for so many reasons: fear of other men, and the knowledge that she is more versed in this area than he is. He also does it so that she can once more name his child, or give him proof that a child is his and for a while at least enable him to name it for himself. Then he tends to give it back to her as he walks away into the busy world again, seldom better off for the interchange. What is remarkable is that there *was* another way of being able to name his child, in both senses of that phrase – and that was to have asked for co-operation from woman rather than practising coercion. The fact that this didn't happen is perhaps an indication of the extent of man's fear.

The revenges exacted for all of this are both simple and convoluted. In personal terms man takes an awful revenge on himself, not just through stress and heart disease, but through continuing loneliness and emptiness. By refusing to acknowledge the child in himself – by refusing, in other words, to remember and accept his past – man defeats himself.

Man exacts an awful revenge on woman, too, first of all by calling her 'other' and less than himself, and by imprisoning her. In the past he also went further than this and raped her. The reason he rapes her now is that he wants to throw her back into line where she belongs, under his control, and because he is furious that she left that line in the first place. He withdraws from her the sex she would like to have – the exploratory, taking-your-time, getting-to-know-each-other-intimately sex – because that threatens all his security systems.

While this happens on a daily, microcosmic basis it is also reflected macrocosmically in other forms of revenge. These revenges are thought of as mistakes or short-sightedness, but in fact have much deeper roots in the male psyche. They are visited upon and against nature, and while nuclear weapons are their most dramatic manifestation, global pollution, acid rain and deforestation are ultimately just as threatening. Phillip Hodson writes:

> In the battle of the sexes nowadays, it is men's behaviour that appears to be anachronistic. We are an old-fashioned conscript army ever eager to obey our leaders' orders . . . Men say they fight for a cause, but that cause is their own identity, an external source of power, which they cannot find in themselves. The wars of virility are without end since those who can learn nothing from history's errors are doomed to repeat them in a cycle of tragedy and farce.[4]

And he argues that 'men who repudiate all emotional dependency actually increase their emotional needs and related hungering'.[5]

That hungering is for recognition of many kinds, and it is arguable that if the child inside had ever been tended then the child outside would not have needed to be coerced through a loaded marriage contract. There is nothing unnatural about wanting to love your own child – it is still considered 'natural' in woman – but man wanted something more from woman. He wanted to be able to clamp his surname on the people she gave birth to. He wanted to indoctrinate such a sense of fear that from generation to generation women would protect their own by chanting time and time again: 'The child looks like his father.' So the child is looked at not to see who he is, but to impose on him a likeness through the paternal line. Without proof of this, in times gone by he would have been not loved but perhaps thrown to the wolves.

In this way the fate of a life came to depend on man. If the child was his, and preferably male like him and capable of carrying on his 'line', he was welcome and would be given advantages. If she was female, or not his, he decreed that her fate was far less certain. So through no fault of his or her own a child could be declared guilty at birth. This is one of the meanings of original sin.

Through the father original sin is introduced as a way of compensating man for his continuing insecurity over the nature of his offspring. Children are not born sinful, because no one *is* in any compassionate appraisal. Original sin is a perverse idea based on man's need to cast out or reduce the circumstances of children who weren't male or whom he felt weren't his. However, it is possible for man to mask his misdeeds by saying that God has declared *everyone* born in original sin. (Those who are high-born choose to forget this because they deem themselves masters and rulers over what they see.)

Alice Miller writes: 'Our culture [is] overshadowed ... by a particular kind of image of the father and the Deity. God the Father is easily offended, jealous, and basically insecure; He therefore demands obedience and conformity in the expression of ideas, tolerates no graven images and – since "graven images" included works of art for the Hebrew God – no creativity either.'[6] Miller believes a jealous God needs the control and security of being the only person who can create. In his footsteps man has sought to impose this, so that, although the child is born of woman, her destiny is named and decided by man. The child is given man's surname because she is assumed to belong to his line, and is trained to act according to his rules. Miller continues: 'He [God] dictates beliefs and imposes punishment on apostates, persecutes the guilty with a vengeance, permits His sons to live only according to His principles and to find happiness only on His terms.'[7]

She sums up her argument about the value of the relationship between children and adults in these words:

> It requires no great effort to identify the apocalyptic features of our century: world wars, massacres, the specter of nuclear war, the enslavement of millions by technology and totalitarian regimes, the threat to the earth's ecological balance, the depletion of energy sources, the increase in drug addiction – the list could go on and on. Yet the same century has also brought us knowledge that is utterly new in human history and that could bring about a decisive change in our lives if its full significance was to penetrate public consciousness. I am referring to the discovery that the period of early childhood is of crucial importance for a person's emotional development.[8]

Miller's argument is that the violence done to children through viewing them as empty vessels to be filled up with our dogma seriously damages them. We should treat children as individuals who are sacred in their own right. In doing this we give them an essential facility, particularly in view of child abuse – the right to say no. The need to control and discipline has taken over from the need to countenance and revere. We should accept the new stranger into our midst not as a blank piece of paper for us to scribble our dated message all over, but as an unfolding book in his or her own right.

The child who pulls out the plug on adult males, making them prone to heart disease, is the child who says no.

11
The Villain
of the Codpiece

The right to say no to sex has not until recently been a man's privilege. The culture which produced the myth that man was 'always ready for it' at the same time proffered the insult that man was sexually undiscerning and therefore slavish. For surely it is only slaves and automata who will *always* do something. Was this why sex was arranged so that woman feared and sometimes hated it? For if woman hated it and man was always on the look-out for it, the fact that *he*, not she, was the sexually 'weaker' partner would be concealed.

It hasn't paid man to make sex interesting and pleasant for woman, for by so doing she would expose his sexual limitations. But a man is only sexually 'limited' if his penis is used as the yardstick for measuring what sex or sexual performance is. If sex is about *whole* people, then a man has just as many fingers and toes as a woman and on average a larger body surface both to give and to receive pleasure. However, since man has so resolutely built up his myths around the notion of penis power it was on this basis that the issue had eventually to be addressed.

And it has been – sometimes kindly, mainly not. Its main instrument has been humour, that dubious medium which, as Freud pointed out, has a habit of revealing more than we know and therefore of rebounding on its messenger. It has certainly rebounded on man, who until the mid-seventies had a practically exclusive contract on public humour. Working in newspapers and television at the time, I heard it said over and over again: 'Women are no good at humour. They're too self-conscious.' The viewing public still doesn't realize how strongly it was felt in media hierarchies, which were male, that whatever else woman might be able to tackle, humour was not female. Standing up and playing comic, which was how men perceived humour, was a male affair. Was this to protect man's image of woman as serene and beautiful, or to protect man from the public exposure that woman telling jokes about him would inevitably bring?

In the decade between the mid-seventies and the mid-eighties female humour was difficult because feminism was a serious business. A man who joked about it ran the risk of being censured, and woman hadn't yet found the means to do so herself. It is only now becoming possible for feminism to join other serious subjects – like politics and sex – as something that can be laughed at for its faults and excesses. But the 'coming out' of female humour has of course made man more vulnerable than woman.

The critically self-conscious male has now been exposed, as he feared he would be. The 'Good Woman's Rules' as handed down by the biblical and Freudian fathers had at the head of their list of commandments: 'Thou shalt not question, ridicule or bring into ill repute the male organ.' The Department of Dirty Tricks said: 'Get 'em where it hurts.'

For every stand-up comic who clawed his way to the top on the back of mother-in-law jokes, the seventies and eighties produced women for whom sex was political and politics was dirty. Thus the potent mixture which feminism introduced – the issue of sexual politics, or the marriage of political and personal – got under way. Man as an embodiment of both sexual and political oppression was under attack.

Victoria Wood said it in lines like: 'Just 'cos they've got willies and can mend fuses it's no reason to go overboard about them.' And of course Mae West had paved the way with lines like: 'Is that a gun in your pocket or are you pleased to see me?' On cabaret stages and in alternative revues woman was out there in the limelight. She turned rapidly from her role as humourer of man's ego to attacker of his cock: 'Oh, don't do it, love, don't do it . . . Get yourself a vibrator instead. Much cheaper . . . doesn't snore. And let's face it, when all's said and done, well – how shall I put it . . . cleaner . . .'

Much of it also went on in women's loos, where the graffiti read: 'When God made man She was only practising'; 'Women who want to be equal with men are lacking in ambition'; 'A man is a long streak of misery attached to a short piece of tomfoolery' and so on. One female executive put down what she describes as a 'pin-striped barbarian' in her office when he was doing a number in his best public school accent on a new junior. As the girl quailed under his sarcastic tongue-lashing, the woman said loudly to someone nearby: 'He wouldn't have to do that if his willie worked properly.'

Although woman by this time had said that sex was not mainly about intromission, it was nevertheless the penis and the link between the penis and the ego which attracted her flak. An apocryphal story went the rounds about a statuesque woman pursued by a short, drunken man. He had been wanting to bed her for a long time, and eventually he got drunk enough to have a real go. He launched himself at her after a particularly boozy lunchtime, and swaying a few inches from her chinline, said in a slurred voice: 'One of these days I'm gonna have you.' She drew herself up to her full height and replied slowly and icily: 'If you do . . . [pause for effect] . . . and I find out about it . . . [another pause for effect] . . . I shall be very cross.' This was all dangerous stuff, and it provoked male humorists like Dave Allen to suggest ruefully that sex between men and women was in such a sorry state that men were now faking orgasms.

Then Gray Jolliffe made his appearance on the bookshelves, and the penis went through a transformation in popular culture from butt of female humour to 'man's best friend'. Jolliffe's books about man and his best friend/worst enemy, Wicked Willie, captured the paradox that the penis is both lifelong friend and arch-enemy. In one picture Willie, condom over head, looking like a bandit with a stocking mask on, points a gun at his owner and says: 'This is a hold-up.' Quite right. It's been the longest hold-up in human history.

Wicked Willie, the bad boy of masculinity, the villain of the codpiece, had at last been exposed *by a man*. All his and his owner's egocentricity, sexism – neither of them likes intellectual women – and many other failings were laid bare. He was portrayed both affection-ately and accurately as leading his owner by the balls, and women along the garden path of male supremacy. Jill Tweedie called him an 'unpredictable hydraulic system'.

Jolliffe pointed out what women had intuited for years – when you meet a man, you are never meeting him alone. Because there are two of him he is quirky in his behaviour, unlikely to be honest and unable to keep promises. He is certainly not a free man, attached as he is to his myths; he is divided and ruled by his boss in the Machiavellian form of penis/ego. A woman therefore is often dating two men. While the troilism could be appealing, Jolliffe told us that the two men take the edge of this by being far more involved with each other than with her. Through the guise of humour Jolliffe told the world that Willie had been causing havoc way beyond his immediate sphere of influence.

In my own work in schools one of my concerns has been that tomorrow's men – today's teenage boys – receive in many cases very little more help than their fathers did in coming to terms with male myths. Their sexual feelings are still obscured by prevailing phallacies. Earlier I described how in many ways the advent of puberty is much more difficult for boys than it is for girls, because a boy is so often abandoned during his teenage years. I came to the conclusion that a boy is deserted, emotionally speaking, because his mother fears she may 'cissify' him and prevent him becoming a 'proper man' if she still behaves warmly towards him. This, coupled with an emotionally absent or invisible father, means that a boy of thirteen is not as warmly treated as a girl of the same age. But there was another conclusion I came to in *Friday's Child*: 'The further key here seems to be that male adolescence is not coped with by adults because it is seen to be the beginning of male sexuality *which is viewed as potentially threatening.*'[1]

I went on to describe how an additional problem with boys is that the penis is not only visible, but may become even more visible through an erection. What if a woman teacher or his mother should cause this through discussing sexuality with, or behaving warmly towards, a boy? 'One of the problems in the classroom or anywhere else,' I wrote, 'is that the penis is so *present*. And this is probably why discussion of it is shied away from. If discussion results in an erection, what then?'[2]

When I was discussing all this in a classroom with a group of sixth-formers a seventeen-year-old boy recognized something about his own 'unattended' puberty. His words showed the other side of the picture from the one described by the journalist in Chapter 2, who talked about pubescent boys suddenly being 'ever so embarrassed' to see their mothers. The seventeen-year-old told of his mother's sudden embarrassment at seeing him. He said: 'You've just explained something that's been a mystery to me for years. I couldn't understand why my mum went funny. It was as if she couldn't look me in the eye any more. It went on for ages. It's only lately it's got OK again . . . It's a wonder *any* of us come out normal.'

One of the first things that becomes obvious from this kind of work is that, as I said earlier, boys have tremendous difficulty in viewing any sex as unwanted. I went on:

This initially brings out some flak from the girls who say, 'Yeah, they're always wanting it. They don't think about anything else.' To which I reply: 'If you had penises which behaved strangely and parents who wouldn't discuss this with you perhaps you wouldn't be feeling so smug.' . . .

When you consider what the penis does, unbidden it seems, it is almost predictable that for a while it is viewed as a cross between the eighth wonder of the world and a hydraulic system it's better to be on the right side of. As both friend and foe, it certainly behaves like and responds to being treated like a piece of equipment. Its antics, unless explained properly in sex education, are only comparable with what they learn about in the physics lab and if men are 'penis-centric' then I'm not at all surprised. There just isn't anyone around at this age to let boys know that their errant willies are not the centre of the universe.[3]

All this discussion takes place against a background in which the penis is viewed either as a butt for female humour or as something to which feminists are still not reconciled. Woman felt that the role of the penis was not to satisfy her but to pander to the male ego. It was not so much a tool of woman's pleasure as an instrument of her downfall. It was the agent through which she became, not person, but interstice between man and his other half – he the mathematician, she the elusive angle. The penis was therefore man's problem, not hers.

While this is not true, what *is* true is that many men view the penis as a possession. Women do not feel the same way about their vaginas, probably because they regard them as something which will be entered and shared rather than as inner sanctums. It's as if the penis, being a possession, is a 'thing', whereas the vagina, being in part a vacancy, is a 'no-thing'. Again, a split between what is obvious and what is hidden. Just like the genie's lamp, the penis comes to life when you rub it, thereby fulfilling its owner's wishes. It is small wonder that the possession of such an obliging 'toy' is seen as proof of superior and indeed superhuman powers.

When I asked a number of men about their wildest fantasies, one replied: 'The commonest I've heard is where you drop your trousers and she says: "Oh my God, what a whopper! You'll never get that in me, guv!" ' And in schools I've been in, including primary schools, pupils have vividly and wonderingly related Tales of the Giant Penis. You might conclude that fables like Jack and the Beanstalk, and Aladdin's Cave had been written with Willie in mind.

The stories are, of course, told by girls – the boys are unusually silent at this serious juncture. Teenage girls will tell you stories of ones which have to be wound round and round the boy's leg and still peep out at the bottom of his trousers. A junior school class of ten-year-olds felt in their heart of hearts that willies were so indestructible that if you chopped them in half they still kept on growing! This is a clear example of the dangers of teaching sex education in biology classes, for these were not the first children I met who had confused willies with worms.

But the myth of the ever-growing, giant, indestructible, all-

132

powerful penis is still ravishing the minds of girls. Culture imposes in this way, for as well as being an aggrandisement of the male organ it is also part of the girl's own fantasies that the bigger the penis the more satisfied she will be. Her vision of riding off into the sunset with the man of her dreams still includes the desire to be taken over, to be entered and to be subsumed by his maleness – of which she knows nothing, for it is a mystery to her.

Regarding the penis as a possession creates exaggerated fears for its safety. What will happen to it if it strays too far from its owner's sight – especially if it disappears into a black hole called a vagina? At its worst, the fear can become a pathological terror in the form of giving the vagina teeth. The penis runs the risk of being bitten off or clamped in place. When Germaine Greer talked of 'cunt-hatred' in *The Female Eunuch* she wrote: 'As long as man is at odds with his own sexuality and as long as he keeps woman as a solely sexual creature, he will hate her, at least some of the time.'[4]

One of the main reasons why man is at odds with his own sexuality is that in adolescence he feels himself to be a slave to his penis. Since male adolescence is so unattended, it is difficult for a man to grow out of adolescent ideas about the penis. It therefore remains a toy, a water pistol, a show-off instrument, something you *do* things with. A male furniture designer in his forties told the following story:

> As men you're brought up to think of your sexuality as some kind of physical thrash. I remember hearing even in school that when you're in the navy you have a blanket and everyone puts half a crown in it and then you all sit round the blanket in a circle and start wanking and the first one to 'come' gets the money. And when we used to make sexual jokes at school at the age of about fifteen it was always to do with how quick we could do it. It was the fastest one to 'come' who was the best.

He explained that the only time he could think properly about sex was when he *wasn't* with other boys. Most boys of his own age didn't think properly about it – they just rolled out one exaggerated or frightening story after another. He said:

> As an adult I've often thought about those men sitting round a blanket with money in the middle of it. I can't imagine any of them saying: 'Ah, wasn't that lovely . . .' the way you do after good sex. It would be more like: 'There it goes', a bit like taking the weight off a pressure cooker.

The trouble is that, having been used to all this, when men now think of ways of slowing it down they're still thinking about *ways* of doing it rather than getting into the feelings attached to sex. It's still mechanical. Oh, yes, pinch the end of the penis and give it a short, sharp shock – rather than: 'I wonder what's in my head and my heart which could help me sink into sex with a woman and really learn how to enjoy it.'

He then made the unusual statement that men didn't have orgasms – the same point that was made by the journalist in Chapter 2 who felt that man had ejaculations rather than orgasms – and went on to talk about his own experiences:

For most men sex is about ejaculation, and these days about slowing that down a bit so that they can be better performers. It's not something they get into, and get involved in with all of themselves, but something which they *do*.

The first time I had an orgasm was when I was about thirty. For the first time in my life I actually felt something that was more than just a pleasurable sensation at the end of my cock. It was wonderful. I felt as if I wanted to go on stroking the woman I was with because I felt so good, not just at the end of my cock, but all over. It was to do with loss of control, and it was the best sexual lesson I've ever learned. I just let go of being in charge of anything, and discovered that my whole body was sensitive and joined in with love-making.

It happened because the woman I was with got me to realize that she didn't want me to achieve anything for her or for myself. She just wanted us to hold each other. So I let go of any purpose I might have had like giving her an orgasm – or maybe a few orgasms – before I came. I just joined in and it was marvellous.

This man had obviously relinquished the myth that the penis has to be powerful for a male to be a really good lover. He had relinquished the idea that anything which threatens the penis, or is perceived as threatening, has to be talked about in condemnatory terms. It is for this reason that the vagina is often unconsciously thought of as a cross between Jaws and the Black Hole of Calcutta.

A man in his thirties who had sought professional help for his attitudes towards sex thought of the vagina as resembling the carcass of a chicken. He considered himself heterosexual and was attracted to women, yet whenever it came to what he called 'giving his penis' he

134

developed a cold sweat and couldn't 'perform'. Therapy in the form of getting him to put his finger in his girlfriend's vagina hadn't worked, because it was the fate of his penis that he was worried about. That was far more crucial to him – and symbolic of his entire identity – than a finger, which could be risked with ease.

In describing his relationship with his penis another man said:

> Initially there was the fear that I might not get it back again. My feeling was distinctly one of ownership. It was almost like boy scout's honour. This is something that is yours and you mustn't let it out of your sight. Of all the things you can give away, this you can't, because it's the ultimate thing of your being. You're a man because you've got this, and if you didn't have this you wouldn't have an identity.
>
> As I grew older I talked with certain girlfriends about it and one of them said she felt that *she* had the penis in certain sexual positions, as if it belonged to her. So we experimented with shifting positions slightly, and she got quite a buzz from letting that happen. In some positions it seemed as if she had more control over moving it than I did. It was certainly a liberating experience.

A banker in his mid-thirties talked of the vagina as petrifying, as containing extraordinary powers, when he described his own early sexual experiences:

> Losing your virginity is terrifying for a man. There's lots written about how frightening it is for women, but it's also frightening for men. There's definitely terror of fathering a child, and for me there was also fear of pain.
>
> I tried many times to fuck, and it took me ages to meet a woman who could handle my terror.

The combination of the mythical power of the penis and the subconscious fear for its actual vulnerability means that much hatred has been projected on to the vagina. Because the penis is thought of as a weapon, it is the vagina that is armed to the teeth. Because the penis is dominant and conquering, the vagina becomes enemy territory.

If the mythology presents the vulnerable penis as powerful, then something even more terrifyingly powerful must be invented to cope with this contradiction that man is both master and slave. The vagina must become tyrant to his slave and mistress to his master. However, until the phallacy was exposed, the nightmare stories of vagina as black hole leading to God knows where could not be contradicted. The long life of the penis in the world of unreason has led to considerable hatred. Woman is balanced between tyrant and mistress, virgin and whore, prim exacter of conditions and gaping hole. Man's need to create something powerful – a flagship of masculinity – out of something as vulnerable as a penis has led to terrible things. In his divided world he tries to rule through terror what he cannot rule – his penis and woman.

It is not unusual for rape victims to have to 'help' the rapist because he cannot 'get it up'. For woman this is one of the cruellest manifestations of man as tyrant on the one hand and inadequate on the other; as someone who is powerful enough to do what he will with her, and yet doesn't have the power to perform at will. Because of man's division the woman is forced, sometimes on threat of death or mutilation, to make her assailant powerful so that he can complete his attack on her. The woman who does so is left not only with having had a serious crime committed against her but with the fact that, however unwillingly, she has helped the instrument of that crime. It is a double revenge, and its message says that if man is going to be at the mercy of his cock then woman will be at the mercy of them both. The twisted irony here is that the penis is both a symbol of violation and flaccid flesh in need of assistance.

If man could have accepted the penis for what it actually is – sexually vulnerable – he would not have had to invent egotistical myths. The link between the penis and the ego is a complicated pulley system in which the cock is the ego's barometer and vice versa. When the cock rises, so does the ego; and when the ego is fed, the cock rises. This unholy alliance has kept man in a state of fragility which he has projected on to woman. It has kept women, either by force or by conspiracy, as tarts and creeps. For ministering to a man's ego through his penis, or to his penis through his ego, breeds handmaidens and groupies. As a youth worker once said to me:

> We're in the 1980s and girls still do it. There are half a dozen girls in this pub who follow these groups round, and they'll perform a quick blow job or a wank in between sets for the singer or the lead guitarist. If they're lucky they get a drink out of it. The big man goes back on stage and struts around a bit more. The girls think they've been involved in some kind of intimacy.

A social worker in her late twenties told the story a different way:

We'd been having trouble with love-making because he wasn't getting erections very often, and then only if I stimulated him, and he'd lose them quickly unless I continued the stimulation. I began to get anxious, because if I wanted him in me I had to 'work for it'. I did for a while, but I couldn't help noticing that he didn't get hard any more from any other kind of love play than me stimulating his penis. He didn't get hard when we kissed or from touching me. Eventually I just burst into tears one day as I was 'working away', rubbing him to get him hard, and said: 'I can't do this any more. I feel like some kind of slave. I feel as if I shan't be given the sex I want unless I work for it.'

This woman wasn't the first to express the feeling that the sex she wanted would depend on how hard she was prepared to work at getting her man to perform through his penis. The links going back are complex. First: man says the penis is all-powerful and the centre of sexual activity. Therefore sex means the penis going into the vagina and performing. Second: man doesn't understand that woman has other kinds of sexual needs and pleasures which can exist independent of the penis. Therefore the penis carries the can for sexual performance, for 'sex' itself. Third: the penis is, however, also vulnerable and erratic. So man decides he will have sex when *it* wants sex, regardless of woman's readiness or needs. Fourth: woman is often not ready when man's penis is. This leads to the myth of the sexually rampant male. Fifth: he wants it a lot (read for that in his own way rather than hers). So the myth of sexually rampant male is reinforced. Sixth: man is in the position of wanting it. Woman is in the position of denying it (quite often because his cock rises at inconvenient times like when she's cooking the dinner or feeding the baby).

In this scenario the rampant penis is the doer and woman the denier. It supports the myth that woman does not like sex. In fact woman does, but is not always prepared to do the tent-maker's bidding. When sex encompasses woman's needs she enjoys it, which makes her threatening to man. She questions his mastery.

The act of intromission is pleasurable for a woman, and not, as some feminists have tried to argue, an intrinsically violent act. The penis is also pleasurable to a woman as itself. It is desired not only for the intimacy of intromission but for the excitement of its arousal through mutual love play, and the confirmation that she turns her lover on. A woman in her mid-forties said:

137

I admit I want his penis, yet in order to 'get it' I must be nice to him because he owns it. That might seem a convoluted way of saying it, but I think we're brought up from little girls with this kind of collusion. A man has what you want so you have to be nice to him. So we're all brought up to be good little girls, scheming little bitches or licensed whores, whichever you like to call it.

This woman explained that feminism hadn't yet come to terms with the penis – and man *never* had. She described how for a while feminism marginalized the penis as well as men by saying that women mainly don't have orgasms through intromission. For herself, she eventually realized that she liked intromission very much because of the way it made her feel 'bonded' to the man she was with. But some men, she said, viewed this as women 'changing their minds', and as proof that they – the men – had been right about everything all along anyway!

Some men are taking heterosexual women as a sign that the feminist ranks are splitting, as if it was only a difference in opinion over a cock which was what the argument was about in the first place. They're standing round saying: 'Thought you could do without us, did you? Well, let's see who really calls the shots.'

It feels as if, as a woman, you're back to square one. You learn the cock isn't the centre of the world, so the blokes go off and sulk. Then you learn you like it more now you understand more about sex, and it's as if the blokes then do you in, and say: 'We've had enough of our willies being rubbished by you lot. If you want to come back again you're going to have to say you're sorry.' It's back to the position of being cap in hand, ever-so-sorry-I-spoke-out-of-turn-sir and crawling again. The chap's upset, and you can only play with his willie again if you rub his ego for a very long time and tell him it was all a mistake and you didn't mean it.

If woman still feels like handmaiden to the combined mythology of penis/ego, then man feels equally but quite differently done in. His terror is of being found out – of being discovered to be not the sexually powerful partner, but the vulnerable one, not the priapic prince but the servant of woman's seemingly unlimited sexual capacity. Since the ego and the penis are so collusive and reliant on each other, any criticism of one is a criticism of the other. Feminism has criticized both: the link between the penis/ego and nuclear weapons was not a difficult one to find. As Michelle Roberts describes it:

Then I saw Ignorance and his children dancing on the battlements high above us, their arms full of engines of death that were shaped like the sign of maleness . . . a sign I had venerated myself many times in the person of the man I loved, and to which I had managed to join the sign of myself, of the female. Now I saw Ignorance waving it aloft as a message of death . . .[5]

The feminist cry: 'Take the toys from the boys', which accompanied so many anti-nuclear marches in the early eighties, was not altogether free of the notion of mass castration. Since the penis is used by young boys as a personal water pistol to play games with, it is not surprising that some men would view taking their toys away as a particularly well-aimed feminist war cry. The other aspect of this slogan is the insulting idea that men are not mature adults but destructive children. It was 'clever' in that it used subliminal ideas and therefore worked on many levels. It reinforced the old idea that the whole lot was man's fault.

The split at Greenham Common between an all-female group and the male weapons they encircled – the phallic symbols of cruise missiles – had far wider significance than the issue of war. It stood convention on its head. As the Falklands War loomed in 1982 I saw one of the Greenham women being interviewed on television. Some of the questions were the usual ones, like how could she possibly leave her husband and children, and she answered something like this:

No one has asked that question of the men going off to war, and they are going to kill. They are leaving wives and children in the name of war, and may well leave widows and orphans. I have left home in the cause of peace. Why am I being asked why I leave my husband and children when it is for the future of the earth – and the men who are going off to war are not being asked why they leave their wives and children?

In this way the women of Greenham challenged accepted reason and so became the focus of more hatred than can be described. By their determination to have no men among them they offended one of the western world's principles – that it is only through men, through Christ and through God that important transformation can take place. The women were asking for paradise on earth – that the planet should be saved, that their children should have futures – without enlisting the visible help, let alone the permission, of men. To the literal, biblical and military mind their offence was terrible.

The women of Greenham took man's Hell, a nuclear arsenal, and said that they would deliver the world from it through the ways of woman, not those of man. They said they would use woman's gift and woman's symbol, the desire to nurture and the circle, to defeat man's warring tendencies symbolized by a penis/cruise missile which penetrated and destroyed. The imagery was powerful and ancient: the arrow and the circle; the male as hunter, the female as gatherer. Dora Russell once described man as being in perpetual 'flight from the body'. The image that sprang to mind is that of an arrow leaving its home, the bow, and travelling outwards without returning to earth. By encircling, the Greenham women invoked the old magical power of the circle.

The kind of hatred shown to the women – excrement was dumped on their tents, for instance – was the measure of how disturbing they were. They disturbed an ancient balance, not only of male/female, but also of beauty. Much of the offence heaped against them was because their temporary living conditions – and, for some, their principles – prevented them from looking conventionally beautiful. They were challenging the phallus by wishing to disarm it, and by refusing to acknowledge its beauty and to give it theirs. Michelle Roberts's book, which credits her debt to the women of Greenham Common, takes up this challenge:

> All my companions in scarlet from the hall of judgment were there . . . We encircled the walls of the city of Ignorance . . . No-one could tell where our circle ended or where it began, for we spun on without end, lassooing the city with love. But . . . the defences that Ignorance had built between him and us did not fall . . .
>
> And then I saw a great sign in the heavens: a woman arrayed with the sun, and with the moon under her feet, and upon her head a crown of twelve stars. She . . . cried out in her birth pangs, longing to be delivered. Angels caught her up, and carried her into the wilderness . . . And there she gave birth to a son. He looked up at her face, and saw who made him, and how they were both part of God. And so she blessed him, and said: your name is Jesus.[6]

The challenge to established Old Testament beliefs – some called it sacrilege at the time – was compounded with this piece of 'heresy'. How dare she suggest that it was woman who did the making – and the naming!

Greenham was a symbol of the penis under siege by women, who named the phallus deathly. So the phallus 'went public' at woman's behest, as part of a drive towards 'manalysis'. Woman had had her share of public exposure through her sisters, her writings and a medical system which viewed her vagina as an unending source of enquiry. She had much to contemplate as she lay around, sometimes with her feet in gynaecologists' stirrups, and learnt that cancer of the cervix killed two thousand women in 1986 in Britain. While some reactionaries tried to lay cervical cancer at the door of female promiscuity, the cause of the cancer in the first place looked surprisingly like the male sexual organ. Women who do not have sexual intercourse – nuns, for example – do not get cancer of the cervix.

Healthwise, it was beginning to seem like the penis was not good news. Sleeping with a man who was not circumcised carried a slightly higher risk, as did sleeping with men who were promiscuous. Women married to men working in certain industries were found to have a higher incidence of cervical cancer than others – working with tar is an example. Men in such high-risk jobs need to wash themselves carefully to make sure they don't infect women. At one stage, sperm itself was thought to be the cause of cervical cancer.

By the time AIDS arrived it was clearly the case that sex with a man presented a much higher health risk for a woman than sex with a woman did for a man. Some graffiti in women's loos consisted of a stick drawing of a man with a skull and crossbones and 'Health hazard' scrawled across it. Other pictures were of a penis/bomb accompanied by the legend: 'It kills you in more ways than one.' The problem was partly caused by the large number of married men who slept either with prostitutes or with the occasional man. On the first few days of a new AIDS switchboard in London more than fifty per cent of the calls were from 'heterosexual' married men. The sexually active people least at risk from AIDS are lesbians.

The penis as health hazard has been underplayed in the popular press, not because of squeamishness or sensitivity but because it erodes the symbol of masculine power and cuts across the mythology of male as sanctified. Part of the power of the penis has been that it has not been publicly discussed by women. Neither has the phallus generally. Antony Easthope writes: 'The masculine myth has always tried to perpetuate its power by feigning invisibility. As soon as masculinity can be seen *as* masculinity, its power is challenged, it is called into question.'[7]

A combination of the penis as object and the phallus as symbol means that man has grabbed phoney power for himself, and by so doing has displaced reality. As a mature student in her late twenties said:

> I feel like an unlicensed sexual being just because I don't have a cock or a boyfriend. No wonder the spinster has been treated so atrociously. I don't have a licence to fuck because I don't own a penis, and when other men want to fuck me they don't understand why I say no when I don't have a boyfriend. They could understand it if I said that my bloke wouldn't like it. They can respect me as someone else's sexual property, but not as someone who has individual sexual preferences.

A book-keeper in her early thirties described her ex-lover in the following terms:

> His base camp was his willie. He told me he was separated from his wife when he wasn't. He was still not only married but actually sharing the same small flat as his wife. As well as having a relationship with me – he even asked me if I would live with him – he was also exploring relationships with other women. He had a very demanding job and he drank and smoked heavily. I don't know how he survived, but it was his willie that kept him going. Whatever else was happening – his wife threatening something or other, me finding out he'd slept with another woman while I was away for a weekend, a row with his boss – he had one piece of magic going for him. The world is falling apart and he musters himself daily round his cock and makes believe everything's OK.
>
> I had no complaints about him in bed. He was a lovely lover, but he seemed to think bed was isolated from the rest of the world. It was his daily fix, and because of it he was able to go on out and do yet another juggling act. He did it until he died. He was only in his late forties.

The penis 'coming out' was discouraged by some women, who thought of it as just another way for men to grab attention. But it was a necessary piece of subversion. As a woman academic said: 'Until you've sorted out the phallic myths, neither men nor women are free.'

12

Rome Is Not Destroyed in a Day

The act of standing back and looking at a man, of examining him to see who he is and what makes him tick, has always been considered subversive. Man made himself unexaminable and unquestionable through a series of ruses which still hold powerful sway.

First of all he invented for himself the extraordinary contrivance of a male God-figure. Devolving from this structure was an edifice built on unnatural and strictly hierarchical rules. I say 'unnatural' because there is nothing in the natural world, from where man has taken so many of his models, to match it. This was always the purpose of the contrivance, since the natural world was not good enough for man and he therefore invented something to 'put on top of it'. In presenting himself as a chip off the old block, a descendant of the male line stretching down from God through Christ, man took on some of the mantle of the God-figure.

It has been considered sacrilegious to question this figure – which is a pity, for there is much to be questioned. Had it not been sacrilegious to question God, His role as a vengeful invention of the darker side of man's psychology could have been examined earlier. To anyone not steeped in Old Testament lore it would be absurd to accept what has been handed down in the name of biblical truth.

This is not in the least to argue that the spiritual and emotional world is not vital: it is where much of life lies. However, in constructing a God who must not be questioned man made the search for spiritual and emotional vitality almost impossible. He set up a system in which he, as God's emissary, was not questioned either. Until recently the very act of a woman questioning her husband could amount to sedition. Women did not question the authority of their husbands or their fathers, which is what helped to make tarts and creeps out of them. It enabled women not to interfere while their husbands beat hell out of their child. Women are not used to the business of standing back and examining a man to find out who he is, whether he is worthy, and where his strengths and weaknesses lie. As one man said: 'Why is it that a woman will stake her future on a man she meets in a pub one night when all he did was lose his way home?'

She has done so in the past because the self-invented system by which man's wanderings and ramblings are sanctified and written down as gospel has been kept going by a veritable garrison. Woman has been on the outside of that garrison, and has longed to enter this place – the heart of a man. In his book *Jung and the Story of Our Time* Laurens van der Post writes of this syndrome:

> Athens, not Rome, still seems to me to be the incomparable light-house of the spirit. It presupposes the vital honouring, in equal proportions, of the masculine and feminine ... that we have betrayed in our own Western history ... We are caught up in another Roman moment of decline and fall in the spirit of man, wherein worship of the material and subservience to the value of power has driven the feminine, and its accompanying love, out of life ...[1]
>
> One searches in vain for a venture in which both the masculine and feminine values, both the man and the woman, have been honoured in their full proportions ... The history of civilisation appears to be a sorry, one-sided history of domination by man ...[2]

Taking up Michelle Roberts's point about the bride with full knowledge of her husband, and the dangers of twice crucifying Christ, a valid way of interpreting the Crucifixion is to see it as the cruel and symbolic death of the feminine. The body of Christ is ravaged at the hands of the one-sided man – the Roman soldier. Symbolically, Christ's death can be seen as the Roman state denying the feminine principle – the world of individual conscience and of true worship. The Roman soldier is the body politic which turns its back on the full scope of reason to satisfy a narrow intellectual order. The Roman soldier finds the chaos of love and the daily miracle of personal insight not to his limited ascetic taste.

This was the beginning of the rule of culture through a hierarchical system which wilfully turns its back on nature and on wonder. It certainly turns its back on the personal transformation which is the discovery of a life lived 'on the pulse' – a life, in other words, of adventure and the search for meaning. Using the term 'adventure' in the sense that Whitehead means it, an adventurous life offers the possibility of toppling tyrants. Myths and fairy stories are full of such longed for adventures – David and Goliath, Jack and the Beanstalk, to name but a couple.

Surely the Resurrection of Christ carries the meaning of true adventure. It is possible to rise above life as just a series of rules and tests and to find in it your own personal story. This is one of life's biggest adventures and mysteries. Van der Post writes of Jung: 'No-one has worked harder to push back as it were the frontiers of mystery which enclose us. Yet no-one has shown so great a respect and reverence for the mystery.'[3] He goes on to point out the unfamiliar forms that individual mysteries take. Unfamiliar forms are what the Roman soldier would banish, and to him the form of the child is especially alien.

In his present form the Roman soldier, who is what I term a linear man, believes that life is a line or a ladder. You walk along it or up it. What you don't do is look back, especially to your childhood. A man, being a man, does not look back over his shoulder, because if he did he might get frightened out of his wits. Linear man works with the ideas of progress and building a future, not of contemplating the past. He doesn't actually inhabit the present, for he cannot stay still enough and peaceful enough to do so. In looking for his pot of gold, he is busy travelling to the end of the rainbow. What he doesn't do is find the 'gold' inside himself, the childhood years which formed him. These are the years he denies.

Linear man believes mistakenly that life follows a direct line from infancy through youth to middle age, old age and then death; previous stages, including adolescence, are discarded along the way. This putting of life into a series of sub-divisions or compartments was described in the following way by a scientist in his early thirties:

> The reason why women are a mystery to men is that they carry all their luggage with them, and when you meet a woman you meet all of her. She comes steaming into the platform, you go to greet her and then realize that, like all long trains, she doesn't stop there. And you stand and watch in absolute amazement as all her carriages roll by you – mother, father, grandmother, old school friends, childhood. They're all there, attached to her. All you ever wanted to do was *get on* – but you're not just dealing with what came steaming into the platform. You have to take on the whole trainload of her. Most men won't do that.
>
> A man, on the other hand, doesn't carry his own luggage. He dumps it. If you meet him the problem with getting to know him is that he's left bits and pieces of himself – whole carriages, in fact – in sidings up and down the country and sometimes all over the world. Which is why the business of reintegrating a man with his real belongings is sometimes a lifetime's work. Half the time he can't remember where he's been anyway.

Because it is linear the train image is actually better at describing man than woman. Man fears that his masculinity will dissolve if he remembers and acknowledges his childhood. But the infant could also be viewed as a vital, affectionate and energetic companion in the world of the imagination. He is man's guide to sensuality and spontaneity. It is in any case erroneous to regard early childhood as just a time of dependency and silliness. The energy used up and the growing achieved by a child between birth and five are so prodigious that they are never again matched. So in one way the infant is a blueprint for growth, development and achievement.

However, linear man is only interested in *his* kind of achievement. As a shop steward in his mid-thirties said:

> It's bloody siege mentality. I'll stand in my castle, my garrison or my army outpost, and I'll suffer heart attacks in my sentry box, and I'll yell and scream till I'm blue in the face – but I won't give in. I won't accept or recognize myself as only human, and since I can't trust myself I certainly won't trust anyone else.

Alice Miller writes: 'The more or less conscious goal of adults in rearing infants is to make sure they will never find out later in life that they were trained not to become aware of how they were manipulated . . . [and] forced into the Procrustean bed of theories.'[4] The Procrustean theory is so apt here because it signifies a society which will deform the person rather than change the principle.

In deforming the man what it has done is to concentrate on his intellect as if that were an entity in itself, not part of a bigger whole. The result is what I call the 'disconnected intellect' – a person who is extremely clever in his chosen field of study, but is not integrated. He is trained as if a human being is a set of separately functioning parts, rather than an accountable whole. As with the splitting of the atom, his division has dangerous results – he cannot place knowledge within context, and he has only a limited understanding of the laws of cause and effect. He is, in other words, short-sighted. He is culture without nature, brain without body. His intellect is developed, not in harmony with the rest of him, but in opposition to it. Compared with his important brain his body, for example, is of little account, and his emotions are irrelevant. He is unco-ordinated as a result of abandoning the child, which is perhaps why so many disconnected intellects are so childish.

However, they do not become like this alone, and women coddle such men and indulge them. When I was a student in Bristol the disconnected intellect to whom my landlady was married forgot to pick her up from hospital after she had given birth to their first child. Instead of being angry or hurt she told this story many times as she patted him on the back and said: 'Of course he's always so preoccupied with his work.'

The disconnected intellect takes many forms – the short-sighted scientist, the dozy professor, the forgetful inventor etc. I once spent an afternoon with a very famous disconnected intellect. He had enough smells coming from him to make me feel queasy whenever I had to be near him, and he scratched whatever part of him was itching at the time. He was quite oblivious to my distress and, more importantly, to his own. Whatever noise came out of his body he either ignored or treated with considerable surprise, like the startlement you see on a baby's face when it can't work out where a sneeze came from.

However, his attention span was also short, and the same expression did not stay on his face for more than a few instants. In the course of that afternoon I came to be immensely pleased that he was petrified of women, because sometimes he also viewed *me* with a startled glance and his reflex action then was to scuttle to the other side of the room. When I left he haphazardly extended a limp arm on which hung a limp hand, a few fingers of which glanced mine before his expression of anxiety suddenly altered and he banged the door shut with relish.

The Roman soldier or linear man has been responsible for a whole way of thinking that operates in straight lines and divisions. The divisions have been as unquestioned as Heaven and Hell. But aren't people a mixture of both? Linear man divides them up, so that you have a long queue behind the 'Heading for Heaven' sign and another behind the 'Couldn't care less – going to Hell' sign. Linear thinking also penetrates relationships, and through it man has placed woman in a vertical line. At the top, the pinnacle from which she must fall, is the virgin. At the bottom is the nagging, boring wife who is man's reason (read for that excuse) for taking a mistress or for staying out late with the boys.

Relationships on which this view is not imposed are cyclical and layered. People fall in and out of love, have periods of happiness, periods of boredom, and moods in which the relationship seems either stale or wonderful. Man finds this reality difficult because it seems suspiciously like covering the same ground. Man the phoney adventurer believes he is an arrow, always travelling on and never returning to home base. In fact the same ground is never covered twice by the same person or in the same way because it is impossible for nature to create an exact replica; in nature, change is unavoidable. It is culture's task to do this, to mass-produce replicas and to fix things by means such as film. But the hand operating the projector or the eye watching the film *does* change.

The Roman soldier's siege mentality is aimed of course at protecting the ego, which, being frightened, would like to pin things down, to make them controllable and safe. The fear is of life itself, of nature, of insecurity and ultimately of death. In other words the fear is of the very processes which constitute being alive. In the preface to his book *The Wisdom of Insecurity* Alan Watts writes:

> I have always been fascinated by the law of reversed effort. Sometimes I call it the 'backwards law'. When you try to stay on the surface of the water, you sink; but when you try to sink you float. When you hold your breath you lose it – which immediately calls to mind an ancient and much neglected saying, 'Whosoever would save his soul shall lose it.'[5]

The Roman soldier sees the ego not as a tyrant but as a poor, battered, heroic figure fighting against life's odds – as culture fighting nature, as order fighting chaos. In the world of culture the ego is not questioned because culture is the ego's manifestation. One of the earliest recorded figures to question culture was Christ, who challenged the Jewish work ethic and the idea that you earned or bought your way to Heaven. 'It is easier for a camel to go through the eye of a needle', goes the well-known verse from St Matthew's Gospel, 'than for a rich man to enter into the kingdom of God.'

Man sees himself as the potential victim of nature, which will bring about his ultimate death. What does hasten his demise is the way he clings to ego – read for that culture – through which he hopes to prolong life and his own individual identity. He feels personally and symbolically threatened, so he increases the fortress of the ego through pursuits like marking the earth, naming children, erecting skyscrapers and escaping earth itself through space exploration. The link between the penis and the ego confounds both man and woman. As an Oxbridge research scientist in his early thirties whom I interviewed said:

> These days technology is the big fuck. You don't have to look far for the connections. Sex is in the same place now as astronomy was in the sixteenth century. At the moment technology is the displaced

148

and ultimate sexual activity. It wasn't wrong to equate nuclear weapons with man's need for sexual power and the ego's need for control. Technology *is* displaced sexual activity. As man fertilized woman – and doesn't need to any more because there's far too many of us – so shall man fuck earth. What else is the ego about but ultimate domination in order to flee actual vulnerability – which is the knowledge that we must all die?

The link between Old Testament attitudes and sex is a way of trying to get round this. It was described by a housewife and mother in her late sixties who said that the reason she and her husband eventually parted was because he regarded his penis as a religious symbol and her body as a kind of prayer mat. She said: 'He would kneel down before we made love and pray a kind of chant I couldn't catch the words of and which he wouldn't tell me when I asked him. And I hated it. I began to feel filthy.' In *The Sadeian Woman* Angela Carter writes:

She [woman] is most immediately and dramatically a woman when she lies beneath a man, and her submission is the apex of his malehood. To show his humility before his own erection, a man must approach a woman on his knees, just as he approaches God. This is the kind of beautiful thought that has bedevilled the history of sex in Judaeo-Christian culture, causing almost as much confusion as the idea that sex is a sin ... The same beautiful thought has elevated a Western European convention to the position of the only sanctified sexual position; it fortifies the missionary position with a bizarre degree of mystification. God is invoked as a kind of sexual referee, to assure us, as modern churchmen like to claim in the teeth of two thousand years of Christian sexual repression, that sex is really sacred.[6]

Ms Carter goes on to make the point that the missionary position, because it exemplifies man as dominant and woman as passive, lends itself to making generalities out of lovers. She explains that lovers themselves become anonymous when they become symbolic of male and female, Heaven and earth, planter and receiver. Subverted by Old Testament churchmen, the missionary position has been turned from a personal sexual act into a general one where man the seeder plants himself in woman the soil.

The spirit and the flesh of it is that man is caught between God and penis, between ego and prick, between symbol and person, and it is woman's body which lies in between. A social worker in her late twenties described the act of love-making in the following way:

> He would gasp when he saw me naked, and say something like, 'Oh, my God' in a tone between reverence and shock. It was as if my body was his prayer, his hope of salvation, and his erection a cross, and through praying me he would somehow be relieved of this cross.
>
> Outside bed he treated me as if I were some kind of permanent itch in his life, and – yes – we've parted now. I remained with him for eighteen months because I was in love with him and because I thought I could change things. I couldn't.

Talking of men and prayer, a woman publicist in her thirties said:

> It's as if a man doesn't say his own prayers. He's invented a God to pray to so that he doesn't have to pray himself. Yes, he'll get down on his knees in church and pray to someone up there, but that's just an old habit, and it gets him nowhere.
>
> When I pray, I pray myself, using to pray as a verb there. I don't know exactly who I pray to – maybe it's God, maybe it's something, someone else – but I actually give myself up when I do it. And then feel better.
>
> But men can't *pray* themselves. They've created something between themselves and true worship, and they call that something God. But the God men have invented doesn't help them find themselves. On the contrary, *He keeps them from it*, because He lets them off the hook of self-discovery and therefore of repentance.

The Roman soldier cannot give voice to longing. He must instead keep a perilous divide between his fragile ego and the seemingly implacable natural world which will eventually have him end. This is something he cannot bear to contemplate, so he must busy himself with other things. But his business/busyness cannot result in what he really needs, for it doesn't address his longing. In his divided state one half of him tries to head for the stars, where surely new opportunities will present themselves. The other half struggles fiercely at base camp to keep the real new world at bay.

In a Channel 4 TV programme called *Mission to Mars*, transmitted during 1987, some technicians and scientists – mainly male Americans – were interviewed about the USA's continuing costly space programme. The interviewer asked why the government should spend so much money on space research when life here could do with a few improvements. In other words, if we can't make life peaceable here, what makes us feel we can do it somewhere else. One of the scientists replied: 'It's [space travel] an incredible engineering feat . . . By the time you'd constructed a place to live on Mars you'd have invoked the mechanism for making it a good place to live.' The words that struck me were 'constructed', 'invoked' and 'mechanism'. The idea that the 'good life' is something that can be constructed out of the will and the ego, and that the bad life can be flown away from, is delusory. It breeds a dangerous separatism.

The self-deluders have convinced themselves that things come in separate boxes, and that as long as your own personal box is OK you can throw things into that floating lavatory, the sea, without ever worrying about them again. This view has resulted in damage which people in the last quarter of our century have begun to be extremely concerned about. University research departments and bodies like Friends of the Earth and Greenpeace have started to make their findings a cause for widespread public concern. The 1980s have seen a decimation of the North Sea seal population, certainly in part due to pollution from industrial waste and sewage. The last half decade has seen a drastic reduction in the numbers of healthy, edible fish, not just through over-harvesting, but from poisoning as a result of mercury and other discharges which are beginning to clog up the world's oceans. It has become painfully obvious that you can't throw something into the sea – at least not at the rate that the heavily industrialized western world has done – without the damage coming back to you tenfold on the next tide.

The separatist approach believes that you can split a person up into parts and educate the intellect without worrying about the emotions; that you can feed antibiotics to the sick part without worrying about the overall immune system. It is a consciousness which tries to separate cause from effect. Through it the Roman soldier thinks he can march straight off the end of the world, or fly to the moon; anything but clear up the shit in his own back yard.

Because of it people send boys in particular to places without mothers and fathers called public schools, and encourage girls in particular into training for hospital care. In this way today's boys, and the next generation of men, are guaranteed to be needy – for their emotional lives will not have been adequately attended to away from home. And the next generation of nurses will still be mainly female, providing the necessary field hospital for the petrified male psyche.

151

In his book *The New Male–Female Relationship* Herb Goldberg writes:

> The traditional male–female relationship is a relationship between a machine and a child. The more closely she resembles the feminine ideal, the more child-like the woman is psychologically. The more accurately he approximates the masculine ideal, the more machine-like the man is in his behaviour and the consciousness of himself and his life. The relationship between the two produces guilt and hopelessness in the male, and the feelings of rage, helplessness and victimization in the female . . . He is a machine, driven by the unending need to prove himself. Therefore, he lives by acquiring *symbols that validate him* [my emphasis], rather than by experiencing the process of his life. He is motivated by how things make him look as a man, not how they actually feel. As a result, he loses his capacity for human connection and intimacy. The male's strength is an illusion, built on the defensive belief that he can transcend humanness to become a well-oiled, perfectly functioning machine.[7]

He becomes in fact the ghost in the machine, or the Meccano man. He is a functioner and a doer – and he may function and do well – but the heart of him is a mystery. He acts out what is reflexively urgent to him rather than considering what it is he feels and taking his actions from there. He is a set of responses or actions rather than a person who responds. The mechanic in him sees woman as a function. Emotions are accidents, and commitment a hole in the road you might fall into if you don't drive fast enough.

The Roman soldier is an invention to subvert the reality that man is not a creature of the gods outside himself but a servant of the only god he will not tend – his own nature. To those who would argue that man *only* tends himself, I would answer that he doesn't tend the person he *is*, but rather the constructs, the fictions, the oughts and the -isms; in other words the machine rather than the ghost.

In *The Sea of Faith* Don Cupitt looks towards tending that ghost and relinquishing the machinery that has so far kept it in thrall. He writes:

> For him [the philosopher Kierkegaard], Christianity demands that we become subjective. The polarities and tensions of life ought not to be pushed away and resolved metaphysically, but should be internalised and experienced subjectively to the highest degree, so

that we are forced to undergo the inner spiritual transformation which is Christianity's demand and promise . . .[8]

The movement from an understanding of religion centred on dogmatic belief to one centred in spirituality and ethical activity may seem irresistible. Why do people then resist it so strongly? Because it is coupled with the admission, at last, that religion is entirely human, made by men for men. This admission is now inescapable, and the next stage in the development of religious thought will have to be based upon it.[9]

At the conference called Men Too mentioned in Chapter 2 the chairman, Paul Boateng, said that men had two tasks, which was why their work was so difficult. Men had first to disempower themselves by divesting themselves of the mantle of tyrant and boss. They then had to re-empower themselves, but in a different way, so that they regained what everyone needs – personal authority. Man has to take off the apparatus, the suit of armour of the old system. He must then find a new wardrobe more appropriate to the late twentieth century and the new emerging woman, or else walk around naked.

This is why talk of the 'new man' has been so alienating and unproductive, for it has often formed the question: 'New man or wimp?' It comes from the concealed fear, on woman's part as well as on man's, that when divested of his old power bases man will have no new ones to go to, and will therefore be powerless – feminism's eunuch. The cry from the fair-minded that man should divest himself of unscrupulously gained power was not in itself enough. The danger lies in man once more looking outside rather than inside himself for answers and therefore for interpretative power.

This danger is particularly acute if he looks to woman, for while her own struggles might make it seem as if she has answers for man, these answers are perilously close to instructions. 'Learn how to feel'; 'Learn how to cry'; 'Learn how to stop being boss', says woman – and these are, after all, commands. The irony of replacing the Puritan fathers with the Puritan mothers might be more than this beleaguered species could withstand. Woman has found that real power lies in working with or through emotions, not against them; and that resolution of pain lies in its acceptance, not in its denial. These are universal truths that are not sex-related. They in fact form the basis of a New Testament Christianity that is concerned with Christ as embodying and sanctifying individual struggle. The Old Testament, by contrast, inflicts an external set of rules.

Man must find his own way towards a definition of masculinity, and it cannot happen without the help of other men. But as Antony Easthope, Phillip Hodson and feminist writers have pointed out, the problem is that man does not have a friend in other men. His emotionally absent father and competitive hierarchical systems have ensured that man has to work hard to find a helper and good role model in another male. The task of finding masculinity through an invisible God-figure, an absent father and the suspicious, fearful silence of other men has been well nigh impossible. Man has not yet discovered the power of a full set of emotions, and because of this is, as Hodson points out, the 'super-sensitive sex'.[10] Hodson also says that 'it is actually only two-thirds of his emotions that a man is enjoined to conceal since the rules of the game permit him to express violent anger and rage'.[11] This is hardly surprising when the background of man's suppression of himself by his constructed mechanisms is understood. While I was interviewing and talking with people for this book a number of men asked if I had come anywhere near discovering what masculinity really is. Not one woman asked the same question about femininity.

13

Astride the See-saw

The essence of femininity and the essence of masculinity are difficult to find, for through the constructs of them as opposites they have become interdependent in a stifling way. Biblical myths, behaviourism and biology have been plaited together to form a Gordian knot in which man is God/intellectual master/penis owner and woman has been constructed to fit in with this scheme. But by inventing her in opposition to this, man guaranteed his dependency on his invention. By depicting woman as mortal/earth mother/penis receiver man made himself *dependent* on this female structure. After all, what use is there in being a god if there is no one to bow the knee? And what use is there in being an intellectual master unless there is someone to indoctrinate?

The whole system is extraordinarily convoluted, because it is ultimately self-enclosing and does not have the power to break the mould or snap the vicious circle. It is like a constantly rocking see-saw, on which you can't budge an inch or even shift your weight without provoking a reaction from the 'other side'. Feminist writers have described that see-saw as being heavily weighted in favour of man, whereas in fact it has been weighted differently and perversely in a complex system of needs and counter-needs. Sometimes the very thing that one side has done to strengthen itself acts against it and does the opposite. As the other side gleefully takes advantage of this, it too realizes there is a sting in the tale. And so the game goes unremittingly on.

This busy see-saw never rests, because neither side will get off to leave the other alone. Neither side *can* get off without denying sexuality: if you are a heterosexual woman you have an interest in man, and vice versa. The see-saw is also a restrictive piece of equipment because – unlike the swing, for example – you must have someone opposite to make it work. However, that someone opposite you must be of similar weight to your own if you want the see-saw to work rhythmically.

The rhythm between man and woman was initially interfered with when man decided to off-load himself of some of the qualities he

155

didn't need. In letting go of beauty, gentleness and receptivity he thought he was making himself more efficient – in other words stronger. He now realizes, of course, that this was not so. Woman would *appear* to be the victim here, as indeed she was to some extent. But in another way she was also given more power, both in the sense of having vital qualities like beauty and receptivity for herself and in being Mistress of the Keep for man.

The scenario of the man who dumps his 'feminine' bits and the woman who relinquishes her 'maleness' forms another piece of sophistry in the pairing of wimp and nag or frightened husband and strident wife. This system of opposites has been captured on many seaside postcards depicting a woman brandishing a rolling pin and – very important – endowed with enormous breasts. She is usually berating a weedy, knock-kneed, diminutive man.

These familiar scenes illustrate man's fear of woman – but why should he fear her if he's really the boss? Man fears his dependency on woman who has been created, as in the bad old days of Hollywood, to be always his screen opposite. One of his fears is that he will not actually be hero without his heroine. The other is that, having dumped part of himself, he knows he was in collusion with the Devil in so doing.

He won't admit this consciously, but present knowledge is making it difficult to turn his back on this inner truth. The knowledge, through Freud, of the power of the unconscious, and, through feminism, of the dirty deeds of patriarchy has made it obvious that man's constructs were not godly but devilish. When he invented his God-figure his pact was not with the holy, but with the unholy. He did not produce a good (God) system, but a bad (Devil) one. Make woman into that Devil and you have the postcard of the henpecked husband and the big, clucking chicken of a wife; in other words, the cockerel brought low.

Woman said that patriarchy's dirty tricks were about as low as you could get. Man invented the God-figure, not from love and reverence of good but out of anger, jealousy and inconsolability. So the see-saw became weighted. Woman, light as a fluffy feather, stayed up in the air in contrast to man's grave, serious, boss position. Then woman sank like a frump to the ground while glorious, righteous, God-empowered man soared skywards. They were always the opposites in play.

Man thought he had put God in the fulcrum position. He hadn't. Old Satan himself was the gleeful straddler. This is why man has built traps in which he ensnares himself. He had wanted to be the strong hero who played opposite the beautiful damsel in distress. Instead he sometimes found himself the emasculated wimp crushed by the female siren.

The clay of gender opposites and stereotypes didn't come from Heaven or from natural soil, but from devilish invention. So masculinity and femininity are terribly interfered with. The invention of opposite sex myths is basically a recipe for dependency and collusion. The penis is dependent on the ego, and the ego is dependent on the penis, so these two collude. Both of them depend on the virgin/whore. The virgin/whore depends on man, man depends on woman, woman depends on and colludes with man. Neither can depend on him or herself. Much of this was set up to hide man's vulnerability when in fact he is both powerful and vulnerable, as is woman. However, the penis/ego serves as a shield to try to make man impervious to his own frailty – and to the strength in woman.

Having created this shield or castle to protect himself, man then has to have an enemy outside himself. He would look pretty daft standing on sentry duty without an Indian in sight. He also, of course, needs someone to service the castle, for like all fortresses it has large and compelling needs. Once you have created a system of superiority it has to be maintained.

The person who will accomplish the opposites needed here, as enemy and provider, as attacker and servant, can only be woman. She, as the opposite sex, is foe and handmaiden, assailant and the-one-who-has-to-be-conquered. The ability to slay and be slain is given to her in the archetypal guise of virgin/whore. This is the combination which most accurately reflects man in apposition, and which most carefully keeps him pinned where he is. It fixes him in an ego drama where he is not free to engage in 'real life' or the daily dynamics of an ordinary relationship.

The construct of the virgin supports the penis/ego system and is controlled by it. The virgin is herself a fortress, and an honourable one, so she reflects man's own fortress. She is also, however, rendered non-virgin – in other words *killed as virgin* – if her defence is penetrated only once. So in order to remain virgin she must at all cost not be penetrated. In this respect she mirrors what man would have us believe he must defend, even to the death, or die *as man* – his own battlements. If his masculine fortress is penetrated, he may indeed survive as wimp, but this is not what he wants. So the virgin and the penis/ego support the fortress mentality for each other.

Put in another way, the ego's biggest fear is that of lacking an identity. The terror of the void, of being without form, of being a nothing or a nobody keeps it in the boss position, and the boss position requires ritual sacrifices. That is why the virgin must die: sometimes literally in the form of sacrifice, as has happened in the past, and metaphorically in losing her virginity and becoming an ordinary woman.

The woman, as opposed to the virgin, presents a problem. Although she has been slain as virgin she still continues as person, and moreover as a person who is palpably alive and kicking. To describe this person the fortress mentality uses the word 'whore', and the vital woman is concealed behind this derogatory label. In order to avoid shame and concealment, in the past woman was offered a contract which would save her face – she was offered marriage. Although it was also a form of imprisonment because of the constraints it placed upon her, it gave her the only choice other than virgin or whore. In this way the fortress mentality contained woman. It had to do so, or it would have been faced with its own shortcomings and eventual surrender.

By constructing a fortress condition for woman called virginity, man mirrored his own state of siege. He also ruled the opposition fortress, because her only way out was into whoredom – or his marriage bonds. Enter the censor, who must keep her strictly tied within these bonds, and make further enclosures even within this corral. How dare she be fallen image and still laugh at the exploits of her children! Is she mad? How dare she enjoy sex again freely! Is she a nymphomaniac? How dare she speak with her sisters! Is she a witch? How dare she in the end love man! Is she not either insolent or blind? Part of man's folly is that his fortress renders other men either strangers or enemies to him, so he will tell woman that most men are bastards and that in loving one she also has no sense. Much of the difficulty which men experience in comforting women friends over the loss of a lover is that on one level they really cannot perceive it as loss.

The hunter mentality says that with one thrust man will slay the virgin. One of the nastiest pieces of work that this cultural construct has produced is the notion that a woman who has been penetrated is less than one who hasn't. It directly feeds the system which holds that a sexual woman is a slut because of sexual experience, but that a sexual man is a fine chap. If man is supposed to be 'doing it' outside marriage to gain experience and prove his masculinity, and woman is supposed to have been intact, who the hell has man been doing it with all these centuries?

The invention of man's myths was always a slippery business. The business becomes even more unstable when the myths have to start sliding around in order to collude with these opposites. In the figures of potent man and passive woman, passionate man and submissive woman, you only have to slither along a bit to exchange 'submissiveness' for 'withholding' and you have woman as bitch. Rape, which is revenge on women, takes its starting point from the notion that there is something to *be* avenged. Woman as bitch, whether in her modern form of having dared to cut loose, or in this ancient form of withholding from man what he needs to make him better, has a great deal to answer for. Antony Easthope describes the situation in these words:

> In a complex organisation, all these elements work together in the dominant culture to produce masculine heterosexual desire as an ungovernable force. Such desire is defined culturally in an imbalanced equation between active and male, passive and female . . . If the feminine is treated as an essence, the Woman, masculine desire must take a corresponding form.[1]

Man made an Essence of Woman which would always suit him. It was as if he took one huge piece of cloth, divided it by the number of women around, and chopped it up into that number of pieces. Yes, all women are different, but uniformly and controllably so, so they are also all the same. Or perhaps man took Essence of Woman and poured it from a large pitcher into prettily shaped bottles on a shelf; again all looking slightly different for his better delectation, but all actually from the same brew. It was nice to know that the bottle was there for special occasions, and that it would stay safely on the shelf when not in use. But when the bottles started popping their own corks and became self-fermenting the 'trouble' was bound to spread further than the shelf.

Woman's attempts to escape stereotyping and feminism's questioning of gender roles have created more than just local difficulty. They threaten to undermine what has so far held traditional hetereosexual relationships – though not heterosexuality itself – together. In fact man's need for sexual dominance and the vicious circle it has created have ensured that relationships between men and women, as well as those between men and men and between women and women, have been difficult, hypocritical and stressful.

The particular strand in feminism that hits the myth of male dominance is the unifying of women, not by men, but through themselves. Woman has in one sense slipped out of the constructs she had of herself remarkably quickly. This is not, however, to deny the enormous volume of work which has been done and is still being done as unrelenting pressure against individual growth continues to push everyone towards stereotype and greed. The relative ease with which woman slipped out of her mould depended on the extent to which her mould could be described as man-made. She was able to turn her back on those parts of her wardrobe which clearly did not fit her because she had not been there in person when such things were arranged. So the clothing of tradition and of stereotype woman has in the main discarded. She was able to do so because when she consulted other women she found that the wardrobe was uniform. With the help of the sisterhood she has discovered the full spectrum of traditional oppression; without this co-operation she couldn't have done it.

In this respect, as Paul Boateng suggested, woman's task has been simpler than man's. She needed to empower herself, and was doing so. Where it hasn't been simpler is in the amorphous area of guilt and superstition. For the fiendish form straddling the see-saw has invaded woman's heart as well as man's. One invasion in particular is the little-revealed corner of woman's heart and soul where man acts as talisman within woman. Woman has been accustomed to staving off man as tyrant, but as a cross between God, Santa Claus and genie his old ghost still lingers. Don Cupitt expresses it like this: 'When we have . . . freed ourselves from nostalgia for a cosmic Father Christmas, then our faith can at last become fully human, existential, voluntary, pure, and free from superstition.'[2]

The superstition remains in the uneasy marriage between 'God' and his self-made child-bride, the female eunuch. Although the bride has come a long way since both the days of the Old Testament and the early seventies, when *The Female Eunuch* was first published, there is still a sense in which woman is fearful. Although it is now true that for every man in Britain who divorces his wife, three women divorce their husbands, there is a lurking nervousness that this uppityness will be punished. The majority – who didn't want the clock to move forward in any case – are lurking ready to swing the pendulum back at the first sign of weakness in the new ranks. Since these people will hire planes to trail the words: 'I TOLD YOU SO' across the sky if women fail, there is a pressure to examine and re-examine.

In her book *The Cinderella Complex* American author Colette Dowling describes modern woman's continuing dependency on man. However hard woman strives to be – and succeeds in being – financially independent and a person in her own right, the old needs are present. She still wants a man to rescue her from the drudgery of daily life and transport her into a better world. This is the area in which the I-told-you-sos are ready to pounce: 'We told you so all along. A woman needs a man.'

Obviously woman wanting man for herself, as a lover and partner, is normal. Wanting him to change her world for her is not, for then he takes on the mantle of abnormal or supernormal. But the fairy stories told her he would do this – he would light up her world.

In order to illuminate a complicated, shadowy area of this abnormal dependency I have taken Ms Dowling's theme and turned it round to call it the Prince Charming Complex. For what Ms Dowling is saying is that woman has achieved the task of slipping out of her Cinderella rags, but has not achieved the disrobing of Prince Charming. Woman has shrugged off the Cinderella Complex by leaving dependent Cinders behind her. What she hasn't done is to leave Prince Charming behind too.

This is the grey area where man acts as talisman for modern woman. She keeps the hope and prospect of Prince Charming alive; she hangs on to him as her good luck charm. So heavy has the mantle of man as provider, prince and God-figure been that woman, who has fought so hard to be properly independent, barely realizes she can't let go of this final piece of fool's gold.

In order to understand this, the fairy stories themselves need looking at for the way in which the handsome, rescuing prince is a ubiquitous God-figure. For the stories that the present adult generation of little girls were brought up on made them believe that life would not be just unpleasant without a man, but would be doomed or cursed. The prince of the fairy stories is not just idealized; he has God-invested powers. For a start, there is the 'colour' of these princes.

The interesting thing about fairy stories is that they seldom describe the prince in technicolour detail. In this respect the prince is somewhat like the invisible God who, in my childhood, I had assumed was married to Mother Nature. Cinderella, Sleeping Beauty and Beauty herself are all vividly portrayed – in other words the fully coloured 'hussies' of the piece. And although they are presented as individuals they are symbols of damsels in distress, of how much women need men.

The princes who rescue the maidens of our childhood reading are, however, mainly interchangeable, and like 'God' and 'father' symbols of power and goodness. These princes are of course handsome, brave, single, high-born and so on, but these are generalities. The particulars

161

of their names, or how they grew to be so exquisitely suited to the awesome task of making our heroines not just happy, but happy ever after, are not provided. Although it is woman who is usually symbol, and still is in these stories, where man is symbol he is either rescuer of beauty (knight and prince) or bestower of power (God and king). The size of Cinderella's dainty feet would not have mattered till the day she died of overwork and drudgery had not the prince made them the object of his search. In other words, a woman is made real, important or meaningful by a *man*, and does not exist in her own right. For our fairy stories to have happy endings a man must appear on the scene; a knight or prince must bless the page and make the story whole.

While the obvious aspects of man's symbolic power have been carefully examined, the superstitious ones have been less so. While woman has worked on the manifest task of becoming independent of man-as-essential-to-life, she has found it less easy to divest herself of the wizardry that says he might be essential to happiness. The condition of woman needing man has been more than just financial or pragmatic, for in all the myths from Genesis onwards man has held the key to paradise.

This is once more where oppositional contradictions appear. For while man has held this key, so, through man's myths, has woman, as the gateway to Heaven. Man holds the key to paradise because – so the myths go – through him woman will enter a state of wholeness. The Christian religion's precedent for this was man – and woman – entering Heaven through the body of the man, Christ.

In wanting to make sure he was needed by woman, man tried to make himself indispensable to her in every way. He tried to impose a system in which her life would literally not be worth living without him. So through man, woman may hope to find paradise on earth – in other words, wholeness – and through God she may hope to enter Heaven. It is hardly surprising, therefore, that she carries around with her the notion of man as lucky charm; hardly surprising, either, that because of this she tries to copy him.

Feminism provided a much needed counter-balance to the busy, fretful see-saw, but the heterosexual heart of the matter is still clouded. This was described by a beauty therapist in her early thirties:

I realized that in order to escape dependency on man I made men and women interchangeable for a while in a sort of asexual way. Men were brothers, and women were sisters. In the end I realized they weren't interchangeable, because I wanted more from men than women. I wanted from a man not just friendship and understanding but also sex, comfort and the prospect of long-term companionship.

And there I really got caught out by the enigma of male–female relationships, because something else became clear. I began to see that I suffered even more when I ended a relationship myself than when one was ended for me – dependency if you like. But it wasn't only that. It was because I feared I would be cursed if I finished with a man. It seemed as if somehow I was pushing my luck. I feared that if as a woman you were ungrateful enough to finish with a decent guy then something, somewhere would punish you for it.

But more than punish – curse. I feared some kind of jinx, and this could only have come from some deep-rooted idea that men have more rights than women – that there was in men some voodoo or magic which I had no right to interfere in.

Fairy stories are the stuff of magic. They often deal in curses and spells, and ingratitude or even just ungraciousness is a punishable offence.

The notion of being either punished or, more than that, cursed for ending a relationship with a man is one that an older woman, too, spoke of as solving for her a long-term mystery. The woman, who is in her seventies, said:

I had two husbands, both of whom suffered very poor health shortly after marriage and until they died. This meant that I spent my married lives nursing them. I accepted this as my penalty for having walked away from a sweet boy when I was sixteen and he was eighteen. I was rather independent for my time and a bit uppity. When life dealt me a number of blows, without realizing it at first I traced my bad luck to that. I thought I had brought it on myself.

The Prince Charming Complex has meant in the past that women have left slippers, rings, locks of hair and various other bits and pieces of themselves lying around for a man to discover. It has given men the power of diviners and women the hope of being divined, alighted upon, or reunited with their lost property and thereby made whole. A prince was not only a husband and a guardian against life's ordinary ills like poverty and loneliness; he was also a lucky charm. Through his auspices little girls have been fed man as talisman with their

163

morning malt and little boys have been seized with the terror of their shortcomings.

After she had waved the magician's cloak aside and found little more than a bag of dirty tricks, woman did a curious thing. It might have been understandable if for a while she had abjured all things male for fear of falling under spells again. It might also have been understandable if in the cooling-off period she had avoided things that were conventionally or traditionally thought of as feminine, like make-up and delicate clothes. What was unexpected was that she sought to become like the tyrant she was claiming to overthrow. Woman decided to weight the see-saw her own way.

The most bizarre example of this behaviour was reported to me by some friends returning from the United States, who talked about 'aspiration parties'. A group of women will get together with specula and hand mirrors and examine their own and/or other women's cervixes. They are able to tell from this, and a rough idea of the date their period is due, almost exactly when menstruation is about to start. Because these women do not want tacky things like periods they then aspirate, or evacuate by suction, the contents of the uterus. This can be medically damaging, especially if it is done frequently.

These cervix-watching parties are indulged in so as to be free of the 'curse' of being female. After all, men don't have to put up with it. The interference makes women more like men, which is an insult to both sexes. Women are more than male castrates, and men are more than non-menstruating beings. A woman may rightly insist on being thought of as more than a person without a penis, and a man may hope to be identified in a more positive way than as a person who doesn't bleed.

At the other end of this biological reductionism, some women switched from 'The Menstruation Blues' (a cabaret song by Robyn Archer) to talking about menstruation so often and so publicly that, as was expressed by a woman who runs an art gallery: 'I secretly longed for the bad old days of suffering in silence. If this is where suffrage had got us, then those who had fought for it must be turning in their graves.' A woman in her forties went on a fortnight's holiday with enough tampons and towels to staunch the effects of a small civil war, and insisted on trying to make her menses the centre of conversation. Another woman handed a tampon (unused) to a freelance writer she had just employed and asked her to keep it in her bag. The writer said: 'Since she had a bag of her own and a skirt with large pockets in it I was nonplussed. Could it really have been her way of letting me know she had a period? She didn't ask for it back, by the way.'

There was certainly a danger that being more honest about the discomfort of menstruation would push women back into the ghetto they had just fought their way out of. Would recognizing PMT (pre-menstrual tension) as a syndrome actually help women in the long term, or would it be used as an argument against employing women on an equal basis? Gloria Steinem gave an answer, though not directly to this question, in her hilarious article 'If Men Could Menstruate':

So what would happen if suddenly, magically, men could menstruate and women could not? . . .

Men would brag about how long and how much.

Young boys would talk about it as the envied beginning of manhood . . .

Generals, right-wing politicians, and religious fundamentalists would cite menstruation ('*men*-struation') as proof that only men could serve God and country in combat ('You have to give blood to take blood'), occupy high political office ('Can women be properly fierce without a monthly cycle governed by the planet Mars?'), be priests, ministers, God himself ('He gave this blood for our sins'), or rabbis ('Without a monthly purge of impurities, women are unclean') . . .

Medical schools would limit women's entry ('They might faint at the sight of blood') . . .

Menopause would be celebrated as a positive event, the symbol that men had accumulated enough years of cyclical wisdom to need no more . . .

In short, we would discover, as we should already guess, that logic is in the eye of the logician . . .[3]

Another mischievous example of the possible results of gender and role reversal can be found in Margaret Atwood's *Murder in the Dark*. In a preamble to reading from it in the early eighties when it was her latest book, Atwood mentioned that a lot of men were cooking these days and that she often went to dinner parties for which the men and not the women had done the cooking. This had been her starting point for 'Simmering', a story set in the future. It describes how men take over the kitchen, making it their preserve, and banish the women in their business suits out of the house to do boring things like earning money. The kitchen becomes the hub of the community. Atwood writes:

A man's status in the community was now displayed by the length of his carving knives, by how many of them he had and how sharp he kept them, and by whether they were plain or ornamented with gold and precious jewels . . . Psychological articles began to appear in the magazines on the origin of women's kitchen envy and how it could be cured. Amputation of the tip of the tongue was recommended, and, as you know, became a widespread practice in the more advanced nations. If Nature had meant women to cook, it was said, God would have made carving knives round and with holes in them.[4]

Logic is indeed in the mind of the beholder.

This being so, the logical consequence of feminism in the minds of many men was that women would become *like* men. Who else was there for them to emulate? The notion that women could become more *woman*-like did not occur to man, perhaps because it was he who had designed the female construct as the opposite of the male one. There was no other direction in which he could imagine woman going. In moving away from her 'opposite' position she would have to come forward to be closer to, or more like, him.

Man's fear ran through many levels, the lowest of which was probably the idea that he already had enough competitors in other men without adding women to the list as well. Man's fear is that woman, having been conditioned to be his foil – his opposite – will in a reverse situation run him through with his own sword.

Woman has also made the mistake of aping the rules of the system she has called tyrannical and oppressive. This phallic woman is a straight leap – in the dark, unfortunately – from the Puritan fathers to the conformist mothers. Swapping the sins of the fathers for the dirty tricks of the mothers was not in fact what reputable women had in mind for the latter half of the twentieth century.

But not all of phallic woman consists of deliberate dirty tricks. Some of her is the inevitable result of overbalancing of the kind that Angela Carter writes about in *The Sadeian Woman*:

If women allow themselves to be consoled for their culturally determined lack of access to the modes of intellectual debate by the invocation of hypothetical great goddesses, they are simply flattering themselves into submission (a technique often used on them by men). All the mythic versions of women, from the myth of the redeeming purity of the virgin to that of the healing, reconciling mother, are consolatory nonsenses; and consolatory nonsense seems to me a fair definition of myth, anyway. *Mother goddesses are just as silly a notion as father gods* [my emphasis].[5]

It is understandable that, in order to invent her own being out of the ghosts, wraiths and ashes of patriarchy, woman would both react against it and copy it. However, since revolutionary change has been and is afoot, then, taking up Don Cupitt's description of a post-Freudian personally accountable religion, the form will be goddess in woman and god in man. The form would consist of personally accountable people – both male and female – with their own identities.

In escaping the bondage of the God-figure men would be able to become more like themselves – in other words, men – rather than caricatures of masculinity or empty cardboard boxes. In escaping the tugs and instructions, women could become more womanly – more centred in themselves – instead of constructs like virgin, whore, slim, buxom, flighty or dumb.

So in a personally accountable religion a woman would become whole – her own goddess – and a man would become whole too – his own god. Neither would act upon instructions imposed by the other sex, or by artificial symbols of the other sex. A grand marriage could then take place – the wedding of the goddess and the god. The difference between this and other 'grand' events is that this one could be daily and normal. But there are still hurdles in the way.

For phallic woman it is business as usual, for she is a clone of linear man. She hasn't understood or indeed wanted to understand anything about serious attempts to change society and world views. She is a deeply conservative person. Change frightens her, unless it is to her direct advantage. She seeks power and wields it as selfishly and ruthlessly as a man. In so doing she confuses the main issues, because she is used as evidence that, with women running things, life is no different from before. If you thought it was bad when man was in charge, the argument goes, you'll welcome him back like a cuddly teddy bear after you've tried rule by woman.

In the period of copying man, woman has been through a complex of habits and transformations. She tried on a few 'boys' tricks' for size, and set some alarming trends. Since the late seventies the number of women who have become heavy drinkers and smokers has risen alarmingly. Research has also shown that men are nine times more likely to leave a woman who drinks heavily than women are to leave a man who does the same.

In 'coming out' on such a grand scale there was an early

assumption that everyone at the feminist party was a friend, and was benign. However, there are dangers in moving away from man as talisman and creator. If woman decides to re-create him and his systems to her specifications, then the goddess has a god complex. The see-saw goes clunking on.

14

Heaven and Hell

If man and woman are to live a better life then they must exercise themselves as *people in the present*, not as symbols representing constructs. While the see-saw has continued, man and woman have not been free to engage in the challenge that is the excitement and adventure of the here and now. The whole business has been so stultifying and bizarre that it gives credence to the idea of God the master puppeteer pulling invisible strings on which we poor mortals dance. In fact mortals dance to the tune of an egotistical system which depicts itself through a God of wrath, a Hell of eternal fire, and the prospect of Heaven to be attained only through a life of suffering and sacrifice.

In the manner in which the picture has been drawn this is self-perpetuating, for the ego must be all-powerful (God), and in order to escape from its own barbarism it must either die or destroy itself. It is both its own worst enemy and its own best friend, and it carries on between Hell and Heaven, for the ego must maintain itself. The egotistical system which has invented Heaven and Hell as constructs of its best hopes and worst fears denies itself any possibility of respite from its own constraints. The see-saw clunks unremittingly back and forth, up and down.

This system looks at the world in order to dominate, and therefore prevents or eclipses a spirit of enquiry or adventure – which is, as Whitehead said, crucial to leading a civilized life. Such a spirit is also crucial to the survival of this planet, for the true adventurer as opposed to the plunderer or pirate travels not to take but to find. It is the ego that is piratical and tyrannical; in the spirit of enquiry or adventure lie both trust and humility. The person who adventures is a learner and a disciple, and the adventurous spirit is a trusting one. It travels not in order to conquer or gain, but in the knowledge that life itself is its own journey and reward.

The ego dare have none of that, so it devises a system in which man dances to woman's tune and woman dances to man's, and so we go round and round. In *What a Man's Gotta Do* Antony Easthope writes:

In so far as men live the dominant version of masculinity . . . they are themselves trapped in structures that fix and limit masculine identity . . .[1]

So, trying to define masculinity is going to be a tricky and speculative venture. However, for this task psychoanalysis provides one valuable piece of extra assistance. It is an analytic not a moralizing discourse . . . To be male in modern society is to benefit from being installed, willy nilly, in a position of power. No liberal moralizing or glib attitudinizing can change that reality. Social change is necessary and a pre-condition of such change is an attempt to *understand* masculinity, to make it visible.

The venture has one clear implication. If masculinity is not, as it claims, normal and universal but rather has a particular identity and structure, then it would be wrong to regard masculinity simply as a source, whether of oppression or anything else, as though masculinity were just there, a given . . . masculinity is an effect, and a contradictory one. In so far as men live the dominant version of masculinity analysed here, they are themselves trapped . . . They do what they *have* to do.[2]

The unbending of gender roles is having a boomerang effect. Man originally wrote a script giving himself all the leading roles, and now he has to continue playing those roles because the script says so. He doesn't question the script because he wrote it, and to question his own rightness is not in the script. So the show goes on.

The boomerang is man's homophobia and his fear of homosexuality, which he sees as the possible consequence of expressing the 'feminine' side of himself. If he becomes more 'like a woman' in that he accepts the gentler, softer aspects of himself, this might make him attracted by and attractive to other men. Easthope says that the 'homosexual side' of man finds its way of expression through activities like sport and war. He claims that these structures are allowable expressions of man's affections for other men. Other, unstructured expressions might lead, man feared, to homosexuality. So he created a system which contains no particle of femininity, and his myths are both a defence against the female side of himself and a defence against attraction to or by other men. This is why man relates to other men in a stereotypical rather than a spontaneous way, which in turn is why he now envies the spontaneity of woman's relationships with other women.

The breaking of the male ranks brought about by women breaking theirs has left man with no male role model around from which he could reconstitute himself. The masculine myth has invented for itself an invisible boss in the form of the Christian God. But this God cannot be a role model for *actual* man because he has qualities that actual man cannot achieve – like omnipotence and the power of universal creativity.

In the person of Christ there is a model of a kind – certainly a model for the qualities that the masculine myth has avoided, like mercy, compassion and the ability to be non-judgemental. But the problem with Christ's story as it has been handed to us is that he is both man and not man, for as the Son of God he is other than man. In particular he has been presented to us as non-sexual. Through his myths man has given himself impossible tasks and no visible role model who is fully male. If Christ did have sexual relationships, as writers like Robert Graves in *King Jesus* and Michelle Roberts have suggested, this fact has been withheld from traditional and popular culture. Where it is presented, as in the film *The Last Temptation of Christ*, a hue and cry ensues. There is, however, a symbolism in Christ's life which has been of tremendous importance to woman, and in its deeper meaning has been ignored by man's culture. This is the fact that Christ carried His own cross.

Whatever her difficulties in shouldering the burdens of the models imposed on her, woman has actually had an ally – although she might call it a dubious one – in the form of her menses. This monthly bleeding both undermines and transcends whatever models are pinned on her. Whether she is virgin, temptress, dutiful housewife, seamstress, politician or airline pilot she bleeds. But the positive result of this bleeding is that woman has retained a closer link with other women. Her bleeding, which she knows was not man- or culture-made, has kept her in touch with the reality behind the myths. It has been a reminder of herself both as an individual person and as a female linked with other females.

One of the reasons why woman has been able to free herself from man's myths – in other words, to find herself – is because she was not as lost to reality as man was. She has therefore retained some of herself in order to ward off dehumanization and depersonalization. In one important sense she has had the cross of her own reality to hold up to the Devil of invention. She has carried her own cross because of her biological function. Christ carried His own cross. Man has not. He has instead invented a system of crosses or hurdles *apart* from himself, thereby evading the essential issue.

Man does this by creating dynamics of tension outside himself, in the form of polarized opposites. He then sets himself the false task of dealing with them. At its most dangerous, man made an almost seamless construct of his myth of male dominance, and if you cannot see how something is made you cannot easily undo it. However, you can completely destroy it, which is what nuclear warfare would achieve.

The story of Frankenstein – written by a woman – is a prophetic one in this context. The Chambers Twentieth Century Dictionary defines Frankenstein as the man who 'forms an animate creature like a man, *only to his own torment* [my emphasis]: hence, by confusion, any creation that brings disaster to its author'. In the story of Frankenstein the man-made monster escapes to terrify innocent people, while simultaneously, like King Kong, tugging pitiably at our heart strings. The further twist is that he can be destroyed only by the person who created him, whom he both loves and hates. This is why nuclear war would be waged by the people who created the myth it will destroy – that man is supreme, that he is a god.

There is, of course, a sense in which opposites – 'natural' opposites – are a crucial part of living an adventurous life which encompasses the possibility of change and the qualities of awe and wonder. For life contains death within itself, and every moment lived is a moment nearer death. Culture's fear of mortality means that it seeks to slow down the process of dying and to put off the moment of death. In doing so it inevitably also atrophies the process of living and the moment of life, the present. But it doesn't of course understand that. It is a paradox.

There are opposites or paradoxes that, if understood in themselves, lead to a more personal engagement in the art of living rather than a preoccupation with the science of controlling. In this science a fundamentalist approach to Christianity puts the last nail in the death-promotion system. For in its final analysis the God-myth states that man is destined to be evil because he is not God. It says that he is destined to destroy the earth one way or another, and that on the Day of Judgement God will come and save those who are His. This viewpoint is linear in that it believes one line of people will continue to burn on this Hell-earth while the other lot go to Heaven. It also produces the paradox that man (not being God) is *destined* to destroy Eden. It gives us the really odd situation in which those who are on the side of 'good' (God) are also on the side of 'bad' (lethal weaponry) – in His name.

The problem for modern man in finding an identity is that since his past myths have rested on impossibilities, it is very difficult for him to find what is possible. The bringing down of the myth has left Adam

172

naked, devoid of the suits of armour, sceptres, robes, crowns and swords which he gathered to arm himself against the reality of his plight – that of being simply human. It is difficult for man to realize now that he is not a hoax, that 'the gods' are not malign. It is equally difficult for him to apportion blame. He still vents his feelings of impotence on nature, not culture, and will say: 'Life's a bitch' rather than 'God's a tyrant'.

Man has difficulty in finding himself, in finding out what masculinity is. He has trapped himself in an elaborate system which encompasses the ideal of technology as foolproof and God as human-proof. But it is now possible to say what masculinity is *not*. For man is not a god, not a prince, not a piece of machinery, not a Roman soldier, and certainly not an essence. Neither is masculinity a system of vying opposites with femininity. What masculinity *is* must lie in some understanding of paradox rather than oppositional forces. Perhaps one of the most crucial paradoxes is that strength is found not by avoiding vulnerability, but by accepting and accommodating it. For vulnerability is absolutely and irrevocably a condition of being human.

In the late twentieth century man suffers a new vulnerability, for, in Britain at any rate, he is no longer a scarce commodity. For the first time men outnumber women, by an overall figure of a million. There are two reasons for this reversal. Male births always exceed female births. Because in the past boy babies were slightly more prone to die in infancy than girls, a balance in the sexes was achieved. Now, with improved standards in health care, coupled with an absence of large-scale death through war, those boy babies are surviving. *Family Policy Bulletin* No. 3, published by the Family Policy Studies Centre in September 1987, showed that not only was there an overall outnumbering, but that males outnumbered females in all age groups except the over-sixties. In the fifteen to twenty-nine age group, for example, there were 238,000 more men than women.

The other factor in play when man was a scarce resource and woman was controlled by him was that woman might be relied upon, or at least encouraged, to fight other women to get herself this prize. The simultaneous combination of feminism and a surplus of men has been devastating to the siege mentality. Women breaking their own ranks and joining with other women in co-operative financial, business and leisure arrangements broke the male ranks in any case. The fortress had to crumble if part of what was holding it up walked away. So once the dynamic of Essence of Woman was broken then Essence of Man cracked too, because throughout the lifetime of that particular cultural myth the dynamics had been inter-dependent.

Man's deep knowledge and fear is that woman has become the crypt of his cast-off shelf. That is his fear of her, and in looking around for support at this time of such profound change man has found that the male next to him is not brother or comrade. He is a fearful assembly of the bits and pieces of a rotting empire.

Resistance to woman becoming a person in her own right runs as deep as the fear of Hell; or, to be precise, it encompasses the fear of losing Heaven. For, in the constructs of opposites which have supported traditional interpretations of male and female, Heaven and Hell are the most dynamic and important. Woman has been represented as earth and as Heaven. She has contained the opposites of the seeds of Hell and the prospect of bliss. In seeking partly to demean her by making her earth-mother, man actually managed to do the opposite as well, for it is through life on earth that either Hell or Heaven are achieved. In this sense woman earths man's current, which flows back and forth between the twin places of Heaven and Hell, or between the twin myths of God and the Devil.

The myths and places are 'twin' because they are different faces of the same seed, or pairings from one source. Through temptation, woman's body can lead man to Hell. However, it also promises, and to a certain extent gives, Heaven and bliss. For the *concierge* of Heaven on earth has been woman. She has been the literal bliss of those rare moments of sexual ecstasy; and she has been the keeper of what is valuable, of children and a peaceful home to return to after the hell of war or of hard work. It has been through woman's body, woman's hearth and woman as the keeper of beauty that man has kept himself in touch with the idea of Heaven – which is another reason why he has needed to keep woman apart from the hell of daily life.

No wonder it was thought that the Furies themselves would be released if woman ever opened her box and stepped out. With woman on the sideline, a conduit conducting through herself as symbol the delicate, vital strands through which the 'better life' is glimpsed, man had hope of comfort. Man has great need of such hope, for the nightmares created in the name of culture need balancing by a safe bit of Heaven. If not, there is a risk of culture becoming completely insane.

Those on the political right who argue that woman must remain the 'moral keep', and that feminism has taken this precious role away from her, are actually arguing deeper morals than they realize. For woman has been the 'moral keep' not of herself as person but of man's dangerous fantasy that Heaven exists somewhere outside himself. She has been the continuance of a split not only between woman and man, nature and culture, but between Heaven and Hell – and therefore between people and the possibility of real change. For Heaven and Hell are indeed constructs, not places. In order for that which they symbolize, the exercise between good and bad, creative and destructive, to be tackled they have to be known as such.

If they are not, they confuse in the area of relationships which is most crucial to human survival – sexuality. The opposite sex theory would have us believe that sexual attraction or sexual magnetism depends on it – that sex itself would not happen if men and women were not opposite. It deludes us into believing that the human species would not continue without God in His Heaven, Satan in his Hell, and man and woman doing the will of these two on earth through the battle of the sexes.

The opposite sex theory would have us preserve the idea that sexual magnetism occurs because he is macho and she is pliant, because he is aggressive and she is submissive. Through this contrivance it makes certain that love-making is often fraught and ultimately disappointing. For it does not belong to us as persons but, as Angela Carter described, to 'them' or 'that' as symbols. These symbols are the inventions that man and woman wear, eat and swallow from birth in the form of prevailing myths. The final paranoia in the realm of the dominant myth of masculinity is the fear that if these myths were dismantled men and women would no longer make love, and the human race would die out.

15
Something Better Afoot

The notion of the 'opposite sex' based on the idea of man and woman as magnets rather than as people is founded in the need for those magnets to meet. In this way sexual union becomes the door through which a person passes from a bleak state of halfness to a paired sense of wholeness. This notion underpins romantic fiction, which couldn't survive without it.

From this perspective Hemingway's question: 'And did the earth move?' may take on a slightly different meaning. It is descriptive not only of the power of sexual union to transport, but of its power to shift one's blinkered half-vision to a whole one. It makes possible a sweeping breadth of view where the world literally moves because the other half of it suddenly leaps into focus before your startled gaze. Traditionally, intromission is the way through which woman becomes at one with the whole world rather than being its half-sister, and man fulfils his prophecy as both hunter and seed planter. This is why sex makes the world go round.

In *The Sadeian Woman* Angela Carter writes about the spuriousness of gender archetypes and the awful romantic slush that they produce: 'These [gender] archetypes serve only to confuse . . . any man may encounter any woman and their personalities are far less important to their copulation than *the mere fact of their genders* [my emphasis].'[1]

The reason why both sex and feminism have come in for so much flak is that they threaten traditional concepts of masculinity and femininity, and the divide created between the two. If in love-making all the sexual parts, male and female, are of equal value and importance, then the big divide between male and female vanishes. Sex threatens the status quo. If sex is explored in an attempt to make it more honest, more meaningful and loving, rather than an automatic, stereotypical activity, it is a force for anarchy. In other words sex as an honest adventure or tender exploration, rather than as a tiresome duty, a furtive affair or a quick poke, could lead to all kinds of personal revelations. These would not be helpful to a system based on coercion and standardization.

Good sex can certainly be worked out in a marriage bed, for

176

example. But it will not support the bed if the male fundamentally derides women, or if the female is bored, unaroused or a sleeping partner. Good sex will not sustain two people just because they belong in an institution called marriage, for it cannot be institutionalized as such. It may well strengthen an arrangement in which two people strive for more than an anodyne agreement. But it certainly cannot be relied upon to corroborate a system in which people wish to use sex to subvert itself, which has been the purpose of some marriages.

In *The Female Eunuch* Germaine Greer writes that 'The sexual personality is basically anti-authoritarian.'[2] And later: 'The implication that there is a statistically ideal fuck which will always result in satisfaction if the right procedures are followed is depressing and misleading . . . Real gratification is not enshrined in a tiny cluster of nerves but in the sexual involvement of the whole person.'[3] A 'whole person' is by definition anti-authoritarian in having authority in his or her own right, and will seem to threaten systems which don't respect individuals. The fear of sex and feminism, which has sought to redraw the sexual map, is therefore pronounced in western society. For this society has followed a set of rules supposedly open to no human questioning, since they come from an invisible God.

In threatening traditional concepts of femininity and masculinity feminism has challenged not only a fearsome tradition, which is powerful enough, but also what is perceived as a natural order of things. If intromission suddenly becomes less important, because we are now overpopulated and because it is not the way through which most women have orgasms, then the whole male-dominated system is in danger. It is, after all, the penis which, in the last resort, has guarded the crumbling fortress of patriarchy.

If men and women are *both* lovers and *both* people who 'do' and are 'done unto', however, the picture looks completely different. It is even open to the mischief of being reversed, as Robert Graves did in *The Golden Fleece*:

She [the Orange Nymph] asked: '. . . How can any tribe worship a *Father*? What are fathers but the occasional instruments that a woman uses for her pleasure and for the sake of becoming a mother? . . . The woman, not the man, is always the principal: she is the agent, he the tool always . . . Is it not the woman who chooses the man, and overcomes him by the sweetness of her perfumed presence, and orders him to lie down in the furrow on his back and there riding upon him, as upon a wild horse tamed to her

177

will, takes her pleasure of him and, when she has done, leaves him lying like a dead man?'[4]

In Graves's mind the dead man who will not lie down is the patriarch whose denial of his vulnerability made him create his own myths. One of these myths is that man is like Priapus, the origin of sexual power, always erect, not only as the dominant sex but as the dominant sexual being.

In his chapter called 'The Idea of Woman' in *What a Man's Gotta Do* Antony Easthope asks the question: 'Why is male heterosexual desire presented as absolute and undifferentiating, as though it were always the same, no matter what the time, the place, or for that matter the person?'[5] This almost rhetorical question depends for its answer on woman being the complement of this description. Unpredictable, moody, volatile, prone to being over-personal, sexually withdrawn and shy are some of the qualities traditionally attributed to her. Man's myths have been so craftily woven that the idea of sexual magnetism has come to be thought of as a natural rather than a cultural formation. It appears that man and woman being opposites, and having opposite qualities, was how nature intended things rather than how culture decided them.

What this phoney picture actually conceals is the idea of a sexually active woman, which would threaten man's sexual absoluteness and supremacy. If woman is presented as meek and compliant, then the beast of her sexuality will be tamed and culture's jungle can keep its fragile balance for another century or two. While heterosexuality can be seen to depend on man and woman as opposites, then fighting to keep them that way becomes a life-or-death affair. The sexually active, assertive and knowledgeable woman is a threat to this system, and man will go a long way to keep her down.

He does this in many ways, one of which is to present the penis as a weapon. Feminism fell into this trap by agreeing with the definition, and by then declaring the penis defunct as far as the female orgasm was concerned. In fact the penis, which feminism has done so little to come to terms with, may be viewed during love-making as shared. Then the phallacy might really begin to distintegrate – because, while feminism may not have come to terms with the penis, the masculine myth has fared even worse. It has presented the penis as a powerful object, ignoring hundreds of centuries of personal evidence that the penis is actually vulnerable. By not accepting this vulnerability, man has done himself out of discovering a richness and joy in love-making which could have been his long since. This is the joy of 'letting go' referred to by the two previous men who stated that men don't have orgasms, but merely ejaculate.

By bringing the penis into bed as shared pleasure and shared responsibility man can learn not only to be relieved of the responsibility of the performance ethic, but how to be submissive. In the sexual relationship that is love-making far more empathy and interchange might then be achieved. The man might learn more of what it feels like to be a woman, and vice versa. By allowing the vagina to be an active part of intromission, and therefore in a sense temporarily giving up the penis, both man and woman have the opportunity to discover greater sexual harmony. This might have the effect of making man less phallocentric and woman less forlorn.

In women who want good sexual relationships there is a desire for the penis, and when it is dissociated from the phallocentric power structure the penis in fact may become androgynous. For the penis when shared is actually both comforter and nurturer. If goal-orientated woman replaces goal-orientated man this doesn't become the case – if she is interested only in orgasms then she will declare the penis defunct.

If, however, she is interested in intimacy she will tell you that the presence inside her of the penis of the man she loves is indeed a comforter. Its sharing is a joining, a pleasure and a union. But phallocentricity has denied both man and woman the penis as comforter – as mother. This is one of the phallacy's crimes. It has denied mothering and nurturing qualities to its own sex. By insisting on the penis as a bold, potentially dangerous cock, the phallacy has almost executed its own downfall. By making the cock the main emblem of desire and of masculinity it has made man a slave. Sex for many has become a mechanical business. But if you take out the performance and put back the human emotions of trust and need, then, as a woman in her mid-forties said about intromission with her husband:

Sometimes when we make love and he enters me what I feel is relief. I feel relief that I am not any more alone. Sometimes I cry a little at the solace of returning again to being vulnerable, human and entered – to the contact. At times like this I gain the repose I seek, not from frantic love-making, which I also enjoy, but from being gently soothed. I know of no better way of being healed, of being repaired, of being put back together again than having the man you live with, who shares all your mundanity, your triviality, lie with you, lie *in* you and be with you like that.

179

My husband knows I like to be 'taken' sometimes by his cock – and that I find it also a source of repair. The two are not incompatible. On the times when we feel like aggressive love-making that is what we have. On the nights when his cock is comforter that is wonderful.

I have understood that women have had to distance themselves from men for a while in order to find themselves. I have done this myself. If heterosexual women now can't find their way back, then the question has to be asked: 'Was the journey worth it?' Was it worth it to be this lonely, and this alienated from comfort and consolation? If men and women can't find the men and women in each other, then I can't see anything ahead but misery.

I have never accepted the penis as intrinsically a weapon. I have always accepted it as possible pleasure. I now accept it as an actual comforter. Feminism hasn't sorted out its relationship to the penis. And of course men haven't either. If women have to teach them, then so be it. But let's get on and learn.

The envies and their corresponding revenges that exist on both sides of the divide are to do with man's initial envy of woman's ability to be mother and with woman's envy, which, I would suggest, is not so much of the penis itself as of the whole way of life which asserted itself as dominant. If the penis is both mother and father then man's envy of woman as mother, and also his fear of this, need not continue for he will have mothering and comforting for himself. But of course woman has to recognize the penis as mother and father too. If she doesn't see it in this way, then man can't give it as such. If woman doesn't recognize man as mother, then he cannot be mother, and if man doesn't recognize woman as father then she cannot give that. He cannot give his passivity, woman cannot give her power.

Full sharing of sexuality would relieve man of another aspect of the phallacy which is extremely insulting – to man himself. It is the picture of man as sexual animal always panting for it rather than man as sentient human looking for love and companionship. The picture of man as a dog with his tongue hanging out is one that describes him as servant, not master. It depicts him as a lackey to his sexual drive. This is the outcome of the man-made myth. Within it man is a servant of God, not master of his own destiny, and is slave to his penis instead of macho stud. These constructs are interdependent, so in assuming the boss position man has done himself down.

In Angela Carter's *The Company of Wolves* one of the messages is that woman will be 'safe' if she refuses to be alarmed and deterred by man's wolfish exterior and instead befriends him. My own interpretation of this fascinating story is that man's own myths do him in. His invented role as sexual predator (read for that wolf) not only eats his victim, woman, but devours himself. He cannot free himself from his wolfishness *unless* he is accepted, not as fierce animal, but as loyal companion. His salvation lies in woman befriending him and letting him know that the monstrous edifice he has created can indeed be transformed by affection.

Looking at this from a different aspect, man is frightened of the beast in himself, as is woman. Sex is extremely alarming, for if it is explored rather than contained it might face one with insatiable and terrifying appetites. What then? How about some trendy consumer sex to take people's minds and hearts away from intimacy as a serious – and anarchical – concern?

In this way, jolly-old-hockey-sticks bonking became as much a vehicle of sexual repression as the Old Testament itself. With the popular press telling the British nation that bonking was good for us, sex in the early eighties was in danger of being nationalized – and under a Conservative government! Any sex that wasn't about intimacy, that wasn't about the charnel-house of longing, fear, old age, disability, ill health, unemployment and straightforward ignorance, was OK. Headlines about boobs, beefy blokes, gutsy guys and sexual performance were all the rage. In fact if you only read the tabloids you would have thought that the whole western world was bonking itself silly – at least those parts of it which were young, agile, good-looking and wealthy.

No, sex did not become respectable. It became mechanical or light relief. And, as always, the forces of repression blamed sex itself for a decline in moral standards, when what they were really experiencing was consumerism. There were sexperts and sexercises, sex foods and sex games. Sex was now the way you 'kept fit', 'toned up' and 'wound down' after a stressful day at the office. It became a performance art for which you groomed yourself.

Pre-AIDS you were cool enough to discuss contraception and not to discuss commitment. Sex happened in a consumer hammock of lotions and potions, handbooks and appliances. In other words it happened in a spiritual vacuum. In Germaine Greer's words: 'We still make love to organs and not people . . .'[6] Bonking became, like youth, a thing apart; or, like football and jogging, a national pastime. It tended to take its toll on knee-joints rather than stretching the resources of emotional lives.

Then AIDS arrived on the scene, and sexual behaviour began to alter, albeit too slowly to prevent the continuing spread of this illness. As mentioned in Chapter 11, its progress has been hastened through the activities of married men who are not able to understand the split within themselves. Some homosexuals have been furious about the fact that 'cottaging' or 'playing off-side' has been the real cause of the spread of AIDS into the heterosexual community. They view with contempt the hypocrisy of married men needing to have a sexual fling now and then with a member of the same sex. For while homosexuals who have declared themselves such have risked public condemnation, these 'heterosexual' men shield behind the respectability of marriage.

It was said by some that the tragedy of AIDS was God's vengeance not on people exploring sexuality, but on them exploiting it. In a recession and under fascism there will tend to be 'high tech' and divided sex. Today, as well as the risk from changing sexual partners, there is the danger that when a man and a woman meet they are like a pair of well-oiled machines. They have read the books on sexual technique and have paid attention to the language. They talk of 'partners' and 'sexual politics', not lovers and desire.

By the mid-seventies some feminists had argued that intromission was violent *per se*. By the mid-eighties that archdeacon of repression, celibacy, was being wheeled in not as a creative agent of discovery but as a blunt political weapon. Its message was that the so-called 'permissive society' was wrong. Sex itself was seen as an indulgent waste of time by some, and as necessary as a good bowel movement by others. So-called sexual awareness reached its consumer peak when you went to bed with a gallon of massage oil, the latest book on 'how to be an exciting lover', and a 'partner' who didn't trouble you emotionally. Germaine Greer's comment about making love to organs or erogenous zones rather than people was illustrated by a wine-bar manageress in her late twenties:

He knew what to do. He pressed all the right buttons and went at me with the assiduousness of someone with a wind-up arm and a tongue working on a long-life battery. It was only our first time in bed and after the first 'shock' I tried to slow him down a bit and explain that my body was not an assault course and no one was going to give him a gold star for getting over it in record speed. When I asked if we could just cuddle a bit and move into cunnilingus in time he was genuinely puzzled.

We went to bed a number of times after that because I liked him and would have liked a relationship with him, but in the end I realized he wasn't *there*. I couldn't find *him*. He was so unused to intimacy that he couldn't get into bed and just curl up and stroke my hair and let our bodies relax while we chatted for a bit. He'd learned to do the 'right things', but in the end he didn't move me.

Once it was discovered that love was not a prerequisite of the act sexuality was soon systematically hived off, usually at punitive cost to the consumer. It became a game of 'How many orgasms can the woman have before the man "comes"?' Technology or know-how certainly became the important issue. Far easier after a long day at the office to get yourselves some soft porn and stick it on the video than spend time explaining what it is that's troubling you.

Things went in 'syndromes' at this time. On a *Kilroy* programme in January 1987 Robert Kilroy-Silk was interviewing older women who slept with or had married younger men. It was called the 'older woman-younger man syndrome'. The danger or backlash of this syndroming of people's sex lives was apparent here in a piece of symbolic revenge: one woman said she slept with younger men because they had nicer skins and more sexual stamina. Presumably this was a side-swipe for all the years when a woman over thirty-five was not only undesirable in men's eyes, but completely invisible.

The homosexual lobby has also had a strong effect on hetero-sexuality. Among aware people nowadays heterosexuality is not *presumed*, which has resulted in a marked lessening of attempts to help single or divorced friends find partners. A woman in her early thirties who had been on her own for a number of years after the break-up of her eight-year marriage said:

Because I'm a teacher in the kind of school where we try not to be sexist, classist and heterosexist, people must have made a number of assumptions – and non-assumptions – about me. I have always had close relationships with women, so it wasn't out of the question, for example, that I might have found out I was not heterosexual after all.

It was a time when it was difficult to say straight out that you missed a man. It was a time when it was assumed somehow that a woman was OK on her own – as if feminism had meant that women didn't need men any more. Suddenly all the ways of meeting men *as lovers* had vanished. I was too old for discos, and the people in my broad social circle didn't presume to introduce me to men friends. There were men around at public meetings and so on, but they were adopting politically clean positions too. They weren't assuming that a woman they met at a meeting might be interested in them as men, or as people, let alone as *sexual* people.

This woman eventually advertised in a magazine and now lives with one of the men who replied. She added: 'I put in that I wanted a long-term relationship, and I received two hundred and fifty responses!'

Certainly the habit of couples in particular introducing single men and women to each other was sometimes tiresome in the past, when it was presumed that a lone woman or man was an offence against some natural law. But the opposite situation has been just as problematical. Since AIDS has made it crucial once more for people to learn a lot about each other before entering into sexual relationships, a certain amount of standing back is important. However, as a man in his late twenties working in the computer industry said: 'Bending over backwards to be politically clean is ridiculous. Where has all the fun gone? I don't mean hopping-in-and-out-of-bed fun – I mean enjoying a woman because she *is* a woman.'

Heterosexual relationships therefore do not just suffer problems from the bad old days. There are also difficulties from what are seen as the bad new days, the blame for which is so often laid at the door of feminism. If women hadn't decided they wanted more, the argument goes, none of this would have happened. (By implication 'this' includes issues like an increase in violence and what tradition-alists call a decrease in moral standards.)

It has been far too easy to pin on to modern causes the blame for man and woman seeming to be enemies. This structure was in truth written into the very system of the 'opposite sex' culture, which had man and woman as poles apart with only sexual activity as a mutual stamping ground. In the sexual arena woman was both the ground man trod on and his mystical prize.

But sex in the past had supposed man's dominance and his doing. Feminism introducing women to themselves as sexual beings and as sexual innovators was welcomed by some men. When I interviewed a number of men in the late seventies for a magazine article about their attitudes to sexually aware, 'liberated' women, one man said he was all for this. It would mean that instead of having to do all the work himself he could wait for women to come knocking on *his* door. Not only would he have more sex for less effort, but he would suffer less bruising to his ego as a result of rejection. He wasn't the first man to say this. And he was, of course, wrong.

A technical artist in his early forties interviewed nearly a decade later had this to say:

There are a lot of women available these days, and you know that if you hang around – put yourself about a bit – there's always going to be an interesting, attractive woman around. In fact lots of them, at least in the circles I mix in.

The problem is that it's almost too easy. It's as if guys have been waiting decades for this to happen, for women to be on the Pill, sexually adventurous and mentally stimulating.

And now that it's here, what's happening? It's almost the classic role reversal. You see these guys going out gung-ho, hardly able to keep the smiles off their faces, and then something goes wrong. They can't handle it. They suddenly find out they weren't feeling quite so randy after all. Or perhaps they'd prefer to spend an evening boozing with the boys.

I've thought about it in my own behaviour as well, and it's got something to do with the fact that blokes are such masochists they can't imagine anything will be that easy.

It's also more devious than that. I don't think men can value something unless they've worked for it. If you give a man an attractive, intelligent woman on a plate the cynic in him wants to know what's wrong with her, and the stud in him is suddenly declared redundant. He's petrified. Only if you've got geared up to go out and get it is it worth having.

Both sexes suffer from the feeling that if you get it on a plate you don't value it. The historical difference is that, until recently, man has never been on a plate: in one way or another he has usually been away from home. Woman has been available in that she has remained in one spot, the home, but she was not always sexually receptive. It was necessary for her to be fixed to one spot, for she was the keeper of certain of man's qualities and of many of his hopes. She was in many respects his bank, and banks have to stay where they are. If *they* collapse, society is really in trouble.

However, the eye/penis/ego doesn't only want security and control; it also needs excitement and adventure. So woman had to be in some way *un*available or tantalizing. Somehow this fraught business called 'sex with a woman' had to amount to more than a rudimentary insertion of something into something else. The woman therefore needed to be hypocritical in order to satisfy the contradictory demands of the eye/penis/ego. She had to pretend that she didn't want it, and allow herself to be chased or persuaded into having it. Then she had to pretend that she enjoyed it – or pretend to be cool about it if she *was* actually aroused. Finally she had to re-form herself afterwards in a denial of it, so that she could become a challenging 'virgin' once more.

The linear thinking in culture is stuck there, with the idea that sex with an intact woman is the most exciting kind and that after the deflowering everything is downhill. Of course modern man will tell you this isn't true – that sex with an honest and knowledgeable woman is as good as or preferable to sex with an actual or 'acting' virgin. But part of man still believes in the thrill of the chase and despises a sexually innovative woman, not only because she denies him the friction of resistance but also because she challenges his myth that he is sexually omnipotent. Modern woman challenges the phallus, and takes the role of adventurer away from man too.

She is an adventurer because she has undertaken the dual tasks, personal and political, of exploring and examining her own inner world and the outer structures of the world systems she has inherited. She has redefined what a woman is, and by definition what a man is. The role of woman as explorer of the inner journey and the outer one, as rewriter of history and as remaker of the present, has shown up man's so-called adventurousness. She has exposed it for what it is – opportunistic, isolationist and shallow. Woman as adventurer, as iconoclast, has brought down the phallus as symbol – which is not to be confused with the penis as personal.

Understanding the myth of the phallacy has revealed all kinds of problems which already existed. It is commonplace to assume that public or feminist exposure of the phallacy *caused* problems. Not so. Man had constructed an intricate set of interdependent problems which will take a while to resolve.

For a start, man has been used to thinking of his penis in terms of its success or failure. It has mattered to have erections when he has wanted them, and in order to conceal the fact that this is not always possible – that he is, in other words, fallible – he has curtailed *himself* within limited stereotypes. While man's myths have wanted him to be priapic superstud, he has also had to invent another series of stereotypes to counter the truth that he isn't. These stereotypes run from young stud, through married man on the lookout for a bit of spare but not prepared to leave his wife, to dirty old man who is still thinking about it. In this way man pins himself to a performance cross which is dependent upon his erection as a sign of manhood. Sexuality itself becomes penis-centred, for both man and woman.

In order for man to be so sexually alert or rapacious he has needed to make sure that woman appeals to his eye/penis/ego, so he has sought to hone her into a constantly desirable shape and pattern. The pattern runs like this. The man marries a virgin, who is the biggest turn-on of all, and everything is downhill from then on. For this reason the man needs occasional dalliances with young, physically attractive women. To accommodate this scenario man has invented the twin clichés of frowsy wife (the woman who runs to seed) and tempting, delectable mistress (who is everything the wife is not, but is not eligible for marriage). The Japanese culture, which is frighteningly adept at creating divisions, formalized this system and produced the pairing of wife and geisha. In Britain it was woman's emancipation that brought to light such a morally dubious system – and was blamed for bringing about the downfall of the status quo. It was a tradition that upheld the idea of woman being valuable only while she was young and not yet 'known' to a man. Once the hunter had speared her she then became so much dead meat and he went off chasing new game.

Man therefore has difficulty relating to the woman who wants to take equal responsibility for getting to know him – with the woman who, in other words, deprives him of the thrill of the chase. For even if he can dismiss 'the chase' in his conscious mind as so much ancient and redundant tradition, it bedevils his unconscious needs. The Puritan and linear man have equated value both with work and with *rarity*, so that in order to be valuable something must be difficult to obtain in all senses.

In this sense nature is not valuable. Although it is unique in producing a different sunrise every day, it is nevertheless boringly predictable in that the sun always does rise, and sunset follows sunrise in a marked pattern. Culture at its worst would like to do away with this pattern and order sunrises and sunsets when it wanted them.

Judging the value of something by how rare it is and how difficult it is to obtain is a consuming notion, for it depends on something being a scarce resource to be consumed by the few. The spot at which the worst kind of Old Testament bigotry and the forces of commerce meet is the hymen. A virgin is valuable (or at least a young virgin who appeals to the eye is valuable) because of the nature of her rarity: she can give herself as virgin only once. She is the apotheosis of the paradox in the masculine myth, for she is both desirable (to be broken) and precious (to be kept in one piece). She is perfectly formed, yet if her form is fully appreciated (and she is sexually loved) she is no longer what she was. The touch of man's magic wand will draw the blood which takes her from the realm of the princess into the ordinary.

But ordinary, daily devotion or affection is not what the masculine myth was constructed to serve. It was constructed to attempt the impossible. It has filled people's minds and hearts with the Hollywood Dream, the Impossible Dream and the Happy Ever After Dream. It has not concerned itself with reality.

Back on the streets, the difficulty man experiences in dealing with woman and with himself is an extremely complicated issue. The Puritan in him believes that something is only of value if he works impossibly, punishingly hard for it. The loner in him can't see sex as a shared responsibility and enterprise. The fearful person in him can't lie back and let her take him, for fear that if she does he'll never achieve the miracle of reconstitution – let alone by nine o'clock in the morning. And the idealist in him adds another problem.

For the idealist – the amalgam of the fundamentalist, the romantic and the anally retentive, commercial man – cannot disengage himself from the yoke that worth and rarity go together. His perfection complex makes him believe there is a summit – always up there, never here and now – and because of this he is used to living in a constant state of being thwarted. Anything that comes close to alleviating that state is terribly threatening and must be avoided at all costs.

The cost in terms of beauty is financially high; and the cost in terms of woman is high, too, but in a different way. It is the notion of her as most valuable because a virgin. Therefore the woman who play-acts the virgin and denies her own experience is still in demand, and she is in greater demand as a recession bites deeper. Her counter-balance, the earth-mother, the woman who stays at home with her children and does not challenge man, is also more in demand both as a revenge against feminism and as the answer, perhaps in twenty years' time, to a declining western population.

Man hoped that he could keep *desire* alive in himself by constructing his myths about women in certain ways. Part of his problem is that his desire as a consumer in the marketplace and as a lover have become mixed up with one another. The possession of a rare commodity has become a simulacrum of a sexual experience, and a sexual experience has become as isolated from daily life as a rare commodity. The control freak in man would prefer his 'highs' to be at his behest, so he will take an expensive substance like cocaine, which is part of the 'new economy', rather than risk losing control with a woman. He will spend money rather than tend emotions.

The woman who knocks on a man's door and lets him know she is ready for equal relationship right across the boardroom through into the kitchen and bedroom can look terrifying. Because she exists in contradiction to the masculine myth – the phallacy – castration can appear to be her game. Undoubtedly for some women it is, but there is a clear distinction to be made between an attack on the phallus as symbol and the penis as personal. The Department of Dirty Tricks, which is an equal opportunities employer with a vengeance, would call woman ball-breaking and man emotionally retarded. A whole spate of women have used men as sex objects, in revenge for the times when men did this to women. Then a deeper revenge was exacted, as women moved from thinking of men as sex objects to thinking of them as lost causes. Counter-revenges followed, as men frowned on any woman who looked independent and some men raped women who were presumptuous enough to imagine they could walk around unprotected.

Even without these awesome difficulties a further problem existed. It concerned the confusion between sexism and sexuality. Many people who want to be more free of stereotype and symbol and to be aware of the pitfalls of traditional assumptions have found themselves trapped as a result.

Sex between trusting adults was supposed to be sometimes spontaneous and always enjoyable. Suddenly, as the eighties arrived, it became hedged about with *new* rules. A man might suddenly stop paying his wife compliments about her lovely breasts: she might think he was using them as a substitute for being mothered. A woman might discover that females could be sexist too: suddenly her interest in her lover's penis might mean she was using *him* as a sex object. A man might be mortified to get an erection while thinking about his absent lover and looking at a poster of a woman with her skirt round her thighs. A woman might have enjoyed dressing up sexily sometimes because it made both her and her partner feel good: now she might think she was letting down the sisterhood by behaving like a wimp and a sex object. The list goes on.

The concern to behave correctly, to be politically clean, has created a formidable list of 'thou shalt nots'. Thou shalt not be sexist, bully a woman, take men for granted, presume sexual interest, flirt, even up the male/female numbers at dinner parties, presume heterosexuality. Both in and out of bed sexual interest between men and women has in many ways become more complicated. Spontaneous compliments, for example, are now much more difficult for a man to pay to a woman, although a woman may compliment a man. This is how a magazine editor in his mid-thirties described it:

I find that I don't any more compliment women I don't know well, and even those I do know well I'm more careful about. Recently I told a woman friend that I thought she'd chaired a meeting really well. I meant it as a compliment, and then afterwards I thought she might have felt it was insulting – as if I was saying that it was unusual for a woman to be good at that sort of thing.

A lot of men are definitely holding back, and there's far less fun around than there used to be. I don't mean women to sleep with. I mean . . . just fun.

There is no doubt that the spontaneous smile, compliment, sparkle, mischief and merriment have been absent from many relationships. That most delicate of instuments, humour, has been one of the first casualties of concerted attempts to redraw the map of relationships between men and women. This is another way in which feminism has been blamed for spoiling everybody's fun. But a woman teacher in her late thirties said she felt things were improving now:

I know it's difficult, what with everyone working so hard and neglecting what I call 'sexual time' in any case, but I really do think it's changing. I've been sensing a huge change in general attitudes. There was a lot of man-blaming, and I think that's stopped now. And there was a time when it was difficult to talk with men about anything else except business. But massive changes in awareness have taken place, and I don't feel at all pessimistic. I used to a while back. I used to think this must be about the worst time in history to be a heterosexual woman. But it isn't. And in fact after the difficulties of sudden change – and did we think it would all be painless? – there is something better afoot.

What is afoot is the possibility of such a fundamental change that the intrinsically warring positions from which man and woman have faced each other for at least two thousand years can be seen as completely unnecessary. The penis as 'mother' is one of these accomplishments in taking male sexuality out of its aggressive, oppositional role into the realm of shared fulfilment. Much has already been accomplished in order for this to happen. One of the remaining obstacles to co-operation is a misunderstanding of and vying for the position of 'victim'.

16

The Victim Position

Woman and man both refuse to acknowledge the other as victim because both feel victim themselves. Woman feels victim of a patriarchal system which has demeaned and denied her, and of rape and violence which, even if she doesn't suffer them, are factors which shape the way she lives her life. In a Granada TV *World in Action* programme transmitted in January 1989, researchers found that modern women's strongest single fear is of being attacked by a man. This fear comes ahead of concern about getting cancer, losing a job or being involved in a car accident.

It is startling and salutary to realize to what degree a woman's choices in life are still clipped by the boundaries of personal and sexual safety if she is unprotected by a man. She has to be much more thoughtful about where she lives, how she lives, how she speaks with people in the street, and who she says what to about her living circumstances. It can make her seem irritatingly guarded and mannered as she struggles to come to grips with what appear to be ordinary daily events – like worrying if the male neighbour who has asked her if she lives alone is just being friendly, is interested in a relationship with her, or could be instrumental in a future attack on her. All this makes her resentful, and she directs her resentment at man as a symbol of what threatens her.

In view of the physical danger to women it seems inexcusable that man should not recognize and respond to woman as his victim. However, it is equally inexcusable that woman should not relate and respond to *man* as victim. After unearthing the masculine myth woman has had a tendency to hold modern man to account for centuries of atrocities and injustice. She has not understood that he too is the product of a system he did not choose. A man born, say, thirty years ago is as much a victim of the script thrust into his hand as is a woman of the same age. But woman is so used to viewing man in general either as boss or as potential foe that it is difficult to accept him as a scapegoat.

It is particularly difficult to do so in view of woman's hitherto chief role as mother or nurturer. Whenever she discovered the frightened

191

child inside a brave man she had both to keep quiet about it (at least in public) and at the same time repair this psychological rip. Modern woman wants to move out of the role of chief repairer, partly because she is angry with the tyrant and partly because her developing public accountability means she doesn't want to collude any more in patching up a child molester, a murderer, a bank robber or a bully.

In her BBC1 film *Stand by Your Man* producer Angela Kaye looked at the syndrome of women who still shield murderers and rapists. They provoked two kinds of reaction from neighbours: sympathy and respect for their loyalty, and bitterness and contempt for their collusion. It is still the case in English law that a spouse is a competent but not a compellable witness, meaning that neither a husband nor a wife may be forced to give evidence against a partner, but will be respected as competent if they decide to do so. In practice this law has related mainly to women, since it has always been men who commit the greater number of crimes, and who certainly commit an overwhelming percentage of serious offences. (The Home Office figures for 1986 show that in England and Wales sixty thousand men were found guilty or were cautioned for violent offences, as compared with five thousand six hundred women.) Despite the fact that the law gives equality of protection to both men and women, it would probably not have been possible in 1987 to make a film called *Stand by Your Woman*.

The ethical problems surrounding women both as potential victims of rape and as possible shelterers of rapists (a position which cannot be held in reverse by men) cloud the issue of who the victim is. It possibly turns women against each other once more. Women who are ordered to stay in at night to protect themselves may well reflect on the popular press headlines and consider that it is another woman, a wife or mother, who is causing this curfew. It deflects the central issue that the person who is really causing the curfew is a dangerous man, and that the people who have asked for the curfew to apply to women rather than men are also male.

Such are the convolutions of the victim position. If it is a corner to be fought for, then both man and woman have many rights to claim it, and within those claims counter-claims have to be parried. If woman wants to become publicly accountable, she cannot at the same time hold on to her general blanket of nurturer. If she loses this blanket she loses certain 'rights' that went with it, one of which is to shield the 'bad man'. However, it is on account of her nurturing skills that woman has done so well in comforting herself in a complex world, so she wishes to keep the positive aspects of this role. Her actual request, when she thinks it out clearly, is not that she should cease to be a nurturer but that man should become a nurturer too. But as most men know deep down, most men have not yet learned to nurture themselves, let alone other people.

This subliminal knowedge, arriving at a time when man is no longer a scarce resource, is terrifying for him. While he was scarce *any* man could find a woman for a partner, and woman's fear of spinsterhood and its lack of privileges further guaranteed this. Man's terror of woman comes to the surface when he can no longer rely upon his myths to suppress her, and a surplus of men is one of the factors which reveal the hitherto concealed workings of man's crude devices.

So the problem with the crime of rape in particular is that man's psychology cannot fully grapple with this manifestation of the lengths to which the masculine myth will go to suppress woman. To understand rape fully man would have to admit the workings of this myth, and would therefore be consciously vulnerable to its implications. The consequence of man being so jealous and frightened of women has been twofold: he has eliminated her as woman and himself as man. He has sought to subjugate woman; and where she will not acquiesce quietly, to do this forcibly through rape.

It is only in the last twenty years that rape has been accepted – and even then not universally – as a serious crime against women rather than the problem of over-sexed men. In other words, it is only lately that rape has been accepted as culture's consequence, not nature's. Man blamed his nature for rape, and thought of himself as a victim of sexual urges beyond his control. In fact sexual urges often don't accompany rape (as with rapists who can't gain erections), and rape is a revenge of culture on nature. It is a last-ditch revenge used when other severe restrictions fail.

Despite this, man's role as a rapist rather than woman's as his victim is still relatively uncharted territory. Although serious work has now begun on examining the reasons why men are violent, it has all been recent. Until the early eighties there were only theories, like this one, as to why men rape. The rapists themselves are barely visible in the millions of words that have been written about this crime. They have not been examinable as such. It is still accepted, therefore, that the victim is the problem. Men who rape are given prison sentences like people who rob or commit large-scale fraud. They are not asked to give definitive answers themselves, which would enable the picture of rape to be *proved*, if you like, to the unbelievers. While women have to describe rape, but the men who actually commit it don't, the rest of the world can still regard it as a woman's problem. It isn't. It is the violent seam where culture is seen for what it is – only we do not wish to look.

One of the present misunderstandings in the relationship between men and women centres around the issue of rape in particular and male violence to women in general. It is extremely difficult for a good man fully to understand rape as a symbolic demeaning and denial of woman. If he does manage to do so he is often isolated in his understanding from other men, and frequently feels himself to be a symbolic threat to woman. It is a lot to take on.

This is one of the areas where men and women see the world with different eyes, and it is tempting to regard this difference as inevitable – which it isn't. For it is a product of crude culture, not of any natural law. In experiential terms the *physical* part of the act upon women could be equated in men to the act of forced buggery. However, the crucial addition to that is what women *feel* from the act of rape; and what they feel is the weight of culture crucifying nature. This is one of the reasons why some women need years of psychiatric treatment after being raped. They are trying to get over not an act of forced intromission but an act of attempted negation. Many women who have been raped also sense the further negation of themselves as people by the realization that for the rapist they are sometimes not personal at all, but mere symbols.

All this hinders woman's understanding of *man* as victim, to the extent that slogans are shouted and written that describe all men as potential rapists. At best these slogans tell only a small part of the story, and at worst they alienate and obscure. They obscure the fact that in their *felt* world the men who are not actually rapists – which is the vast majority of men – see rape as a small corner of the picture and women in general as powerful. After all, man constructed his entire myth to make himself invulnerable to the female side in himself and the woman outside himself. He knows that woman has emotional articulation within her that can run rings round him. He also knows, in Freudian terms, that his mother 'abandoned' him. By investing beauty in woman he also gave her the added power to slay him. In sexual terms, yes, he wants the cock to rise – but at his bidding, not hers; and by freeing herself of his bidding modern woman terrifies the masculine myth.

For man, therefore, woman is a possible tormentor. As a man in his late thirties said: 'They have power over you – of course they do. And what's more they know it. Women have always had power over men.' Even if man realizes that he is vulnerable because of his own

194

constructs over the years, and not because of woman's designs, this renders him in the short term even more vulnerable. He doesn't even have the 'other side' to blame. It's his own fault – not woman's. Man readily blames himself, as if he was responsible for the whole mess rather than its recipient and its scapegoat. In all of this woman, as the subject of his yearning for companionship and his wish to give and receive love, is also his possible persecutor.

The man who feels guilty because of patriarchy, rather than angry, then feeds into another system in which modern woman on the warpath can do him in and give the whole victim/tormentor syndrome another painful turn of the screw. For the mainly insulting search for the 'new man' can definitely be seen as a piece of revenge by women on a system which has always publicly exposed *them* as objects and concealed them as subjects. In fact the search for the 'new man' has been, more than anything, a product of other men working to demean possible growth by clinging on to slogans and the status quo. The 'new man' as an object of people's gaze, as a manufactured product, as a commodity good for a few tabloid headlines, is an insult to both the men and the women who are trying to improve the quality of relationships.

Man as the victim of the masculine myth is actually a chronic depressive, which is one of the reasons why the condition of depression has been so frequently and perversely ascribed to women. In depressing the female both within and without himself man has suppressed, thwarted and hindered his own vitality. Qualities like spontaneity, eagerness and a capacity for joy have not been his, so the myth goes. He is not sensitive and responsive; he is strong and determining. He is not keen and aware; he is bold and aggressive.

What the masculine myth has done, through the invention of the God-figure, is to make sure that there are only a few men with enough personal definition within themselves to know who they are. It is the reason why, during the preparation of this book, so many men asked me the question: 'Have you discovered what masculinity is?' Having invented one construct in order to hide his vulnerability, man discovered he had to invent another, then another, and the whole edifice has come to resemble a gigantic hurdle – truly a depressing situation.

In the act of rape man is at his most depressed, most depressing and most destructive. For it is through this act that he strives, with forces he hardly knows, finally to batter the myths down. In his eyes, modern woman rather than his own constructed myths has become the hurdle to his supremacy. If she won't willingly allow him to overcome her whenever he feels like it, then he can't afford to let her be free-standing against his will. The perpetrator of rape is himself the victim – hard though it is to accept when some rapists are so unrepentant of their crimes.

Intrinsic in the victim position is the need to find someone to blame, for if there is a victim of a crime, then society needs to balance the books by having the perpetrator brought to justice. Linear thinking is accustomed to the idea of there being two people, the done-unto and the brought-to-account. The position of man as both perpetrator and victim has therefore been difficult to unearth from its burial ground. The linear system that finds it untidy to accept the good and bad in everyone, but would prefer a column of goodies and a column of baddies – especially if the total at the end of each column is identical – prefers to talk about good men and bad men, rather than good/bad men. If it is accepted that both men and women are victims, then the need for the split between a good man and a bad man disappears.

So does the split between men and women, particularly at a time when it is convenient in some feminist circles to equate women with goodness and men with badness. The issue of violence against women exacerbates these appalling generalizations. It is too simplistic to call all men potential rapists, and in any case men have maimed and killed far more of their own gender in the name of war than they have women in and out of wartime. Just because it is not a woman who will cosh you in a dark alley it is not good enough reason to call men violent, as if women are not.

However, woman will continue to feel resentful towards man if he doesn't really understand that her life in the public eye is difficult; and man will maintain his resentment towards woman if he perceives her as having more 'advantages' than she names. Although, for instance, man accepts that woman runs certain risks, he also thinks she is spoiled and paid attention to in a way he is not. This makes him jealous. The reason why men in general do not appreciate the threat to women of unwanted attention from a certain kind of man is that they themselves crave more attention. They watch the clerk at the bank treat the woman ahead of them as if she brightens up his day, and then barely glance up when their turn comes. Man will not say it in so many words, but he too wants to be 'darling-ed'. Because his own sexuality and physical well-being have never been under threat of attack by woman, he imagines it might be quite nice to be 'chatted up' by a member of the other sex. He fails to understand that you can't switch the roles like that.

Another fact of life that many men don't realize is that, while they themselves wouldn't dream of molesting a woman and don't know any man who would, there is a certain kind of male who behaves in a certain way *only when he is with women*. Other men don't know him as the threat that women do. In fact they may often think of this fellow, from their own experience of him, as harmless and inoffensive. It is no wonder, therefore, that some men imagine that if women are attacked, or are the butt of insulting remarks, it is basically the woman's fault. Men behave all right with them, they argue, so the women must be doing something to attract trouble.

Man therefore thinks woman is exaggerating (and certainly some do) when she talks of the threats to her, and of the contempt of certain men which makes her afraid. Or he thinks she secretly enjoys the attention (as he would), and is only recounting the incident as a way of getting even more notice taken of her. Man knows enough about the 'hardness' of other men to realize that his personal need for the kind of attention he perceives women as receiving – the spontaneous smiles and light moments – cannot be talked about. It would make him seem ridiculous. But man's age-old grumble that women do the complaining while they have the easier lives has a modern counterpart. He is tired of the sex which gets noticed anyway being 'spoiled' even more by the so-called threats they undergo.

One possible way of rectifying this situation is for women to report every case of assault and attempted rape. Then perhaps the official statistics might be recognized in all their gravity. Although Home Office figures for 1987 showed that in seventy per cent of reported rape cases in England and Wales someone was apprehended, the number of reported rapes was only two thousand five hundred. The rape crisis centres say that this figure is only a tiny percentage of the women actually raped.

Man, too, has to play his part by taking issue with the 'bad man' outside himself. For the more women are frightened on a daily basis the more they will tend to herd themselves, both publicly and privately, into ghetto situations which exclude men. And the more women do this the more inconsolable men will become. In any case, this is no answer for a heterosexual woman, for within a system which filters out men she would be leading a life that contained no prospect of finding a sexually intimate partnership.

The blaming that has gone on since public criticism of man became possible through books, journalism, radio and television has created a stand-off position. Now both men and woman can be heard expressing the sentiment that it is not a good time to be heterosexual. Since it cannot be described as being a good time to be homosexual

197

either (has it ever been?), the real meaning of this statement is that it's not a good time to find sustaining and committed relationships. There is both a tug and pull within man and woman themselves, and what might be called a tug-of-war between them. Man and woman have their own internal dynamics in an incredibly 'new age', in which both Freud and feminism have in their different ways sanctioned individual enquiry, and in which fission threatens an end to anything that can be called adventurous.

The microcosm and the macrocosm intermingle in this perplexing way. The vital knowledge uncovered, and the connections formed, by Freud, Jung and feminism, have contributed to changing the lives of women and men beyond what could have been imagined only fifty years ago. However, these people and influences have not in the main been credited with beneficial change. Fundamentalist man has chosen to forget that the nuclear arsenals and entrenched political positions are the results of his heritage, not of this century's concern with the seriousness of individual enquiry. The search for individual meaning has unfortunately been bedevilled with trendy, narcissistic overtones. It has been confused with the personal pleasure principle. In fact the search for meaning is serious and carries with it the wish and need for individual responsibility.

Man and woman's internal worlds are already fraught with important issues of a personal and political nature. They also seek to relate in an age in which consumerism, not Freud, has offered up the idea of sex as a national sport and feminism has unveiled the clay feet of the masculine myth of supremacy. When you add to this the fact that the need for partnership has a defensive ambivalence about it, the tensions become even more acute.

It is now possible for the first time in history for both man and woman to have rich lives *without* partnership, and to *choose* companions rather than fall into relationships automatically. Never have human relationships been quite so riddled with choice. This has brought a kind of despondency as well as elation; as a midwife in her late thirties said:

> Why didn't God just put numbers on our backs and get us to find the person with the corresponding figure? How do you decide these days whether someone is good enough? Do you wait in case there's somebody better round the corner? And if you do, will the opportunity have passed you by? Have you any idea what love is, having fallen in and out of it two or three times? And if you think you know this time round, can you – or it – be trusted?

Now that the need for commitment has lessened, the fear of it has set in. There is an ambiguity both generally and personally, and the tug and pull of it means that one is often dealing not so much with a person as with a rope-trick. One minute a woman is being hauled in on a rope made taut by a man who knows he wants to give and receive tenderness, and will cradle her to sleep as if both their lives depended on it. The same man then suddenly goes all slack around breakfast time and doesn't call again. When she phones him he is nonchalant and non-committed.

Reversing the roles, there is the woman who is vibrant and strong with her new lover and hauls him in with her sense of purpose and vitality. Then she lets go of her rope as, glimpsing the little boy within the thirty-five-year-old who tries solo dancing for the first time, she fears his awkwardness and drops him. She can't shake off the Prince Charming Complex, even if she cast out Cinderella two decades ago. While the man in this scenario may well feel victimized himself, the woman who finds it difficult to relate to a man who is trying to extend his limited boundaries is also a victim of myths. Now that she has agreed, in fact *asked*, that men should discover and share their vulnerabilities, why does she flinch when this happens?

While these kinds of questions are being asked and struggled with, the people who want to return to traditional archetypes and forget the whole sordid, selfish, late twentieth-century experiment are on the move. They are making concerted efforts, particularly in the sphere of education, to destroy the many positive aspects of modern knowledge and thinking. It is extraordinary that reactionary forces should be advocating not the importance of being an individual witness but the necessity of re-establishing a set of rules which negates this. These rules would return us to the Victorian melodrama of woman as victim of birth and man as victim of his puritanical, unloving nature.

The victim position, which is so intrinsically divisive, has roots which go back to the Old Testament. These roots make all people victim through the concept of original sin; for this original curse is foisted on everyone. Only Christ is exempt.

The next piece of victimization is the error of opposites, so that everyone is the victim of war. This can be either an internal war between good and evil, God and the Devil, or the externalized war of fighting the 'other' side, religion, colour, sex or persuasion.

Through these struggles and torments vital energy is sapped from the individual, who becomes prey to a superior force – in this case biblical morality. This has not stopped the forces of repression blaming sex, the swinging sixties and feminism for what it calls declining moral standards. Moral standards in fact declined a long time ago, when man invented the God-figure and abdicated personal responsibility.

The Old Testament would have us believe that a person is prey to the Devil through his or her own nature, and destined for Hell unless she or he turns to the superior power and judgement of a God who ordained it thus. In this tortuous way a child's right to be born innocent and 'holy' is taken away even before birth. So from the very beginning of a life the power and vitality that are intrinsic to being human are subverted and perverted in a colossal struggle with the edifices of biblical doctrines.

The heroic man's work (and in the past it has been only man) is therefore cut out for him even before he is born. He has to fight Goliath, Satan and his own essentially flawed nature. If he doesn't, he is doomed to the torments of hellfire. This highly charged, romanticized form of heroism is the reason why man today has more of a problem than woman in adjusting to a world which is beginning to view heroism in a different light. In any case the Goliaths are here today, and the heroes who sling rocks at them are characteristically unfeted in their time. The giants, in the form of major industries and governments who drown the sea in poisons, come up against heroes in small boats who sometimes get killed for their trouble.

This time, though, the battles are being fought *for* nature, with the understanding that without the earth human culture cannot survive. In itself a remarkable turn-around. It leaves us poised to see how much nature and culture need each other. Now a possible resolution of the victim position exists through understanding it, not as an unavoidable, hierarchical structure, but as a mistake.

17

The Holy Child

The Old Testament is a glorious myth whose deeper meaning we have buried. In it are the workings of the male mind at its most fearful, most hopeful, most punitive and most imaginative. The length, breadth and depth of the male psyche, a psyche afraid and envious of woman, pops up from the pages in resplendent technicolour. When seen as the possibility of understanding the nature of man rather than the eccentricity of a God-figure, the messages of the scriptures are startlingly clear. They are as relevant to life today as the pages of this morning's newspaper. They say this: man's fear of his own frailty and vulnerability, especially in exercising himself in the face of moral dilemmas like woman, caused him to create a superhuman God-figure.

Such was the need among men for a collective voice that this super-ego figure soon attracted myths and stories of a most fantastical nature. A set of moral rules followed, loads of exercises – sorting out the Devil and things like that – and a system of opposites to make sure no one was ever short of a fight. It was a sort of exclusive club, but with a large membership drive. Naturally it got out of hand, but not before the linear beginning-of-the-earth and end-of-the-world theories had taken hold. God became a legend feeding on His own myths. Those who were with Him were saved, and those against were damned.

However, there was some knowledge tugging away at the coat-tails of biblical man. He needed hope, perhaps variety, and a small but insistent voice said there had to be more. Consequently another story arose, and it went like this . . . All was not lost by the construction of original sin. There is something which transcends the rule of kings, which crosses all known frontiers and which is miraculous – a child. So, according to the story, monarchs and wise men travelled through dangerous lands and shepherds left their sheep to follow, not a set of rules, but a star which led them to the infant Jesus.

He was loved, respected and adored by people of both noble and humble birth, and was brought up by parents who knew His worth. The child grew into an integrated man. He embraced all human qualities and hopes. He wept, felt pain, achieved miracles – and mixed easily in the company of women. He was essentially non-

201

conformist. Those who met Him were jealous as well as revering, and in the end He was crucified, both by the state of Rome and by the Jewish elders who pressed for His death when Pontius Pilate could find no error in Him. It was a woman, Mary Magdalene, to whom He appeared after death as a symbol of resurrection.

When it is told thus, the story bears this possible meaning. If children are brought up 'holily' – as individuals to be respected by their elders, rather than indoctrinated with our own rules and prejudices – they will become people of vision. At its simplest, the child is father of the man. It is possible to suggest from the resurrected Christ's appearance to Mary that women are the silent witnesses whose stories need telling and believing. Fundamentalist man's denial of the female perspective was therefore a mistake. It can also be inferred that the edifices of state and of prejudice in the minds of children who were – like most of us – not brought up respectfully, but treated as property, will destroy a holy child.

But the story is not gloomy, for it says that a change of heart, a resurrection – even as an adult – can give meaning to the cliché that while there's life there's hope. It happens through redeeming the lost child within and caring for the child without, in a devoted instead of an imperious manner. We shall never know what difference it might have made to the course of history if the Protestant Church had taken as its central symbol the adored infant figure instead of the painfully crucified man.

The reason for the use in this book of words such as Old Testament and fundamentalism, rather than Christianity, lies in the argument that the big division between authoritarian parent and wise child has its genesis in the difference between the Old and New Testaments. The Old Testament fights the child as the enemy of established order, which is what the infant is. The New Testament suggests that peace can come about only through tending the child both within and without. Good tending means that the adult is both a wise guardian and a humble observer.

It is hardly surprising in the end that the forces of fundamentalism, which value accountancy more than love, order more than vitality and hierarchy more than companionship, would lead us, like Herod, to destroy all children. This is what the hell of nuclear holocaust would bring about, and what the slower death through poisons and pollution is already doing.

Between the Old and New Testaments is a tale of two authorities. It is the battle between the impossible God-figure (the ultimately bad parent) and the possible child. As the world stands now it has the weapons to make all children impossible, to deny them through killing them, and to ensure that for the foreseeable future there are no births. In order for a culture to allow the child to survive, it must believe not only in childhood, but in *childhood for every child*. This is my own interpretation of the Christian message, and one does not have to be religious or a Christian to wish to find meaning in the scriptures which inform so much western thought.

Childhood for every child, not just the biblical one or the European or the American one, means having faith. It means understanding the reality that what exists outside the microcosm of the self is reassuringly similar and at the same time intrinsically different. In other words, all people are unique. This is the quintessential nature of relationships, and it is what inert forms like pornography cannot capture. The nature of desire between men and women lies in the marvellous paradox of understanding both the essential difference in each person and the recognizable sameness.

My understanding of the meaning of faith is quite simply to believe what is true. This means searching for and supporting reality rather than fantasy. The reality is that one person's life is her or his own and that everyone else's is theirs.

The Old Testament viewpoint, however, argues in opposition to this. It says that everyone's life is somebody else's – God's. It says that the child must be indoctrinated with the rules of the fathers, and that this must go on from generation to generation. If not, it would have us believe, all hell would break loose. All hell is about to break loose anyway, brought about by precisely the tortuous psychological structures which invented it.

Christian doctrines as I interpret them are not much practised. However, the traditional Old Testament forces are incredibly powerful: they fear and seek to quash the natural chaos contained in a new life, a new idea or a revolutionary act like a change of heart. This philosophy so underpins our present morality that we hardly notice it exists. It was present from the mid-seventies to the mid-eighties in the form, oddly enough, of women's voices.

These are the people I call born-again feminists. They were the women who wanted to use Old Testament arguments for their own ends – to replace the Puritan fathers with the Puritan mothers. They decided that 'rightness' was synonymous with femaleness and that men, by (un)virtue of their gender, were incapable of morality. These voices are now seldom heard, for the argument used by patriarchy – that rightness is gender-based – is obviously a fallacious one. It is especially so when used by women who argue against patriarchy.

The infinitely more worrying and immensely powerful group of people who encourage false values are called the Moral Right. They consist of people on the right of the political spectrum who associate themselves with 'decent values', and are deluded in doing so. In an article commissioned by the now defunct *Daily News* I wrote about the damage these people cause. They say they are Christians but in fact they practise fundamentalism. By claiming to be decent citizens, however, they fool a large number of people. I wrote:

> In the cluster of attitudes which accompanies the Moral Right its members are likely to think that sex is dirty, but money isn't. In a fascinating juxtaposition they are likely to be pro life *and* pro hanging, but anti ecology and sex education. Its members are anti my own definition of education altogether, but are pro indoctrination . . .
>
> There was a time when children were relatively safe at school. Then the headlines told us Loony Lefties were turning them into homosexuals. They didn't tell us that by the time a child gets past the hurdles of performance tests, the application of market forces and a standardised curriculum her very core might be rigid with fear. She might be terrified in case she has tendencies to be a musician, an artist or something even more 'deviant' like a non-right-wing philosopher.
>
> In the psychology of the Moral Right one of the most dangerous, potentially subversive possibilities of all is a free child. She might make up her own mind.

In *Friday's Child* I described how members of the Moral Right suffer from a form of paranoia which makes them see everyone who doesn't agree with them as dangerous – therefore in need of discrediting. Their views are not so much sincerely held as fanatically so – a condition which, as a result of suffering it themselves, they project on to their opponents. They are frightened of the full spectrum of human nature with all its attendant complexities. The dread of the beast of chaos coming crashing through the undergrowth would make every man and woman of them retreat to the security and order of a well-defended, symmetrical nuclear bunker. For these people rage against sex outside marriage and support a nuclear defence policy.

What further distresses me is that they have hijacked the words 'morality' and 'decency' and taken them away from common behaviour. The rest of us they then proclaim immoral and indecent because we do not have what they have stolen from us. They have tried to hijack love itself, and put it up for a terrible ransom which the rest of us cannot pay because we are not their version of God-fearing, law-abiding citizens. They have dressed themselves in the clothes of modesty but in fact they are wolves of a kind. They certainly devour children.

At the end of *Friday's Child* I described my concern at the way these 'decent folk' talk of morally 'policing' children in classrooms and wrote: 'A child will only contribute uniquely to society if given the opportunity to be unique – i.e. allowed to have a mind and heart of his or her own. This will only occur if children are encouraged to think for themselves *against the day when they will have to*.'[1]

In describing the crucial difference between indoctrination and education – the fact that they are opposites – I suggested that indoctrination of the political right or left had no place whatever in a classroom. I ended the book by writing, of education:

> In the end it's about love; it's about difficult times and the sharing of difficulties. And it's about whether we're big enough people to accommodate the reality that our hopes are our own and that other people's minds are not our property. I do not think any child's bundle of circumstances, fantasies, dreams and disappointments should be 'policed'. I think it should be respected as belonging to that child, who is like no other, and who shares and needs to find much in common with us all.[2]

The exercise of a morality based in Old Testament values is dangerous because it denies the 'whole' child and through this the possibility of a hopeful future. It rests on a system of opposites, is founded on the travesty and hopelessness of original sin, and confuses culture with nature. It says that God is nature, when in fact He is an invention of culture. Old Testament values prevent the true affinity between nature and culture, between man and woman, and between man, woman, child and children. For by presenting culture and nature as opposites, and by confusing the two in any case, the fundamentalist philosophy conceals the fact that all people comprise both culture and nature, male and female, and that a battle between the two forces will end in the annihilation of both.

Alice Miller was quoted in Chapter 10 as describing the 'utterly new' knowledge this century possesses, that early childhood is crucial to a person's development. In writing of what she calls 'the apocalyptic features of our century', she says:

The more distinctly we come to see that the most ominous events of the present and recent past are not the products of mature rationality . . . the more urgent becomes the need to investigate the origins and nature of the human destructiveness whose helpless victims we all are.

The magnitude of destructiveness . . . represents only the last chapter of long stories we are usually ignorant of. We are victims, observers, reporters, or mute witnesses of a violence whose roots we do not see, a violence that often takes us by surprise, outrages us, or simply makes us stop and think, but we lack the inner ability (i.e. parental or Divine permission) to perceive and take to heart the simple and obvious explanations that are already available.[3]

I differ here only with the notion that the knowledge is utterly new, for while fully accepting Freud's part in unearthing it, my own interpretation is that this knowledge *has* been available to us through the life of Christ, whether read as a story that actually happened or as a parable. We chose to ignore and bury it.

The violence that Miller writes of has its apotheosis in the destructiveness of nuclear weapons. The possibility of unlimited carnage is at last ours. I say 'at last' because my argument is that a culture based in Old Testament beliefs, as western culture is, would fight nature to the death and would eventually annihilate vitality. It would produce a situation of excruciating irony in which crime and punishment meet face to face.

The victim position has the ironic consequence that we are now placed to make victims of all living people – and of the planet as well. The further irony is that in the west a massive arsenal of death-heads has been assembled not by evil men, but by decent citizens. Most people try not to think about these waiting weapons. This is a mistake, because they are definitely present in our culture and are carefully tended by the likes of us. They are not, like God, invisible. Their concrete place in our world could spur us to drop the God-figure and pick up the Christ-child so that, as Margaret Atwood writes in *True Stories*, we can expect

> . . . the coming
> down to the wrecked & shimmering earth
> of that miracle you sing
> about, the day
> when every child is a holy birth.[4]

The paternalistic structure which says that God will put it right in the end – when God is an invention of that structure – is self-defeating. A morality which rests on an invisible God-figure as the supreme judge, the final arbiter of human affairs, would in the end punish the inquisitive Adam, who toyed with fission, as it has punished the inquisitive Eve. The depth of Miller's message is this: the invention of the God-figure means that none of us will be allowed to *know* without being punished – hence *Thou Shalt Not Be Aware*. At the end of her book, in the afterword to the American edition, she writes:

The truth about our childhood is stored up in our body, and although we can repress it, we can never alter it. Our intellect can be deceived, our feelings manipulated . . . But some day the body will present its bill, for it is as incorruptible as a child who, still whole in spirit, will accept no compromise or excuses, and it will not stop tormenting us until we stop evading the truth.[5]

It was the invention of the external God-figure which led to the ditching of morality and made us answerable not to individual conscience but to a set of rules. The authoritarian parent destroys the vital child, and with the child the hope for present repair and future hope. As I wrote in 'The Inconsolables', a society which does not remember the child will crucify the man. A man who does not remember the child will crucify himself. These two together will crucify everyone.

Paradoxically, the construction of a God-figure who supposedly provides consolation of the most absolute kind – Heaven – is the mechanism which produces utter inconsolability – Hell. By Hell I mean the Hell on earth which war has always produced, and which nuclear war would unleash on an unprecedented scale. In his introduction, called 'Thinkability', to *Einstein's Monsters*, Martin Amis writes of nuclear weapons: 'They make me feel sick to my stomach; they make me feel as if a child of mine has been out too long, much too long, and already it is getting dark.'[6] He describes how 'our moral contracts are inevitably weakened, and in unpredictable ways'[7] by the very presence of nuclear weapons, and talks of the dangerous link between the fundamentalist mind and the nuclear holocaust:

Nuclear weapons are mirrors in which we see all the versions of the human shape . . . Incomparably the most influential religious body on earth, the New Evangelicals ... warmly anticipate 'a holy nuclear war' ... These people are Born Again; and they seem to want to Die Again ... Nuclear weapons could bring about the Book of Revelation in a matter of hours ... *Like God, nuclear weapons are free creations of the human mind* [my emphasis]. Unlike God, nuclear weapons are real. And they are here.[8]

As an allegory of a world in which these weapons exist Amis ends his introduction with a striking account of a multi-racial children's tea party where slightly subdued children play in the shadow of 'Keepers' – weapons that they don't want to think about:

For the Keepers are a thousand feet tall, and covered in gelignite and razor-blades, toting flamethrowers and machineguns, cleavers and skewers, and fizzing with rabies, anthrax, plague. Curiously enough, they are not looking at the children at all. With bleeding hellhound eyes, mouthing foul threats and shaking their fists, they are looking at each other. They want to take on someone their own size ...

If they only knew it – no, if they only *believed* it – the children could simply ask the Keepers to leave. But it doesn't seem possible, does it?[9]

Speaking at an anti-nuclear rally in Trafalgar Square in October 1980, the actress Susannah York also tugged on the rope which ambivalence and lack of faith would keep slack and unvigilant.

I look into the air and find the spaces where our children's children might be; among the rain and sun and the leaves those bodies are realizable; and I feel with a terrible hope how lovely life is – and how unbearable is the thought that by our own blindness, by our lack of memory and courage, *by our slackness* [my emphasis] we could end it.[10]

It is slack to imagine that a return to past archetypes can achieve anything useful. They have produced a system of sexual opposites, personal warring between good and evil, and the lure of Eden versus the promise of nuclear destruction.

In *Beyond God the Father* Mary Daly writes:

It will, I think, become increasingly evident that exclusively masculine symbols for the ideal of 'incarnation' or for the ideal of

208

the human search for fulfillment will not do. As a uniquely masculine image and language for divinity loses credibility, so also the idea of a single divine incarnation in a human being of the male sex may give way in the religious consciousness to an increased awareness of the power of Being in all persons.

Now it should become possible to work out with increasing realism . . . the creation of a community that fosters the becoming of women and men. *This means that no adequate models can be taken from the past* [my emphasis].

The point is not to deny that a revelatory event took place in the encounter with the person Jesus. Rather, it is to affirm that the creative presence . . . can be revealed at every historical moment, in every person and culture . . .[11]

In the mid-eighties I wrote an article about Soho after spending an afternoon and evening looking at sex shows and sex shops. My purpose was to try to make more sense out of the narrow exchange between male punter and female titillator. I felt outraged a few times. One of the most notable instances was at the Raymond Revuebar, where a gorgeous-looking woman sat faking orgasm astride the vibrator to end all vibrators – a cruise missile. On the side of this particular weapon were painted the words: 'Love Bomb'.

Where there is such evident confusion between the natures of joy and genocide, intimacy and annihilation, it is difficult to feel anything except despair. What this illustrates is that a new morality is needed which accepts sexuality as intrinsic to the condition of being human, and rejects the separation of it into pornography and consumerism. In the modern world, this is where sex and the bomb meet.

This new morality contains Daly's vision that revelation and transformation are not in the past, but with us at the moment. For this to be realized, there needs to be a marriage of the visible mother and the visible father both within and without. Unless this happens, the blind side of human culture will do us all in. It would have us believe that God is in His Heaven when in fact Eden is ringed with missiles. There needs to be a marriage of morality and aesthetics, a symmetry of need, so that both women and men honestly seek intimacy with one another. And this honest seeking of intimacy could bring about the ending of a final taboo – loneliness.

In western culture you may now talk about sex and politics, and even about how much you earn. But watch someone's eyes glaze over, watch a room empty, if you talk about loneliness. It is one of the prime human conditions and, along with death, the one we are least reconciled to. In the modern world we have both contained and exacerbated the condition of loneliness. You now seldom have to be alone, but may often feel lonely. But loneliness is something that nobody is supposed to suffer from any more. We have television, clubs for the elderly, pubs, neighbours, those worse off than yourself to visit, causes, work, voluntary organizations and holidays. Because some intrinsic acceptance of loneliness is crucial to a full under-standing of being human we have rendered ourselves less human and, paradoxically, more lonely through avoidance tactics. Too many modern activities are set up supposedly to do the impossible – to banish loneliness so that it does not have to be countenanced or suffered.

It could be argued, therefore, that the invisible God was created to defend man against loneliness. A God who is always present, always powerful, always listening, always compassionate seems a foolproof defence against the agony of loneliness. It is extraordinary that the invention of such a complete impossibility should not have been questioned. Human beings may let you down – and they often do. But God will be there for every single person the same, forever and forever. And what's more, He is completely inside us, so that we carry Him around. He never leaves us alone.

This seemingly infallible mechanism against loneliness must fail. For the paradox is that you cannot try to avoid something without spending your whole life involved in it. The God-figure has ensured that loneliness and the conditions most likely to cause it are built into our social structures.

If the ritual of the God-figure *was* invented as a security blanket to prevent loneliness, then Christ did indeed die in vain. So that this doesn't happen there needs to be a balance of male and female, and also of the child within and between each. If the inner child in the form of childhood memories, or the outer child in the form of offspring, are treated as perverse, then perversion will ensue.

The nature of desire does not depend on opposites, or on the shadow boxing of symbols, but in the reality of keeping faith with being a unique person. It is uniqueness which is ultimately the most desirable quality of all. It is the mystery of that much sought after 'essence' which people hunger for.

But as well as keeping faith with being unique it is equally important to keep faith with other people's uniqueness. In order for this to happen man must offer woman his considered protection and take issue with the bad man who is on the rampage. Then woman would not be disadvantaged by the bad man, and would not in turn seek revenge on men who are not bad.

This new morality would also take issue with woman. For a small minority of women have felt it is their right to have children as they see fit, without consulting men at all. I do not include here women who have children alone by accident, through hardship or other unforeseen circumstances. I am referring to women who feel they are entitled, by the natural law which enables them to give birth, to decide that men have no part to play in child-rearing. They outcast men from fatherhood, and think they need pay no more consideration to man than a visit to the sperm bank. This revenge on the dirty tricks that culture has played can only result in counter-revenge in the future – especially, sadly, from the children who are produced in this way.

Any person who is a mother or father in the 1990s should know that the moral and physical development of children is the equal concern of men and women. The moral position of anyone born post-Freud and feminism may be freely chosen, but it should no longer be possible to blame a visible mother and not an invisible father for the care or lack of it that children receive. If man chooses to call himself moral, present knowledge denies him the ignorance of claiming that the rearing of children is only a woman's concern. Likewise, the move to blame the plight of 'latchkey' children solely on women doesn't hold water if those children also have a father. Fathers, too, hold keys to their children's well-being. The move to include men as well as women in the care of children would prevent either sex being unfairly praised or blamed for the kind of people today's children become.

18
The Blind Side of Eden

The loss of Eden and the prospect of paradise are two of the strongest forces which still influence and undermine relationships. The tainting of Eden was originally blamed on one symbolic woman – Eve – and then, post-feminism, on all men. It must be rescued by both.

The blind side of Eden is the place where Eve does not see Adam, where Adam does not see Eve, and where neither sees the other within themselves. It is a place where north/south, east/west, goodies/baddies, white/black, male/female and culture/nature are divided. What these divisions do not afford is the reality that the full spectrum of human nature is contained within each person.

Rescuers face a difficult task because major divides have been western culture's personal and political norm. They are the result of a dominant culture which portrays opposites as separate entities rather than as two facets of the whole person or of the whole political picture.

The danger of there being a species, sex or race which is seen as 'other' instead of 'familiar' is that, if curiosity doesn't kill the cat, then paranoia certainly will. Human destruction of animals like rhinos, grizzly bears, elephants and tigers has shown what curiosity can lead to. The wonder of looking is soon replaced by desire to govern for one's own ends – to hunt or to put behind bars. Paranoia sets in when differences are exaggerated – Hitler's attitude to the Jews is an example – and become actually or perceptually threatening. Between woman and man the division – into opposite sexes – has created so much despair and unhappiness that harmonious relationships are exceptional rather than usual. Something, however, has now come full circle, and offers a chance to examine relationships in a new light – to grasp the whole picture.

Through reliable contraception, together with changes in the law and in accepted social customs, women may now have children when they choose, and many women are financially self-supporting. In their new-found role as adventurers, women are also much freer than they were only half a century ago, and fly round the world to prove it. This

212

means that man is once more in the position of not knowing who his children are.

He is vulnerable, as he was in ancient matricentric societies, to the natural condition that women bear children. Women may now have babies on their own, they may have abortions against his wishes, and they may keep children to themselves if they do not live with the father. They may even take themselves and their children thousands of miles away. Since male psychology is petrified of the strong, sturdy, smiling woman it is even more petrified of this woman with a child in her arms. She was present thousands of years ago and she is present once more. In the interim centuries man did his best to govern her through marriage, religion and punitive laws; but she has come back.

This situation presents him with a dilemma and an opportunity. He either has to continue the fight literally to the death, because short of blowing up the planet there is little ground left to fight on. Or he may realize instead that the task of twenty-first-century man will be to *save the child*. The work of saving children in the Sudan, Ethiopia, India and South Africa has become an occupation of the late twentieth century. Whether under the auspices of Live Aid, Sport Aid, War on Want, Oxfam or Save the Children itself, the work of raising money to inoculate, feed and care for children has gathered pace.

But as well as a far broader knowledge of the nature and dimension of world-wide grief, modern awareness also carries vital knowledge of grief on a personal scale. This grief is the division between the adult man or woman and the emotional stock which is their own childhood – and that of others.

In a Channel 4 programme entitled *Evil*, transmitted in June 1988, the subject of division was discussed. Speaking about men who commit hideous murders, the philosopher Mary Midgley talked of the 'fatality of disowning the shadowy, evil or darker side [of self] which if not owned or integrated will become destructive'. She described how this casting out of what belongs inside will mean that the shadowy self will roam the streets without a home, without ownership and without responsibility. Being homeless, it will be wilful and inconsolable (my word) and will strike randomly. She said that what keeps evil at bay is not pushing it aside, but the exercising of moral choice – the vigilance of seeing the bad and deciding against it. She concluded: 'Where there is lack of vigilance there is danger.' In other words, morality is concerned with the personal and public exercising of choice. If people did not contain the propensity to commit evil deeds there would be no need for this choice – no need for morality.

In the same programme an American serviceman who had been in Vietnam described the syndrome which operated at My Lai, when US troops took leave of their senses and massacred innocent civilians, including children. He explained that the soldiers were encouraged to regard the Vietnamese as less than human – as 'other' – which was one of the factors which made the massacre possible. He then likened it to a 'blood sport', the ultimate hunting experience, and said: 'You're not killing people, you're hunting game.' An American psychologist who had investigated My Lai said that one thing was essential to the avoidance of evil – the acceptance that it is general to everyone and not a question of the good 'us' and the bad/evil 'them'. This split was not only wrong because it was untrue, he continued, but it also allowed 'general and generalized – or corporate – evil to continue unabated'.

If man is to find heroism in the modern world it is ironic that a modern morality would ask him to save the child. It would ask him to save any more children from being massacred at My Lai, Hiroshima or Dresden. It would ask him to stop children being poisoned by lead, or killed in the third world by measles. It would ask him to find the child within himself so that he does no more damage to the children outside. It would ask for public and personal reconciliation at a time when this might be his way of 'saving face' anyway. For if he has returned to a situation where he cannot name his children, then, to adapt a computer term, he had better become 'child-friendly'. If he doesn't, his oppositional tendencies will lead him to destroy what he doesn't recognize or own.

So, having always been terrified of the child, modern man would commit the heroic act of facing what he most fears, the child within – in other words his own childhood or his complete, unified self.

This is not his divided self or his compartmentalized self, but the self which contains all his experiences, and is therefore accountable for them. Here he has a problem in modern woman, because, having well nigh demanded at one time that man 'shape up' emotionally, she has proved herself somewhat squeamish when he has done so. She has asked for his tears, and then fled in panic once the floodgates which hold back man's hurt have opened. She wants man to display a full set of emotions, but hasn't quite faced up to exactly what that constitutes. It is such a radical and revolutionary concept that even those who seek it are simultaneously fearful.

The fear, deep down, is still that a man who cries is not a proper man. It is based on the fear of emasculation. For if a man becomes 'soft' (emotionally speaking) might he not then become physically –

214

which means sexually – soft? Will he become a eunuch? On the face of it this fear is ridiculous – so ridiculous that it has shored up the 'male myth of supremacy', to use Easthope's words, for centuries. This male myth, put crudely, was that a hard man had a hard penis, and that this was good for woman. The status quo operated on this basis, with the 'soft' woman to complement the hard man.

However, feminist argument has pointed this out as a phallacy. Feminists have written that the act of the penis entering the vagina is not crucial to love-making, and may play only a small part in it. It is possible for love-making to occur without it happening at all. While intromission for many is comforting and exciting, it does not usually produce orgasm in the woman.

So although intromission is satisfying, and indeed extremely special in being the act of union between bodies, a man only needs to be hard *occasionally* for this to happen. The fear of emasculation is unfounded, and derives from the myth that the man had to be, to use Easthope's words again, 'on red alert' *all the time*.

The other fear was that a man would become less of a man in an indefinable way, that he would lose some of his essence of masculinity. In fact the essence of masculinity is the same as – and different from – the essence of femininity. It is simply that a man should become as much self-realizing – in other words unique – as possible. For the essence of desire or attraction lies not in stereotype but in individuality, which finds its home in self-realization. Likewise the essence of femininity will take as many forms as there are female bodies. For the essence of attraction, of an attraction which grows and develops, is uniqueness.

What man lacks at the moment is something that woman has found – co-operation between people of the same sex, which will make his search for individual identity easier. It is doubtful at present that there is even tacit agreement among men – whose ancestors wrote the parable of Christ's life as a clear example of the importance of individual conscience – that this is where the answers lie. Not out there, but in here. Not in corporate strength, but in co-operation.

There is another difference between man and woman which impedes their reconciliation. It is what I call a difference in the register of need. It has been customary for an elaborate game to be played round the business of needing, and around the business of who needs whom and for what purpose. Traditionally woman was forced into needing man through marriage and property laws, but man also wanted woman to assuage his falsely presented sexual appetite. Intrigues of the most convoluted kind revolved round the business of who caught whom. Surely this doesn't matter any more? For the days of relationships being a necessity for woman and a bit of spare-time sport for man have gone. While they haven't *long* gone, such is the weight of evidence to discredit them that their burial shouldn't be far off. The truth is that man needs woman as much as woman needs man, and that between them they have equality of need for each other. Any man who is still going round pretending he is self-sufficient is indeed a dinosaur.

From a woman's point of view, her modern task contains, ironically, something that was once required only of man – sheathing a sword. This concept carries two meanings. The obvious one is that woman, with her generally better balance in the emotional world, must not demean or slay man because he is weaker than her. Nor must she seek revenge for the sins of patriarchy, for woman was complicit in them. It would be wrong to slay *man* for patriarchy's sins, for – like woman, he was both conspirator and victim. The mistake of confusing patriarchy as a system with man as a person is a dire one. It is a similar mistake – the same in reverse – to confusing the symbolic, powerful mother-figure with woman as a person.

There is, however, a problem inherent in woman 'sheathing her sword', for if by this she hides or denies her power, she is not being true to herself. And the modern self to which she is being true is still, like man's, somewhat unresolved. For the speed of her growth in the context of human history has been like lightning. So woman needs to be sure that the myths are properly unravelled before she knits something to her own, heterosexual design.

As the Garden of Eden story tells us, the myths revolve, in essence, round woman in opposition to man. As God created Eve in the light of man's needs, so man, through culture, created woman in the light of his so-called knowledge. He created woman as dark to his light, light to his dark, good to his bad and bad to his good. She was the virgin/whore, mother/child, field hospital/wounded victim. She was man's shadow, for even if she was light to his dark – say Beauty to his Beast – she was still moved around by his constructions. The crucial way she was shadowed was that she was the invention of his knowledge, and could not behave, to use an old saying, 'according to her own light'. Man saw the light of meaning and formed a culture which enabled his knowledge to bear this light through the world. In the beginning was the word, and the word belonged to man. He named himself knowledgeable and woman not needing knowledge because he possessed it on her behalf.

The *knowing* woman is therefore a particular threat to man. The *sexually* knowing woman is a near catastrophe, because she knows man and the penis to be vulnerable. This is why knowledgeable women have been so derided. The intellectually knowledgeable woman has been called 'bookish', 'mannish' or 'ugly'. The religiously knowledgeable woman is still not fully allowed. The sexually knowledgeable woman has been branded a whore or a nymphomaniac. The latter is a projection of man's fears that he does not have the penis power to satisfy a woman at all times. The cultural nympho-maniac was invented to make it seem as if woman was insatiable, rather than man fallible.

While the patriarchal system operated a kind of lockjaw on female sexuality the sexually vulnerable, weaker male was not apparent. The fact that a woman may accommodate a penis for far longer than the penis can stay hard was kept from public knowledge. This conceal-ment is now unnecessary, since people know that the female orgasm doesn't generally happen during intromission. However, the male myth wanted supremacy, and woman's orgasms were far from a man's mind. In fact the lack of them helped contain her in a position of fidelity, for if sex was boring she wouldn't want to practise it with other men.

In the past, the sexually, politically or intellectually knowledgeable woman was a threat to man's supremacy. The best woman, therefore, was an innocent one, and a sexually innocent one at that – a virgin. With this in mind, modern woman has a tightrope to walk. She has to be knowledgeable without denying it, and at the same time she must bear in mind that a part (sometimes a large part) of man is still bound up in his myths and is frightened by a knowledgeable woman. But as man should not act under instruction from woman, neither should woman be cowed by the left-over fears in man. To use Mary Daly's phrase, they must both be their own 'becoming'.

The creative act of becoming (an individual) would do something very important for and with beauty. Not only would man reclaim an aspect of it which is his, but woman would find her own beauty too instead of being prey to its cultural dictates. If both sexes had their own beauty, it would then be possible to demolish the tyranny of the eye. For in the sense that beauty is in the heart as well as the eye of the beholder, if the beholder possesses his or her own beauty, cultural eye-rule would be replaced by individual appreciation.

The other condition of owning beauty for oneself is that it would then make beauty in others more discernible and therefore more likely, since more acknowledged. Beauty would then, indeed, come home. Since only a few people have conventional physical good looks, beauty is in any case more a question of relationship than anything else. If it were not, then 'ordinary-looking' people would never find partners.

The perfection complex and the need to make things ordered, linear and governable have colluded to allow minimum room for variety and vitality. The life-defying wish of the fascist is to replace beauty with style or image and to limit that subversive entity – the individual – in so doing. The idea that culture in the form of stylized image can substitute for nature in the form of uniqueness has its genesis in the God-figure. That figure was invented to make culture, through scripture, rock-solid. But relationships cannot be conducted behind the façades of stereotypes and symbols, only in the company of people. They are concerned with intimacy, of which symbolism is a dead form. And the acceptance and discovery of reality is the basis of intimacy. A person can only be *known* through this – his or her reality. A person is unknowable, untouchable and ultimately lonely if hidden behind a symbol.

At the end of *Monuments and Maidens* Marina Warner writes that Eve 'has her part to play in the break with the seamless past into the new, accidented era of event and awareness'.[1] That awareness is that culture and nature work together in a relationship that has not yet been understood. To my mind Warner is alluding here to the fact that both Adam and Eve contain within them culture and nature. Instead of accepting this concept, the story of Eden as it is writ has split the two and placed them on separate pages, where they have fought each other for recognition. In describing this fight, a woman friend who is a feminist wrote these last lines in a poem:

> Oh war fought out so dearly
> that makes me slay the man I love
> to make him see me clearly.

Man's demise as hero means his relationship with death has lost a creative or romantic outlet. In the past he could die 'gloriously' on the battlefield or in 'true grit' style, pitting his wits against the elements. He could explore the Nile or climb the north face of the Eiger. In all this he faced the possibility of premature and heroic death. Death now seems far less heroic to man, especially since the person holding the sword, metaphorically speaking, is woman. In all his wildest nightmares he never imagined that his eventual fate might be to be run through by the creature who once lay in his trap. He might literally die at her hand in a car or plane crash, or he might die slowly from disease or old age – all traditionally unheroic ways to go.

On the other hand he may *live* more fully instead, by becoming a whole, moral person instead of a schizophrenic one. He may, for instance, take more than a passing interest in being a parent – which would give him, like woman, a real stake in the future. This in turn would achieve something very important with two myths in one go. The myth of the invisible father would be vanquished if the actual father became visible. And so would the myth of the powerful, ogre-like mother. If children were a shared moral responsibility it would put an end to the spurious notion that it's 'all mother's fault' if they turn out badly, and would give children less chance of doing so by offering them and their mother an emotionally present father.

Male need is circumscribed at the moment by the fact that man still wants to be the transcending, transcendent warrior of the old days, when men were men . . . He hides his needing, vibrant, vital self behind the myth of invincibility and simultaneous mother-blaming. He feels victim of his mother's abandonment, and therefore will not let another woman see the wounds inflicted when he was young. Instead he lays on her the far greater wounds of his raging, festering anger. If he were to become an ordinary, vulnerable, 'good enough' father he would achieve the twin benefits of helping his children and himself. He would stop the rot where man plays dead (emotionally) and blames mother for the shooting, and where woman blames man for the state of the world. Mother is responsible for the state of the male psyche, and man is responsible for the state of the nation. The battle has been pitched here, twixt the Devil and the Deep.

It is now clear, however, that the battle is not primarily about gender at all. It's about attitude. The new man is a man of morals, a man of conscience and not a man of guilt. The new woman is a person of power and compassion. The world has become a far more complex jungle than the original Garden of Eden was hundreds of centuries ago. It needs a moral woman and man to tend it.

The story of the banishment from Eden has contributed more than any other to the myth that man and woman are doomed and need salvation: and were meant to find this – not within themselves, which is where it lies – but through a system of endless, opposed opposites. The Happy Ever After syndrome is based on the guilt of Eden and the yearning to return or go forward to a state of bliss. It prevents discovery of the reality that life is this minute, that it is changed in this minute, and that this is a constantly shifting paradox.

Adam and Eve were not banished from the garden, for they – we – were never in it. The mythical betrayal did not happen, but the continued telling of the tale makes sure that the Eden that *does* exist is not grasped. Our actual Eden is the opportunity life presents from moment to moment for living, for compassion – and for change. This is the attitude which has been hidden by the myths.

The attitude which blames the loss of Eden on one woman (Eve) or on all men (through patriarchy) is an outdated one. Because of it, paradise is in jeopardy. For the blind side of Eden is ringed with weapons.

Change will happen through man and woman accepting the truth that they are equally responsible for themselves and for children. By believing the myths, we have banished Heaven from earth – Heaven to the hereafter and Eden to the long-gone. Poised thus, between two unavailable ecstasies, it is hardly surprising that we have faltered.

Either Eden is now. Or Eden is never.

Bibliographical Notes

Chapter 1

1 Germaine Greer, *The Female Eunuch*, Paladin, 1971 (first pub. 1970), p. 249.
2 Janet Radcliffe Richards, *The Sceptical Feminist*, Pelican Books, 1982 (first pub. 1980), pp. 13–14.
3 *The Sceptical Feminist*, pp. 17–18.
4 *The Female Eunuch*, p. 331.
5 Paul Auster, *The Art of Hunger, and Other Essays*, The Menard Press, 1982, p. 94.
6 Phillip Hodson, *Men: An Investigation into the Emotional Male*, BBC Books, 1984, p. 23.
7 *Men*, p. 3.
8 *Men*, p. 7.
9 Antony Easthope, *What a Man's Gotta Do: The Masculine Myth in Popular Culture*, Paladin, 1986, p. 66.
10 Mary Daly, *Beyond God the Father*, The Women's Press, 1986 (first pub. 1973), p. 195.
11 Marina Warner, *Monuments and Maidens: The Allegory of the Female Form*, Picador, 1987 (first pub. 1985), pp. 224 and 225.
12 *Men*, p. 5.
13 *Men*, p. 6.
14 *Men*, p. 3.
15 Jill Tweedie, *In the Name of Love*, Granada, 1980 (first pub. 1979), p. 72.

Chapter 3

1 Susan Griffin, *Pornography and Silence*, The Women's Press, 1981, p. 22.
2 Alice Miller, *Thou Shalt Not Be Aware: Society's Betrayal of the Child*, Pluto Press, 1985 (first pub. 1981), p. 95.

Chapter 4

1 *Monuments and Maidens*, p. 222.
2 *Monuments and Maidens*, p. 224.

3 Margaret Walters, *The Nude Male: A New Perspective*, Penguin Books, 1979 (first pub. 1970), p. 8.
4 *The Nude Male*, pp. 16–17.
5 *What a Man's Gotta Do*, p. 43.

Chapter 5

1 Edwin Mullins, *The Painted Witch*, Secker and Warburg, 1985, p. 223.
2 *The Painted Witch*, p. 223.
3 *The Painted Witch*, pp. 223–4.
4 *The Painted Witch*, p. 224.
5 *The Painted Witch*, p. 224.
6 *Pornography and Silence*, p. 73.
7 *Pornography and Silence*, p. 74.
8 *Pornography and Silence*, pp. 74–5.

Chapter 6

1 Carol Lee, 'The Inconsolables', printed postcard, The Menard Press, 1983.
2 *Thou Shalt Not Be Aware*, p. 95.
3 *Thou Shalt Not Be Aware*, p. 95.
4 *Thou Shalt Not Be Aware*, pp. 121–2.
5 *The Female Eunuch*, p. 45.

Chapter 7

1 *Monuments and Maidens*, p. 240.
2 Yves Bonnefoy, trans. Anthony Rudolf, *Things Dying Things Reborn*, The Menard Press, 1985, p. 50.
3 The Doctrine Commission, *We Believe in God*, Church House, 1987.
4 *Thou Shalt Not Be Aware*, p. 93.
5 *Thou Shalt Not Be Aware*, pp. 98 and 99.
6 *Monuments and Maidens*, p. 325.
7 *Monuments and Maidens*, p. 333.
8 Peter Biskind, *Seeing is Believing: How Hollywood Taught Us to Stop Worrying and Love the Fifties*, Pluto Press, 1984 (first pub. 1983), p. 347.

Chapter 8

1 Carol Lee, *Friday's Child*, Thorson's, 1988, pp. 98 and 99.
2 *What a Man's Gotta Do*, p. 42.
3 *What a Man's Gotta Do*, p. 52.
4 *In the Name of Love*, pp. 67 and 68.

BIBLIOGRAPHICAL NOTES

5 Michelle Roberts, *The Wild Girl*, Methuen, 1984, pp. 170–3.
6 *The Wild Girl*, p. 174.

Chapter 9

1 *Friday's Child*, pp. 60 and 61.
2 *Friday's Child*, p. 61.
3 *Friday's Child*, p. 62.

Chapter 10

1 Angela Carter, *The Sadeian Woman*, Virago Press, 1979, p. 9.
2 *What a Man's Gotta Do*, pp. 120 and 121.
3 *Men*, p. 6.
4 *Men*, p. 135.
5 *Men*, p. 139.
6 *Thou Shalt Not Be Aware*, p. 221.
7 *Thou Shalt Not Be Aware*, p. 221.
8 *Thou Shalt Not Be Aware*, pp. 99 100.

Chapter 11

1 *Friday's Child*, p. 59.
2 *Friday's Child*, p. 58.
3 *Friday's Child*, p. 63.
4 *The Female Eunuch*, p. 254.
5 *The Wild Girl*, p. 176.
6 *The Wild Girl*, pp. 176 and 187–9.
7 *What a Man's Gotta Do*, pp. 167–8.

Chapter 12

1 Laurens van der Post, *Jung and the Story of Our Time*, Penguin Books, 1978 (first pub. 1976), p. 165.
2 *Jung and the Story of Our Time*, p. 161.
3 *Jung and the Story of Our Time*, p. 224.
4 *Thou Shalt Not Be Aware*, pp. 19–20.
5 Alan Watts, *The Wisdom of Insecurity*, Rider, 1974 (first pub. 1954), p. ix.
6 *The Sadeian Woman*, pp. 7–8.
7 Herb Goldberg, *The New Male–Female Relationship*, Coventure Ltd, 1984 (first pub. 1983), pp. 7–8.
8 Don Cupitt, *The Sea of Faith*, BBC Books, 1984, p. 229.
9 *The Sea of Faith*, p. 265.
10 *Men*, p. 139.
11 *Men*, p. 9.

Chapter 13

1 *What a Man's Gotta Do*, p. 141.
2 *The Sea of Faith*, p. 271.
3 Gloria Steinem, *Outrageous Acts and Everyday Rebellions*, Flamingo, 1984 (first pub. in this version 1983), pp. 338–40. (Earlier versions of this article appeared as a CBS *Spectrum* broadcast, 1977, and in *Ms* magazine, October 1978.)
4 Margaret Atwood, *Murder in the Dark*, Jonathan Cape, 1984 (first pub. 1983), p. 32.
5 *The Sadeian Woman*, p. 5.

Chapter 14

1 *What a Man's Gotta Do*, p. 7.
2 *What a Man's Gotta Do*, p. 7.

Chapter 15

1 *The Sadeian Woman*, pp. 6 and 7.
2 *The Female Eunuch*, p. 44.
3 *The Female Eunuch*, p. 43.
4 Robert Graves, *The Golden Fleece*, Hutchinson, 1983 (first pub. 1944), pp. 8 and 9.
5 *What a Man's Gotta Do*, p. 134.
6 *The Female Eunuch*, p. 46.

Chapter 17

1 *Friday's Child*, p. 157.
2 *Friday's Child*, p. 157.
3 *Thou Shalt Not Be Aware*, pp. 100–1.
4 Margaret Atwood, *True Stories*, Oxford University Press, 1981, p. 57.
5 *Thou Shalt Not Be Aware*, p. 318.
6 Martin Amis, *Einstein's Monsters*, Jonathan Cape, 1987, p. 8.
7 *Einstein's Monsters*, p. 11.
8 *Einstein's Monsters*, pp. 25 and 26.
9 *Einstein's Monsters*, pp. 27–8.
10 Quoted in Nicholas Humphreys and Robert Jay Lifton (eds), *In a Dark Time*, Faber and Faber, 1984, p. 159.
11 *Beyond God the Father*, p. 71.

Chapter 18

1 *Monuments and Maidens*, p. 328.

I have kept excellent company in researching this work. I would like to

BIBLIOGRAPHICAL NOTES

acknowledge the following books which, although not directly quoted from, have been instrumental in forming ideas and feelings:

Margaret Atwood, *The Handmaid's Tale*, Jonathan Cape, 1986 and Virago, 1989.

Paul Auster, *The Invention of Solitude*, Faber and Faber, 1988.

John Berger, *Ways of Seeing*, BBC Books, 1972 and Penguin Books, 1972.

Bruno Bettelheim, *The Uses of Enchantment: The Meaning and Importance of Fairy Tales*, Thames and Hudson, 1976, and Peregrine Books, 1978.

Marie Cardinal, *The Words to Say It*, Picador, 1983.

Angela Carter, *Nights at the Circus*, Chatto and Windus/The Hogarth Press, 1984 and Picador, 1985.

Susan Dowell and Linda Hurcombe, *Dispossessed Daughters of Eve: Faith and Feminism*, SCM Press, 1981.

Colette Dowling, *The Cinderella Complex*, Michael Joseph, 1982 and Flamingo, 1983.

Luise Eichenbaum and Susie Orbach, *What Do Women Want?*, Michael Joseph, 1983 and Fontana, 1984.

Marilyn French, *Beyond Power: On Women, Men and Morals*, Abacus, 1986.

Sigmund Freud, *Two Short Accounts of Psycho-analysis*, Penguin Books, 1962.

Erich Fromm, *Beyond the Chains of Illusion: My Encounter with Marx and Freud*, Simon and Schuster, 1962, and Abacus, 1980.

Erich Fromm, D. T. Suzuki and Richard de Martino, *Zen Buddhism and Psychoanalysis*, Souvenir Press, 1974.

Maggie Gee, *The Burning Book*, Faber and Faber, 1983.

Sandra M. Gilbert and Susan Gubar, *The Madwoman in the Attic: The Woman Writer and the Nineteenth-century Literary Imagination*, Yale University Press, 1979.

Carol Gilligan, *In a Different Voice*, Harvard University Press, 1982.

Robert A. Johnson, *We: Understanding the Psychology of Romantic Love*, Harper and Row, 1983.

J. Krishnamurti, *The Urgency of Change*, Gollancz, 1971.

Jean Liedloff, *The Continuum Concept*, Duckworth, 1975.

Mary Lutyens (ed.), *The Penguin Krishnamurti Reader*, Penguin Books, 1970.

Juliet Mitchell, *Psychoanalysis and Feminism*, Allen Lane, 1974 and Penguin Books, 1975.

Juliet Mitchell and Jacqueline Rose (eds), trans. Jacqueline Rose, *Jacques Lacan and the Ecole Freudienne*, Macmillan, 1982.

Marge Piercy, *Woman on the Edge of Time*, The Women's Press, 1979.

Oliver Sacks, *The Man Who Mistook His Wife for a Hat*, Duckworth, 1985 and Picador, 1986.

Larry Tifft and Dennis Sullivan, *The Struggle to Be Human: Crime, Criminology and Anarchism*, Cienfugos Press, 1980.

THE BLIND SIDE OF EDEN

Fay Weldon, *The Life and Loves of a She-Devil*, Hodder and Stoughton, 1983 and Coronet, 1984.

Alfred North Whitehead, *Adventures of Ideas: A Brilliant History of Mankind's Great Thoughts*, Macmillan (New York), 1933.

D. W. Winnicott, *Playing and Reality*, Tavistock Publications, 1971 and Pelican Books, 1974.